# PRAISE FOR THE FIRST EDITION

"Very useful to anyone interested in the field of stress."
—HANS SELYE, C.C., M.D., PH.D., D.SC. (1907–1982)

"The most informative and practical book on stress to date."
—American Academy of Behavioral Medicine

"One of the few books on stress management that
offers comprehensive self-training procedures . . .
an unusually clear and useful presentation."
—ALBERT ELLIS, PH.D.,
co-author of *A New Guide to Rational Living*

"Excellent . . . should be required reading for every
human being."
—*Today's OR Nurse*

"Drs. Charlesworth and Nathan are to be congratulated on
accomplishing a difficult task. The book is an accurate,
systematic, and practical text for college students."
—BERNARD LUBIN, PH.D. (1923–2003)
Curators' Professor Emeritus of Psychology and Medicine
University of Missouri at Kansas City

# STRESS
## MANAGEMENT

*A Comprehensive
Guide to Wellness*

Completely Revised and Updated

EDWARD A. CHARLESWORTH, Ph. D.,

AND

RONALD G. NATHAN, Ph. D.

BALLANTINE BOOKS
NEW YORK

A Ballantine Book
Published by The Random House Publishing Group

Copyright © 1982, 1984, 2004 by Edward A. Charlesworth, Ph.D.,
and Ronald G. Nathan, Ph.D.

Published in the United States by Ballantine Books, an imprint of The
Random House Publishing Group, a division of Random House, Inc., New
York, and simultaneously in Canada by Random House of Canada Limited,
Toronto. Originally published in 1982 and subsequently revised in 1984 by
Simon & Schuster.

www.ballantinebooks.com

Library of Congress Cataloging-in-Publication Data
is available from the publisher upon request.

ISBN 0-345-46891-0

This book published by arrangement with Simon & Schuster

Manufactured in the United States of America

This 2004 edition has been extensively revised and updated.

9   8

First Ballantine Books Edition: November 1985

Text design by Susan Turner

*To our parents*

AND

*To my wife, Robin, and children, Brittany and Allison;
and to Rotary International on the 100th anniversary of
helping the world manage stress through its Health, Hunger
and Humanity initiatives, and through a sense of purpose
and meaning for life*

E.A.C.

*To my sisters, Susan and Vivian*

R.G.N.

*Therefore say of me that in this book I have only made up a bunch
of other people's flowers, and that of my own I have only provided
the string that ties them together.*
—Montaigne

Special recognition is given to the following scientists, writers,
and original contributors to the foundations and applications of
stress management training. Those in italics are from the most recent twenty-five years.

Robert E. Alberti

*Aaron Beck*

Herbert Benson

*Ken Blanchard*

*Richard N. Bolles*

Barbara B. Brown

*Deepak Chopra*

Kenneth H. Cooper

*Norman Cousins*

*Stephen R. Covey*

*Barbara Deangelis*

*Larry Dossey*

*Wayne Dyer*

Albert Ellis

Michael L. Emmons

Meyer Friedman

*John Gray*

Thomas H. Holmes

Edmund Jacobson

*Spencer Johnson*

*Suzanne Kobasa*

*Harold Kushner*

Alan Lakein

Arnold Lazarus

Wolfgang Luther

*Philip G. McGraw*

Neal E. Miller

*Dean Ornish*

Norman Vincent
Peale

*Kenneth R. Pelletier*

*James Campbell
Quick*

Richard H. Rahe

*Tony Robbins*

*Paul J. Rosch*

Ray H. Rosenman

Johannes H. Schultz

Hans Selye

*Shelley E. Taylor*

*Georgia Witkin*

Joseph Wolpe

# PREFACE

*The only constant in life is change.*
—Denise McCluggage

*The more things change, the more they stay the same.*
—Alphonse Karr

Twenty-five years ago we wrote the first book to use the term "stress management" outside of structural engineering. The winds of change were blowing through every area of life then, but they are now approaching hurricane force. Such dramatic change is inherently stressful. In response, self-help books have exploded from a handful about stress reduction to over two thousand listed under "stress management" as a subject heading on Internet bookstores.

We consider it an honor that our general readers have kept the first edition of this book in continuous demand for over two decades and that medical and nursing schools, as well as colleges and universities, continue to use it as a resource to train future generations of health care professionals. It is a privilege to share what we knew then and what we have learned both personally and professionally over the last quarter century.

We believe that people want to do more with their lives than merely cope with the overwhelming costs of ever-mounting stress. They are seeking the newest and most effective ways of taking control of their lives, preventing disease, and enhancing their well-being. Those who are successful in managing stress seem comfortable in almost any situation. Their lives are full and yet unhurried. They look relaxed and confident, even when they are making critical decisions or meeting important people. Physically fit and seldom tired, they project a sense of optimism and quiet strength. They are also preventing the very diseases that pose some of the greatest challenges to modern medicine.

More and more twenty-first-century illnesses have been shown to be related to the "lifestyles of the stressed and harried." These lifestyles often include overeating, undernourishing, smoking, drinking in excess, underexercising, hurrying, and worrying about everything from work to world crises. It is estimated that as many as 75 percent of all medical complaints are stress-related. The list of these disorders is long and still growing: migraine and tension headaches, high blood pressure, rapid and irregular heartbeats, immune dysfunction, insomnia, back pain, muscle aches, and skin disorders, as well as many psychiatric disorders.

> *Clearly, if disease is manmade, it can also be man-prevented.*
>
> —Dr Ernst Wunder,
> President,
> American Health Foundation

We are all grateful for the advances in medical technology. It was unimaginable when the first edition of this book was written that major surgery using microscopic instruments and tiny incisions could be performed in virtual reality, lasers correct our vision, and new devices scan our bodies for disease. When the Human Genome Project mapped our DNA, the potential for preventing and treating disease expanded enormously. It is a wondrous time of scientific advances.

But designer drugs for disease, incredible surgical procedures, and genetic or molecular modifications of tissue are all colliding with the reality of skyrocketing health care costs, and the need for prevention. The challenge is still to find, promote, and maintain lifelong skills to replace pills.

Our goal is to help you achieve maximum well-being and enjoy a richer and more rewarding lifestyle. Many of our patients come to us for psychosomatic problems and leave not only symptom-free but with a far greater sense of self-confidence, self-esteem, and involvement in life. They are no longer the victims of stress but victors over stress.

This book provides ways to assess your stress so that you can begin to understand and change your response to it. In this way, your stress response can be used in creative ways to make use of energy that would otherwise be lost through distress and disease.

We will present techniques that can be learned through self-guided exercises in a short period of time. To this end, we have provided self-assessment forms, charts, and case examples. Part of this book will help you to establish goals and rehearse their attainment.

Through a series of muscle relaxation exercises, we will teach you how to be more relaxed in even the most stressful situations. To augment these more conventional biobehavioral approaches to relaxation, we have added a chapter about mind-body fitness to promote physical and mental relaxation.

In addition, you will find a new chapter on complementary and alternative medicine (CAM) approaches to stress management. These models may optimize stress management by fostering wellness as a state of balance between the spiritual, physical, and mental/emotional "selves."

In these pages, you will learn how to overcome fears or phobias and reach out for experiences you might otherwise avoid. Furthermore, we want you to find new and rewarding goals, such as those of Dag Hammarskjöld, a past secretary-general of the United Nations, who wrote, "If only I may grow firmer, simpler, quieter, and warmer."

> *For every minute you are angry, you lose sixty seconds of happiness.*
>
> —RALPH WALDO EMERSON

In another part of this book, you will learn the hazards to your heart of anger-inducing, time-urgent living and get an update on the Type A personality. We will also introduce you to a Type C personality, one that is very productive and free of the harmful stress effects from the driven and angry Type A personality.

Our earlier edition reflected the many stresses of dual-career couples and the changing roles of men and women, but health psychologists did not dicover the gender differences in the stress response itself until recently. This edition is among the first self-help books to present these exciting new findings.

Our time management section has been brought up-to-date by adding a chapter about the use of computers, PDAs, wireless communication, and the Internet to help us manage the times of our life. Our goal is that you will be able to increase work productivity and also have more quality time for family and recreation. Again, the goal is to enhance not only your health but also your life.

In the section "Planning the Days of Your Life" we have also included a chapter on laughter and leisure. The research of the last decade has clearly established the importance of our ability to play and enjoy humor in strengthening our immune system and

> *All of the animals, excepting man, know that the principal business of life is to enjoy it.*
>
> —SAMUEL BUTLER

protecting us from the harmful effects of stressful living.

We have outlined the latest findings and guidelines for exercise and nutrition, but more important, we have shared how to begin making them a permanent and pleasurable part of your lifestyle. We hope that you will learn enjoyable ways of more fully developing and maintaining your body. Doing so may well add years to your life and most certainly will add life to your years.

> *Health can be squandered, but not stored up.*
>
> —MASON COOLEY

Another part of this book will help you learn about assertiveness training. Too often we clamp a lid on our true feelings until we are ready to explode. Assertiveness training provides new skills for expressing yourself to others honestly and without intimidation or confrontation.

> *I wish you'd stop yelling, I can't hear myself shout.*
>
> —JOHN OSBORNE

To update this book, we have introduced several new concepts and tools for understanding and managing stress, but stress remains multifaceted, and a comprehensive approach remains the most powerful way to manage it.

When personal changes and stress are both intense and prolonged, depression is a common result. The acceleration of change in so many areas of life is one of the reasons depression is more common than ever. To help you understand, prevent, and lift depressed feelings, we have added a new chapter about depression.

> *Life is like playing a violin solo in public and learning the instrument as one goes on.*
>
> —SAMUEL BUTLER

We have expanded the section on special sources of stress. Recent world events have led to frequent and sustained trauma and terror. Appearing nightly on our living room screens, those events affect everyone empathically. These horrifying changes called for a chapter about acute and post-traumatic stress disorders. We have also added a chapter about money stress, a major source of stress in many of our lives. Employment has changed dramatically in the last few decades. In response to this we have added a chapter about job stress.

Some psychologists have proposed that happiness involves having more pleasant thoughts and images than unpleasant ones. Abraham Lincoln foretold this

> _Happiness is an inside job._
> —JOHN POWELL

when he said, "People are about as happy as they make up their minds to be." If this is true, then happiness is available to each and every one of us at almost any time. We cannot and would not want to promise you unending bliss, but this book will help you learn new, healthier ways of thinking about things.

We have collected stress management quotes for many years. We were delighted when the _West Coast Review of Books_ praised our first edition, emphasizing, "The authors have completely avoided the use of psychobabble and technical jargon, opting instead for quotes . . . witty, relaxed yet disarmingly effective." Shortly thereafter, we began calling these quotes "copelets" because each one briefly, poetically, and powerfully expresses the essence of a valuable strategy with which to cope.

> _It has happened many times—no one knows how many—that a simple saying has drastically altered the course of a life._
> —EARL NIGHTINGALE

For most of us, coping is just surviving in an increasingly stressful world. For some psychologists, however, coping represents the most effective of ego processes. Coping allows the person to handle events realistically and flexibly in such a way as to maintain and promote mental and physical health. We hope our copelets help you cope.

Shakespeare wrote, "There is nothing either good or bad, but thinking makes it so." A crisis or a mistake may be stressful but can be accepted as a part of our journey and even viewed as an opportunity to learn and grow from the experience of life. Thus, by taking on the challenge of stress in our lives and approaching the journey in new ways, we can learn about ourselves, accept our strengths and weaknesses, and grow from both our successes and our failures.

> *It was the best of times, it was the worst of times.*
> —CHARLES DICKENS

Research and resources on spiritual interventions for stress have been of such importance that we offer you a new chapter introducing spiritual stress management.

Those thought-provoking words from Dickens are relevant for our health care system today. Patients around the world with burns, injuries, or unusual diseases come to the United States for emergency treatment of a kind that is unsurpassed. A major disadvantage in our model of medicine is that it is based on disease, trauma, acute care, and emergencies. As a country, however, we are struggling with chronic illnesses from lifestyle choices, aging, and stress. A recent article in the *Journal of the American Medical Association* reviewed the status of health care here and called attention to the fact that "of 13 countries in a recent comparison, the United States ranks an average of 12th for 16 available health indicators."

The application of an acute care model to chronic illness does not lead to lifestyle changes that the individual can responsibly implement. In the late 1970s we saw the growing need for individuals to take responsibility for their wellness, but at that time health care insurance was not in a state of crisis, pharmaceuticals were affordable, and doctors could invest more time in treatment and less in practice management.

Now more than ever, the responsibility for much of your health and happiness rests squarely on your shoulders. You cannot wait until the health care delivery system is healed. You have to start with yourself, your lifestyle, and your body. Let the health care crisis motivate you more than ever to take charge of your life.

We hope that you will use this book to think new thoughts, feel new emotions, and undertake new activities that will not only reduce distress and disease but also bring you pleasure and wellness in every area of your life.

> *There are many truths of which the full meaning cannot be realized until personal experience has brought it home.*
>
> —JOHN STUART MILL

EDWARD A. CHARLESWORTH
Houston, Texas

RONALD G. NATHAN
Albany, New York

*January 2005*

## ACKNOWLEDGMENTS

MANY PEOPLE HAVE CONTRIBUTED TO THIS BOOK AND HELPED TO bring it to press. The first edition of this book would never have become a Book-of-the-Month Club selection and been published internationally if it were not for the commitment and expertise of our outstanding agent, John Ware. In addition, we must thank John for recommending this completely revised, updated, and expanded edition to our publisher. We also wish to acknowledge our editors, Neil Nyren and Susan Leon of Atheneum (Scribner's) and Tim Mak of Ballantine Books (Random House), for their vision, guidance, and hard work to help us refine the final editions to be both more concise, readable, and understandable.

We thank all the doctors, counselors, ministers, and educators who have recommended the first edition of this book to their valued patients, clients, parishioners, and students. We hope this edition is as worthy of your continued support.

There are many individuals we need to thank for making this first revised edition for the twenty-first century become reality. First, we would like to thank Brittany Charlesworth for the countless hours typing and retyping the original drafts and proofreading our numerous changes. Robin Charlesworth, M.A., not only proofed our chapters but also made numerous suggestions that reflected her insights as a truly gifted therapist. Many sections were greatly enhanced by her wisdom.

Special and deep appreciation is extended to William Braud, Ph.D., and Eugene Doughtie, Ph.D., for their early inspiration, research, and academic guidance in exploring the physiological and psychological aspects of stress management. Both Paul Baer, Ph.D., and Ben Williams, Ph.D., gave countless hours of time in developing early research and clinical materials that allowed us to explore the effectiveness of our techniques. Nema Frye, M.S., R.D., shared her expertise and collaborated with the authors in writing the first edition's chapters about exercise and nutrition. The basic outline of the first edition reflects their contributions, which deserve full acknowledgment and are sincerely appreciated. Beverly Graves, R.N., and Carol Loggins, R.N., were also highly instrumental in helping to test our materials for the first edition in a corporate setting.

We are truly in debt to Shirley Hickox for her painstaking editing and proofreading of several drafts of the first edition. If this book is readable, much of the credit belongs to Shirley and Robin Charlesworth, M.A., who generously volunteered hundreds of hours to help our readers. Various drafts were also read and critiqued by Sue Crow, R.N., William Day, M.D., Sharon P. Davidson, M.S.W., Marilyn Gibson, M.A., Fred Kotzin, Ph.D., Mary Lou McNeil, M.D., Gregory Lees, Bill Myerson, Ph.D., Art Peiffer, Ph.D., and Dean Robinson, M.D. Thank you for your valuable comments.

More recently, we have been blessed with people who have been especially helpful. Dr. Charlesworth would like to thank Dr. Thomas DeBauche, cardiologist, and Dr. Dale Hamilton, endocrinologist, who have both, over many years, helped shape an appreciation for the intricate influences of mind and body and helped facilitate the application of these techniques for lifestyle changes with patients with serious endocrine and cardiac diseases. Dr. Dennis Smith has been influential in helping refine techniques for use with chronic pain patients and those recovering from life-threatening and debilitating injuries. Dr. Robert Galloway, director of the Galloway Wellness Center, and Susie Bruce, YMCA director of health and wellness, gave us numerous excellent suggestions to enhance the chapters on exercise, nutrition, and complementary and alternative medicine to ensure they reflected the current knowledge of these incredibly fascinating, and ever-changing, sciences. Dr. Ernest Charlesworth, brother and board-certified allergist and dermatologist, has been a true blessing and helped influence the areas of mind-body understanding in his specialty areas. Bud Hadfield, founder of Kwik Kopy International and the International Center for Entrepreneurial Development, and his lovely and talented wife, Mary, have been supportive and helpful, as many of the techniques were refined to empower the businessmen and businesswomen who form the foundation of the American economy. A special thanks to the Reverend Joe Gossett for the many hours of conversations and exchanges to help start the foundation of weaving a spiritual component into the practice of stress management. A special thanks must also be extended to Rotary International and the many Rotarian friends of Dr. Charlesworth who, through their emphasis on "service above self," have helped provide a foundation for the importance of finding a meaningful and purposeful lifestyle through service as an important facet of a successful stress management program.

Dr. Nathan would like to thank an outstanding attorney, judge, and friend, Arnold W. Proskin; deeply valued colleagues Gene Bont, M.D., Phyllis Bont, R.N., F.N.P., Jose David, M.D., Howard Malamood, M.D., Larry Malerba, D.O., Mary Malerba, R.N., Michael Piplani, M.D., and Randall Taubman, M.D.; spiritual brothers David Hitz, M.D., Skip MacCarty, D.Min., David Miller, Rick Marsan, the Reverend Fred L. Shilling, and Billy Watkins; the staff at the Guilderland Public Library, especially the interlibrary loan and reference librarians; Peter at PLV; Poci's talented pit crew, Jason, Jeffrey, Jitterbug, Malibu, and Sue; and the many other people who have gone the extra mile for him, especially Bruce Barnaby, Patricia Kuehfus, George Conway, Raymond Eggert III, D.D.S., David Juneau, C.P.A., Lee Vinson, and David Wood.

A few words of acknowledgment are hardly sufficient to indicate the importance of the many hundreds of participants in our stress management groups. These people are the true authors of this book. They have been some of our best teachers. Only through their work have we been able to sift through the effective and ineffective techniques and suggestions that we have presented over the last thirty years. A sincere thank you to each and every one of you.

Finally, a very special thanks to our families for their consistent support, encouragement, and love: to our parents, who worked so hard to give us a head start on the road of life; to Susan Nathan, Ph.D., Vivian Campbell, E.M.T., and Ronald Campbell, who have always been there for their brother; Brittany Charlesworth, who devoted many hours in support of this revision; Allison Charlesworth, who is the greatest cheerleader in the world for her dad; and Robin Charlesworth, M.A., who endured many weekends of "work without play." They have sacrificed much, and we are grateful.

# CONTENTS

### SECTION IV
## *Attacking Your Stressful Behaviors, Thoughts, and Attitudes*

### SECTION V
## *Communicating Your Needs and Feelings*

### SECTION VI
## *Planning the Days of Your Life*

### SECTION VII
## *Enhancing Health and Preventing Disease*

# STRESS
## MANAGEMENT

# SECTION I

## Learning About Stress and Your Life

*The real voyage of discovery consists not in seeking new lands, but seeing with new eyes.*
—MARCEL PROUST

ONE

# How Do You Respond to Stress?

*The awareness that health is dependent upon habits that we control makes us the first generation in history that to a large extent determines its own destiny.*
—JIMMY CARTER

## STRESS AND OUR ANCESTORS

WE LIVE IN A NEW AGE OF ANXIETY, CENTURY OF STRESS, AND ERA of terrorism. Once the name Columbine brought to mind only a beautiful mountain flower and September 11 was just another day on the calendar. The history books that our grandchildren read will speak of the alarming increases in health and social problems related to the tensions and stress of our times. You may well ask, has man always been nervous and anxious? The plays of Shakespeare included many examples of the stress response. One of the most respected medical textbooks of the 1600s gave excellent descriptions of anxiety states. In fact, our nervous responses can be traced to the prehistoric cave dweller.

Imagine a cave dweller sitting near a small fire in the comfort of a cave. Suddenly, in the light of the fire, up comes the shadow of a saber-toothed tiger. The body reacts instantly. To survive, the cave dweller had to respond by either fighting or running. A complex part of our brains and bodies called the autonomic nervous system prepared the cave dweller for fight or flight. This nervous system was once thought to be automatic and beyond our control. Here is a partial list of the responses set up by the autonomic nervous system and how you may recognize them from your own experience.

1. Digestion slows and blood is redirected to the muscles and the brain. It is more important to be alert and strong in the face of danger than to digest food. Have you ever felt this as butterflies in your stomach?

2. Breathing gets faster to supply more oxygen for the needed muscles. Can you remember trying to catch your breath after being frightened?

3. The heart speeds up and blood pressure soars, forcing blood to parts of the body that need it. When was the last time you felt your heart pounding?

4. Perspiration increases to cool the body and release a scent signaling preparation for a fight. This allows the body to burn more energy and warns others of danger. Do you use extra deodorant when you know you are going to be under stress?

5. Muscles tense to prepare for rapid action and form muscle "armor" to slow tooth, fist, or spear. Have you ever had a stiff back or neck after a stressful day?

6. Chemicals are released to make the blood clot more rapidly. If injured, this clotting can reduce blood loss.

Have you noticed how quickly some wounds stop bleeding?

7. Sugars and fats pour into the blood to provide fuel for quick energy. Have you ever been surprised by your strength and endurance during an emergency?

The cave dweller lived in the jungle or the wilderness and faced many environmental stressors. Often these were immediate, life-threatening events involving dangerous animals or human enemies. For the cave dweller, this fight-or-flight response was very valuable for survival.

## Stress and Our Modern World

We have the same automatic stress responses that the cave dweller used for dangerous situations, but now we are seldom faced with a need for fight or flight. If a cat is threatened, it will arch its back. A deer will run into the bush. When we are threatened, we brace ourselves, but we often struggle to contain our nervous reactions because the threat is not usually one of immediate physical harm. Bosses, budgets, audiences, deadlines, and examinations are not life-threatening, but sometimes we feel as though they are.

Smaller stressors and briefer stress responses can add up to hundreds a day. These can be parts of our lives that we hardly notice and almost take for granted. If you work in an office, stress may accumulate with every ring of the telephone and every meeting you squeeze into your already busy day. If you are a homemaker, all the endless tasks you alone have to complete can mount up just as quickly and take just as much of a toll as those faced in the office.

Our ability to think of the past and imagine the future is still another way in which stress responses can be triggered at any time and in any place. In addition, distance is no longer a buffer. Turning on a television or a computer makes us instantly aware of wars, famine, disasters, political unrest, economic chaos, and frightening possibilities for the future.

The rate of change in our lives is accelerating. We need only to read Alvin Toffler's classic *Future Shock* or James Gleick's *Faster: The Acceleration of Just About Everything* to realize that the unexpected has become a part of our everyday lives. These unexpected situations are not ones we can overcome physically. Tigers are seen primarily in zoos, but it is as if we see their stripes and sharp teeth manifested in all too many ways in our everyday world.

Not only do we seem to trigger our stress response more often, but also most situations do not provide an outlet for the extra chemical energy produced by our bodies. The fight-or-flight response is not useful for most of the stress situations in modern life because we have few physical battles to fight and almost nowhere to run. In the past, the demands for fulfilling basic needs for food and safety made good use of our heightened arousal. Today, few of these outlets are available.

> *We are influenced not by "facts" but by our interpretation of facts.*
>
> —ALFRED ADLER

## PHYSICAL STRESS VERSUS EMOTIONAL STRESS

When we think about what has happened or what might happen, we cannot run from our anxieties or physically attack our fears. We are undergoing emotional stress. The body has only limited ways of using the output of its various stress reactions to cope with emotional stress.

Physical stress is different from emotional stress. Even exercise triggers a stress response. In fact, for many years, scientists relied on the research in exercise physiology as a basis for understanding the effects of both psychological and physical stress upon the body. Although the effects of physical and emotional stress are similar, we now know that there are differences between them.

Many hormones are elevated during the stress response. Three of them are norepinephrine, epinephrine, and cortisol. Norepinephrine and epinephrine are more commonly known as adrenaline. In response to a physical stressor, such as extremes in environmental temperature or stress induced by exercise, there is primarily an increase in norepinephrine. There is also a small increase in epinephrine. In response to a psychological or emotional stressor, there is also an increase in cortisol. To understand the effects of stress, we need to study the effects of each hormone that is secreted in response to a stressor.

In general, norepinephrine has the greatest effect in increasing heart rate and blood pressure. Epinephrine has the greatest effect in releasing stored sugar. All of these actions tend to aid in preparation for vigorous physical activity.

Cortisol acts to aid in preparation for vigorous physical activity, but it is also triggered by emotional stress. Unfortunately, one of its functions is to break down lean tissue for conversion to sugar as an additional source of energy. Cortisol also blocks the removal of certain acids in the bloodstream. When cortisol is elevated in the blood for prolonged periods of time, it causes ulcerations in the

> *Man, once the victorious predator, is now preying upon himself.*
>
> —HANS SELYE

lining of the stomach because of increased acid formation. In addition, cortisol strains the brain's cellular functioning, or, as one doctor explains, "it fries the brain."

## OTHER EFFECTS OF EMOTIONAL STRESS

Even if we could somehow burn off all the chemicals produced by emotional stress, upsetting psychological distress can interfere with productivity, learning, and interpersonal relationships. If our stress reactions increase, we become less and less able to handle even minor stress. Usually our ability to interact with and understand other people is also disrupted. We can exhaust our adaptive energy reserves and become more susceptible to diseases. It is clear that for life in the twenty-first century, our fight-or-flight and emotional stress mechanisms are often both unnecessary and harmful.

## BALANCING EMERGENCY AND MAINTENANCE SYSTEMS

The autonomic nervous system has two divisions. One division is called the sympathetic nervous system and the other is the parasympathetic nervous system. Let's return to the caveman sitting in front of his fire. The caveman's response to the tiger included increased heart rate and breathing. These responses were automatic and controlled by the sympathetic nervous system. The parasympathetic nervous system influences the body in ways that are almost the exact opposite of those of the sympathetic nervous system. For example, the parasympathetic nervous system decreases heart rate, slows breathing, retards perspiration, and accelerates stomach and gastrointestinal activity for the proper digestion of food.

> *Caesar did not merit the triumphal car more than he that conquers himself.*
>
> —BEN FRANKLIN

If the sympathetic division can be thought of as an emergency system, the parasympathetic division can be thought of as a maintenance system. This maintenance system is responsible for the conservation and replenishment of energy. Scientists have evidence to suggest that our parasympathetic nervous system can be activated through relaxation procedures such as are used in stress management training programs. Maybe we can all learn to replace fight-

or-flight responses with what have been called stay-and-play responses.

## Hans Selye and the General Adaptation Syndrome

Dr. Hans Selye is often referred to as the "father of stress research." His pioneering work demonstrated that every demand on the body evokes not only physiological responses specific to the demand but also the nonspecific and uniform stress responses we have already discussed. Selye called the nonspecific reactions to stress the general adaptation syndrome. It consists of three stages: alarm reaction, resistance, and exhaustion.

During the alarm reaction, the stressor activates the body to prepare for fight or flight. Both electrical and hormonal signals are involved in mobilizing the energy needed for an emergency. Heart rate, breathing, and perspiration increase. The pupils of the eyes dilate. Adrenaline and cortisol are released. Stored energy floods the bloodstream.

According to Selye, if the stress is strong enough, death may result during the alarm reaction. In fact, the immune response is suppressed as energy is devoted to fight or flight.

During the resistance stage of adaptation to stress, the signs of the alarm reaction are diminished or nonexistent. The immune system bounces back and resistances to noxious stimuli and illnesses such as infectious diseases increase above their normal level. Hormones that reduce inflammation from injuries also increase.

If the stressful stimuli or responses persist, the stage of resistance is followed by a stage of exhaustion. By this stage, the exposure to a stressor has nearly depleted the organism's adaptive energy. The signs of the initial alarm reaction reappear, but they do not abate. Resistance decreases, vulnerability increases, and illness or death may follow.

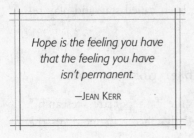

*Hope is the feeling you have that the feeling you have isn't permanent.*

—JEAN KERR

The general adaptation syndrome has great importance as an early theory linking stress and disease. It stimulated much research contributing to our understanding of stress and resistance as factors in every illness. Stress may interfere with our ability to resist most diseases, but we now also know that the ability to manage stress adaptively can be learned. When this skill is used, stress is enjoyed as a challenge rather than dreaded as a threat.

## FEMALE STRESS AND THE TENDING INSTINCT

Most of our biological understanding of the stress response is based on research using male rats because the hormones of female rats fluctuate rapidly and complicate the results. Prior to the government's mandate in 1995 that human research studies had to include both sexes, less than 20 percent of the participants in biological stress research were women. In addition, men conducted most of this research. Shelley E. Taylor, a UCLA psychologist, recognized that this male bias might be one of the few "big mistakes left in science."

The fight-or-flight response might describe the male's life-saving response to attack, but this arousal might be only part of the solution for females with offspring. Flight by a mother would be impaired with children in tow and could be fatal for children left unprotected. The fight might be necessary but could be fatal to the mother and her young. Evading detection and creating a community with strength in numbers might be far safer.

Taylor proposed a "tending instinct" for women that is revealed in a biologically based "tend-and-befriend response." This nurturing and protecting response is principally supported by oxytocin, a hormone that is best known for prompting labor and milk production. Other hormones include endogenous opioid peptides, popularly known for initiating the "runner's high." On the other side, androgen hormones, such as testosterone, regulate male aggression. Joining forces and watching out for one another is important for survival of both men and women, but it may be more critical for the "nurturer sex."

After reviewing thirty scientific studies of what men and women do in response to many different kinds of stress, Taylor concluded that all research revealed women turning to friends, neighbors, and relatives more than men did. Primitive behavior reflects the same bonds. Female primates share their food, groom each other, babysit, and join to defend their young.

The tend-and-befriend response is an exciting new discovery. Research about the response is in its infancy compared to that on the fight-or-flight response, but the implications for stress and its management are many. We have already seen how the fight-or-flight response can help or harm. It may surprise you that the tend-and-befriend response can also help or harm. Thus, women reap the benefits but also pay the cost of both stress responses.

## STRESS AND DISEASE

If your doctor has recommended that you relax or take it easy, you may be suffering from a stress-related disorder. It is estimated that up to 75 percent of all visits to physicians are from people with a stress-related problem. Stress may be a major factor in causing hypertension and coronary heart disease, migraine and tension headaches, and immune and asthmatic conditions. Stress may lead to harmful habits such as smoking, drinking, or overeating, which have been shown to cause or intensify still other diseases. Stress is also suspected to aggravate chronic backache, arthritis, allergies, diabetes, hyperthyroidism, vertigo, and multiple sclerosis.

Dermatologists find that stress is a factor in many skin disorders such as hives, eczema, and dermatitis. It has also been strongly associated with many gastrointestinal disorders, including irritable colon and gastritis. Some of the excess hormones that the adrenal glands release during repeated stress responses can interfere with your body's immunity to infection. You may then become more susceptible to bacteria and viruses such as the flu virus.

## STRESS AND MENTAL HEALTH

Stress not only affects our bodies, but it also affects the way we think, feel, and interact with others. Have you ever come home after an unusually stressful day feeling irritable and still thinking about problems at work? At such times, your family already knows without asking that you had a hard day.

Sometimes we pass our irritability along to others. The stock market drops, for example, and the boss blows up at her secretary for not doing enough work. The secretary goes home and screams at his children for being too loud. The children scold their dog for being bad, when the dog just wanted to play. Do you have any idea what happened to the cat when the dog finally caught it? Stress can disrupt our lives as it ripples from person to person and even person to pet.

The gender we chose for the boss and secretary in the last paragraph may seem an awkward attempt at political correctness, but in this edition the change was necessary to reflect fascinating new research results. A study questioned children about their parents' behavior toward them and compared their answers with reported workday events by their parents. It showed that on days when one or both of their parents were stressed at work, the children felt picked on or left alone by the fathers and hugged or played with by their mothers. The results support that the gender differences and stress responses, with men fighting or fleeing and women tending or befriending the children, are real.

The effects of long-term stress on our mental health can be devastating. Most of us can bounce back from a bad day at work, school, or home, but we may be unable to do so if stress continues day after day. Under long-term stress, our personalities may change.

We may suffer from depression and feel hopeless, helpless, and worthless. Occasionally we may feel tense and explosive. Sometimes we find ourselves compulsively repeating meaningless tasks in an attempt to control our lives. At times, we act impulsively without thinking about the consequences. At other times, we have exaggerated fears of such simple acts as leaving our house, traveling by airplane, or riding in an elevator.

The changes we experience after long-term stress may have many causes. These causes may be very complex or as simple as learning an unhealthy response. Whether the cause is simple or complex, the problem physical or mental, stress can intensify our difficulties.

Some of the disorders initiated or intensified by stress may affect women more than men. One explanation is women's tend-and-befriend response. For example, twice as many women suffer from depression as men. Women are especially prone to depression after a death of a child, when children leave the home, and during separation, divorce, or other isolating events. In addition, there are dangers for women in caregiving. Women tend to the aging, ill, and disabled more often than men. Over half of caregivers work outside the home, and many need to quit their jobs to allow for the more than ten hours a day caregiving consumes. For elderly caregivers it can put their lives at risk, especially if they can't ask for help and time off. Almost 60 percent become depressed, develop cardiovascular diseases, or become vulnerable to illnesses such as the flu. In fact, a University of Pittsburgh study showed that the chances of an elderly care-

> *The healthy, the strong individual, is the one who asks for help when he needs it. Whether he's got an abscess on his knee or his soul.*
>
> —RONA BARRETT

giver dying in a four-year period were 60 percent higher than those without such responsibilities.

## THE CURRENT SCORE IN THE STRESS ARENA

We have begun to tackle the age of anxiety, but we still have an enormous task ahead. Stress is clearly winning at this time. Here are some of the current scores in the arena of stress. They may be categorized as the three D's: disorders, drugs, and dollars.

### DISORDERS

*67 million* Americans have some form of major heart disease or blood-vessel disease.

*1 million* Americans die from a heart attack every year.

*69 million* Americans have high blood pressure.

*18 million* Americans are alcoholics.

*31 million* people have diabetes associated with obesity and physical inactivity.

*108 million* adults are either obese or overweight.

*300,000* preventable deaths annually are caused by modifiable, behavioral patterns.

### DRUGS

*6 billion* doses of tranquilizers are prescribed each year.

*4 billion* doses of muscle relaxants are prescribed each year.

*4 billion* doses of antidepressants are prescribed each year.

*5 billion* doses of painkillers are prescribed each year.

*4 million* people are abusing prescription drugs (pain relievers, stimulants, sedatives, or tranquilizers).

### DOLLARS (AND DAYS)

*$300 billion* is lost annually by American industry from stress-related reasons (lost time, extra costs for health insurance, and the costs of replacing employees).

*$246 billion* is lost annually by American industry from alcoholism and drug abuse.

*$200 billion* annually is spent for treatment and lost productivity from obesity-related illness.

*$100 billion* is lost annually to American businesses (through health care expenses and lost productivity) from chronic pain.

*132 million* workdays a year are lost because of stress-related absenteeism and lost productivity.

*Sources: Office of Applied Studies, Substance Abuse and Mental Health Services Administration, U.S. Department of Health and Human Services, Centers for Disease Control and Prevention, and National Center for Health Statistics*

These numbers may seem impersonal. They do not reflect the pain and suffering of the victims of stress and their loved ones.

## HEALTHY STRESS

Not all stress is harmful. As a source of motivation and energy, stress can spur us on to creative work, and it can enrich our pleasurable activities. Hans Selye made this clear in his book *Stress Without Distress*. We even pay for stress when we go on a roller coaster ride, go to the track, or see a scary movie.

> *Never face facts; if you do, you'll never get up in the morning.*
>
> —MARLO THOMAS

There is an important difference between life's stimulating thrills and its overwhelming anxieties. This is why it is best to manage stress responses rather than try to remove them. Let's begin the journey.

## How This Book Is Organized

Each chapter in this book introduces information or a technique that research or clinical work has shown to be an effective way to understand or manage stress. We have selected stress management concepts and skills that people have been able to learn in relatively short periods of time. In fact, the hundreds of people whom we have helped to become successful stress managers chose the skills you will learn. Some skills are more difficult to learn than others and are best learned after some easier ones have been mastered. We have arranged the material to help you build on skills that are found in the earlier chapters of this book.

> *I know well what I am fleeing from, but not what I am in search of.*
> —MICHEL DE MONTAIGNE

## How to Use This Book

Most of the individuals and groups that we counsel and train are taught one technique each session. We explain the method and give participants instructions so they can practice the skill during the session. Most of the relaxation procedures, such as those in Section 2, have immediate positive effects. After the session, the participants are encouraged to practice the new technique every day during the next week. This practice usually enables them to learn the skill and begin receiving some of its benefits by applying it in stressful situations.

To get the most from this book, we recommend that you progress through it like a workbook and practice one procedure at a time. Many hospitals and clinics now teach stress management to individuals or groups. You may be using this book as part of such a program. If a psychologist or other qualified professional is guiding your training, follow his or her recommendations. Basic mastery of this stress management program from start to finish takes several weeks to several months of practice. Very few people can learn to use and enjoy stress management skills effectively in less time.

On the other hand, as psychologists, we know that people vary widely in the way they learn and change. Perhaps you have already learned ways through earlier training or experimentation to recognize your stressors and to relax your body quickly and deeply. If so, you may want to skim the next chapter as well as the chapters in Section 2 and start learning some of the skills in the remaining chapters. Some people will want to practice a few skills while reading through this book and come back to master the skills

> *You can only cure retail, but you can prevent wholesale.*
>
> —BROCK CHISHOLM

they found most useful. If you decide not to follow our recommendations to practice one skill at a time, try to look back over what you have learned successfully in the past and use the same approach in learning to manage stress.

Some people may prefer to read this material as a book rather than using it as a workbook. If you enjoy reading a book from cover to cover, we invite you to do so. In some ways, this would be like reading a good cookbook. Perhaps you would try out some of the recipes for stress management or save one for a special occasion. Maybe you would put some of the recipes in a convenient place and at a later time plan your strategy for coping effectively with a stressful situation.

# The Challenge of Stress
# and the Benefits of Wellness

*The first wealth is health.*
—RALPH WALDO EMERSON

HAVE YOU EVER WONDERED WHY SOME PEOPLE SEEM TO BE COM-
fortable in almost any situation? They seem calm and collected
even when they make the most important decisions. They project
a sense of quiet confidence and seem to have overcome the fears
most of us associate with modern life.

Many of these people have felt the same anxiety that others
feel, but they have cultivated ways of relaxing in the most difficult
situations. Instead of focusing on the fears or anxieties of life, they
view life as an opportunity for more than just coping. They see it
as a challenge, but one to be enjoyed.

These are the winners in the game of life. There are signs that more and more people are enhancing their enjoyment of life and not just coping with the status quo. Men and women are the most adaptive creatures on the face of the earth. We can live in almost any environment, even in space and under the sea.

The people who are most likely to survive and succeed in this and future generations will be those who can find enjoyment in adapting to a rapidly changing world. Before we talk about the skills of the winners in life, let's talk about some of the approaches that have failed to work.

## BOTTLED TRANQUILIZERS

To help overcome excessive and chronic stress responses and to relieve feelings of being uptight, many people turn to a variety of tranquilizing medications, narcotic drugs, and alcohol. These external agents have helped many through periods of trauma, but they do not modify the fight-or-flight response mechanism.

> These drugs and chemicals cannot think for us. They cannot decide what stress is good and what stress is bad. A tranquilizer cannot decide if a stress response comes from healthy excitement or debilitating anxiety. Ill habits gather by unseen degrees, as brooks make rivers, rivers run to seas.
>
> —JOHN DRYDEN

Over time, many users actually increase their stress by fighting the sedative side effects of the drugs in an effort to maintain alertness. Instead of increasing their internal control over stress, they become more and more dependent on drugs to offset its effects.

## THE BENEFITS OF WELLNESS

Because of the shortcomings of drug therapy, much scientific research has been directed toward finding alternative means of stress management. From this work, a number of effective procedures have emerged. Some of these teach you ways to relax and gain control over stress, tension, and anxiety. Other techniques teach you how to change stressful attitudes, beliefs, and actions. There are also procedures that help you release the emotional and physical effects of stress.

It's clear that we're willing to take on this challenge. More and more people are exercising and practicing relaxation and stress management skills. Large companies are building wellness centers for stress release, physical fitness, and relaxation.

When companies build wellness centers and promote lifestyle changes, their costs can be repaid through improved employee health and decreased health care costs, as was demonstrated in a major study reported by Dr. Charlesworth and his colleagues at Baylor College of Medicine. After ten weekly lunch hour sessions of stress management training, using the techniques in this book, a group of forty hypertensive employees had significantly reduced their blood pressure beyond the results of standard medical care. Three years later, their blood pressures remained lower or in some cases had decreased even further. In addition, the program decreased the costs of their health insurance claims by over 60 percent. More and more studies are showing the many benefits of wellness.

## WELLNESS: ENHANCING YOUR HEALTH

These changes are signs of progress, but we are just beginning to understand the psychology of stress. There are truly vast frontiers to explore in regard to the physical and psychological health-enhancing properties of stress management and relaxation. Thus techniques such as the ones you are about to learn have the potential to go beyond the treatment or the prevention of disease and into the frontiers of health enhancement. If these techniques can truly enhance health, a stress management program could not only help prevent some diseases but also make you healthier and more productive. This is what we mean by "wellness."

Nonpharmacological approaches to the management of stress and the enhancement of health are nonaddictive. They can be set aside until they are needed and can readily be called up as situations demand. For many people, this program will help replace tranquilizing pills with calming skills.

Stress management training is not a cure-all. Instead, it is a change in lifestyle and a new way of viewing the world. You acquire the habit of relaxation and trade the stress and strain of daily living for a relaxed and enjoyable way of seeing and doing things. You might be able to reduce your stress by dropping out of society, but you would be throwing out the good with the bad. Stress management is another alternative. You can learn to manage your stress and enhance your wellness by changing your responses to modern society.

> There is no cure for birth and death save to enjoy the interval.
> —GEORGE SANTAYANA

# THREE

# Discovering Where Stress Comes From

*Kites rise highest against the wind—not with it.*
—SIR WINSTON CHURCHILL

STRESS HAS BECOME A HOUSEHOLD WORD, BUT WHAT IS IT? HOW does it affect you? How can you recognize stress in your life?

Stress has many meanings, but most people think of stress as the demands of life. Technically, these demands are called stressors, and the actual wear and tear on our bodies is the stress.

The demands or challenges of life can come from people and events around us, as well as from our inner thoughts and struggles. When these demands increase, people often feel that they are under excessive stress.

One of our goals is to present better ways not only to help you learn to live with stressful situations but also to help you find more enjoyment in meeting and mastering the challenges of our changing world. You should not have to give up the challenges of life that you enjoy and want to keep. You might be bored if you were forced to spend your days sitting in an easy chair or meditating on a mountaintop. When you live successfully in a stressful world, you will neither burn out nor rust out.

Most people are not aware of their minute-to-minute stress responses. For better or worse, we learn to ignore, overcome, or accept them as part of living. What are these important stress responses?

## Short-Term Stress Responses

At times, we are all too aware of how stress affects us. Have you ever felt that your stomach was jittery or full of butterflies? Maybe you had a lump in your throat or your chest felt tight. Perhaps your pulse raced and your heart pounded. You may have felt pain in your neck and shoulders from tension. Maybe you felt sweaty or all wound up. Thoughts may have raced through your mind, but when someone asked a question, your mind went blank. You may have flown off the handle about something minor. Can you remember getting upset and having any of these responses? Most of us have experienced some of these feelings at one time or another.

## Long-Term Responses to Stress

The short-term stress responses are physical, emotional, or behavioral warning signs. If the stress becomes chronic and incessant, the short-term warnings become more serious stress responses. Some people work longer and harder but actually become less productive. For many, the words "I don't have time" become a way of life. Dangerous stress disorders can follow changes in the way we feel and in the way we act. For example, some people become withdrawn or depressed.

Smoking and drinking may become problems. One's sexual life may suffer. Pain associated with headaches, arthritis, and other chronic diseases may increase. Some people eat more and gain weight, while others eat less and lose weight. Sleeplessness and sleepiness may become problems. Daydreaming and difficulties with concentration are common. Feelings of suspiciousness, worthlessness, inadequacy, or rejection may become prominent.

Too many of us have some of these experiences too much of the time. We find ourselves anticipating the worst and being nervous before anything has happened. We may not recognize how our personality has changed. Even if the change is pointed out to us, we may not believe we have changed.

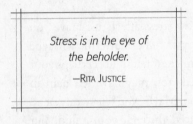

*Stress is in the eye of the beholder.*

—RITA JUSTICE

The following explanations and diagrams will help you to understand what your stressors are and how you respond to them. Notice that no matter where stress comes from, if the short-term effects occur intensely and frequently, the long-term costs are the same—the quality of your life suffers. On the other hand, if you increase and fine-tune your coping skills, your life and health actually improve.

## STRESSORS: WHERE DOES STRESS COME FROM?

We broadly define stressors as the external demands of life or the internal attitudes and thoughts that require us to adapt. Stressors can include traffic jams, pollution, the latest bad news on CNN, that fifth cup of coffee, the pushy salesman who will not take no for an answer, or the angry boss. Stressors can also include the work that never seems to get done, the children who never seem to listen, or the way some people put themselves down for their shortcomings. Notice that some of these stressors come from our surroundings and others from our inner struggles. Some stressors come from both sources.

Many elements contribute to a stressor being stressful. There are certainly individual differences among us. Hans Selye said, "You can't make a racehorse out of a turtle." How much control we have over the stressor and whether we feel we have a choice in our exposure to it will determine our response. If you "have to" work late because your boss "made you," for example, you will respond differently than if you "choose to" work late because you want to finish the project and take the weekend off. The compatibility between a person's background, aspirations, and interests and his or her work will also determine how stressful the work seems.

Reviewing stressors in different categories will help you become more aware of the varieties of stress in your life. As you read the brief descriptions that follow, think about an average day and consider how each stressor may be reducing your enjoyment of life.

## EMOTIONAL STRESSORS

Emotional stressors include the fears and anxieties with which we struggle: "Can we prevent terrorism and nuclear war?" "What if I lose my job?" "What if I get ill with a deadly virus or an antibiotic-resistant germ?" Additional emotional stressors include worrying about unpaid bills, fretting about your children, or taking an exam.

The messages we silently give ourselves about our actions and the actions of others are also emotional stressors. Telling ourselves how awfully we are going to do in some activity is an emotional stressor that may lead to poor performance. On the other hand, consistently denying that we need to be prepared and do our homework may also be an emotional stressor and can lead to failure. Both "awfulizing" about tomorrow and procrastinating about today's activities can trigger stress responses.

## FAMILY STRESSORS

Interactions with family members can be stressful. The family structure has been changing drastically. The institution of marriage was once a strong, supportive force that could help family members cope with other stressors. Now, nearly half of all marriages end in divorce, and an estimated 40 percent of children born in the last decade will spend at least part of their youth in homes with only one parent.

Families go through various stages of stress even if divorce is not a factor. The birth of a child places new demands for adaptation on a family. The striving of teenagers for independence can lead to struggles between parent and child. In addition, families must adapt as the teenagers become adults and move away. Finally, families must cope with aging parents and grandparents. Some adults are even in a "sandwich generation," caring for their children and their parents at the same time.

## SOCIAL STRESSORS

Social stressors involve our interactions with other people. Asking a person for a date, giving a speech, and expressing anger are common social stressors. Attending parties may be stressful for the person who likes quiet evenings at

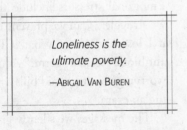

*Loneliness is the ultimate poverty.*

—ABIGAIL VAN BUREN

home. On the other hand, the outgoing person may find staying at home every night stressful.

Social stressors vary widely from person to person. What brings relief from stress for one person may contribute to the stress of another person.

## CHEMICAL STRESSORS

Chemical stressors may include any drug a person abuses, such as alcohol. Chemical stressors also include the pesticides or sweeteners in foods we eat. Caffeine is a common chemical stressor. Nicotine in tobacco is another. Some chemical stressors are less under our control. For example, we may live in a city where the water we drink contains chemicals. Likewise, many foods have chemical additives.

## CHANGE STRESSORS

It has been said that there are discoverable limits to the amount of change that humans can absorb. Since 1900, the rate of change has been accelerating at a speed previously unimagined. In the decades since the first edition of this book we have seen dramatic changes in almost every area of life. We may be subjecting masses of people to changes that they will not be able to tolerate.

We experience change stressors when we alter anything important in our lives. When we leave a job, a house, or a relationship, part of our adjustment to our loss or to our new situation involves stress. When we move from one part of the country or city to another, we experience the change of uprooting. The loss of our social network and supports can be very stressful. Technological advances and the shifting framework of traditions and customs are also stressful changes.

Children, adolescents, and adults with attention deficit disorder (ADD) are especially challenged and struggle when dealing with change stressors. Those individuals experiencing depression will also find it more difficult to cope with life changes.

## THE TWO STRESS CYCLES

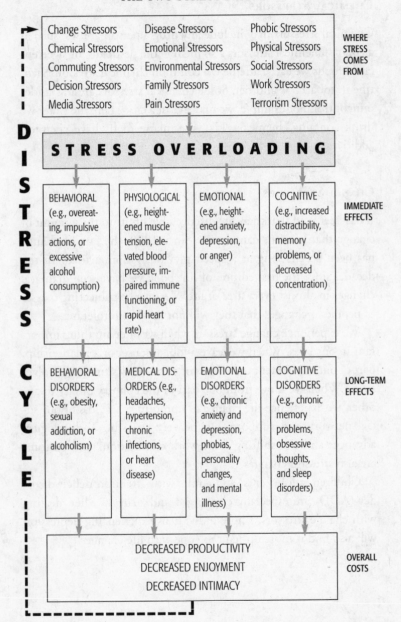

## DISTRESS AND WELLNESS

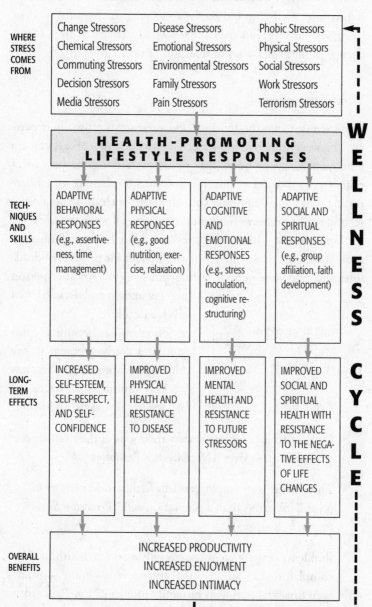

Stress management training is a change stressor because training requires giving up old habits and thoughts. Stressful ways of living are harmful, but they are also comfortable and hard to exchange for healthier ways of managing stress.

## WORK STRESSORS

Work stressors are the tensions and pressures we usually experience between nine and five o'clock at our place of work. If you are a homemaker, your hours may be longer. Asking the boss for a raise, trying to meet impossible deadlines, explaining an embarrassing mistake, disciplining your children, or cleaning the floor a second time to remove fresh mud tracks are all work stressors.

Work stressors, like social stressors, differ from individual to individual. One person may work well under the pressure of deadlines and find slow periods boring and stressful. Another person may get uptight and stressed when given a deadline.

> *The art of life consists of learning how to be obedient to events.*
>
> —MARIA MONTESSORI

Job stress has become a common and costly problem in the American workplace, leaving few workers untouched. For example, studies report the following:

- One-fourth of employees view their jobs as the number one stressor in their lives. (*Northwestern National Life*)

- Three-fourths of employees believe the worker has more on-the-job stress than a generation ago. (*Princeton Survey Research Associates*)

- Problems at work are more strongly associated with health complaints than are any other life stressors—more so than even financial problems or family problems. (*St. Paul Fire and Marine Insurance Co.*)

The gender composition of the workforce is also changing. Over 50 percent of adult women are now in the labor market. This group includes well over half of all mothers with school-age children.

Other changes have occurred in the working world. More than 50 percent of the labor force is white-collar. Fewer jobs are linked to end products such as merchandise, food, or the consumer. It has become more and more difficult to see the value of our individual contributions.

The importance of work stress in predicting life span was demonstrated in a government task force study on longevity and the workforce. The study found that "more so than any measure of physical health, the use of tobacco, or genetic inheritance, the number one predictor of longevity in this country is work satisfaction."

> *Work consists of whatever a body is obliged to do, and play consists of whatever a body is not obliged to do.*
>
> —MARK TWAIN

## DECISION STRESSORS

It has become more and more difficult to make decisions both on and off the job. Rational decisions depend on our ability to predict the consequences of our actions. Now our ability to make the best predictions is often compromised by more alternatives and less decision time. A good example of vocational decision stress is reflected in the occupational alternatives available to us. There was a time when a man became an apprentice to his father and a woman became a mother. A brief look at the thousands of jobs in the *Dictionary of Occupational Titles* confirms the potential confusion.

Decision stress on the job is also increasing. Certain jobs carry too much responsibility with too little authority. People experience ambiguity and conflicting job demands. Predictability and control in our rapidly changing world are increasingly unattainable. There are more possibilities to consider, but humans have only a limited capacity to push beyond certain limits; do so, and your stress response may sound an alarm.

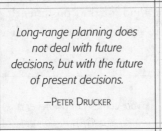

*Long-range planning does not deal with future decisions, but with the future of present decisions.*

—PETER DRUCKER

## COMMUTING STRESSORS

Many people commute long distances to work. Some people drive in rush-hour traffic daily. Others spend hours on a bus or train. Depending on your distance from work, the amount of traffic you encounter, and your mode of travel, commuting may or may not be a major stressor.

## PHOBIC STRESSORS

Many people have exaggerated fears of certain animals, places, objects, or situations that they know pose no immediate danger. These intense and recurrent fears are called phobias. The range of phobias is unlimited, and there are Greek names for almost anything a person can fear.

A dog bit one of the authors at the age of six. For eighteen years, he was afraid of dogs—not just the dog that bit him but most dogs, chained or unchained! This is an example of a conditioned fear. Many people have learned their phobia through such conditioning. Many of these people do not remember the connection or link that caused the phobia. The author realized that his fears were exaggerated and how they started, but by carefully avoiding dogs, he had never learned to overcome his phobic anxiety. Using the techniques that will be presented in this book, the

author not only overcame his phobia but also began enjoying the
companionship of "man's best
friend." This is an example of how
a stressor can become a source of
pleasure and recreation.

> Our doubts are traitors and
> make us lose the good we
> oft might win by fearing
> to attempt.
>
> —WILLIAM SHAKESPEARE

## PHYSICAL STRESSORS

Physical stressors are demands that change the state of our bodies. Physical stressors can be the strain we feel when we physically
overextend ourselves, fail to get enough sleep, lack an adequately
nutritious diet, or suffer an injury. Pregnancies, menstrual dis-
comforts, and menopause are examples of physical stressors that
are specific to women.

Physical stressors often involve increased physical demands.
Working eighty hours each week without getting adequate rest
can place a physical demand on the body. An abrupt change from
sustained high levels of activity to the boredom of low activity can
also be a stressor. For example, some heart attacks occur immediately after a busy period of time when a person finally has a chance
for rest.

## DISEASE STRESSORS

Disease stressors are those we experience as a result of long- or
short-term disorders. Many disease stressors are short-term and
place us under immediate but time-limited stress. We will concentrate here on chronic diseases, particularly those that may have
been inherited and last a lifetime. For example, some people are
born with a predisposition to develop headaches, arthritis, asthma,
allergies, ulcers, high blood pressure, diabetes, dermatitis, hyperthyroidism, multiple sclerosis, or hyperkinesis.

These conditions may or may not be caused by stress. None-theless, they can be aggravated by stress. With stress, the disease may increase in intensity. The attacks of the disease may last longer, and the frequency of the episodes may increase.

There is a theory that each person has genetically one or more weak systems within his or her body. For example, a young man may find that one or both of his parents had hypertension. He should monitor his blood pressure more frequently than a person without a family history of hypertension. He may have a predisposition toward manifesting stress through increases in his blood pressure. Knowing your weak system could enable you to use your body as a barometer of stress.

> *Financial ruin from medical bills is almost exclusively an American disease.*
>
> —ROUL TURLEY

## PAIN STRESSORS

Pain stressors are the aches and pains of new and old injuries, accidents, or diseases. Pains that cause people stress over a long period of time are particularly important. Old traumas to the joints, for example, can leave a person with painful osteoarthritis. This condition, like a chronic disease, can flare up in times of stress.

A person with headaches may be plagued by chronic pain. In periods of stress, the pain may become more severe, last longer, and occur more frequently.

Part of the stress of chronic pain may result in a decrease of both physical and social activities. Thus the stress of chronic pain may lead to still more stress through isolation and inactivity. Ultimately, it may lead to depression.

## ENVIRONMENTAL STRESSORS

Environmental stressors include aspects of our surroundings that are often unavoidable, such as noise, smoke-filled rooms, cramped offices, choking exhaust fumes, the glare of the sun, and the burning heat of the summer or the chilling cold of winter.

The extreme conditions to which we are exposed can be either too much or too little. Loud noise is stressful, but studies in special sound-insulated rooms called anechoic chambers have demonstrated that total silence is also highly stressful. In such sensory deprivation, people may experience boredom, perceptual distortions, and even hallucinations.

## MEDIA STRESSORS

Media stressors involve all the news that comes to you in printed, auditory, or visual formats. It can include newspapers, radio and television broadcasts, movies, or other electronic presentations such as the Internet or e-mail. We are overloaded with information, much of which is of the "bad news" type. Once miles and time distanced us from stressors over which we had little control. Today our journalists are "embedded" into wars so that in your living room you can see tragedy and terror as it happens thousands of miles away. Our movies are so real that what is fiction and nonfiction is sometimes hard to differentiate.

> *Television violence affects youngsters of all ages, of both genders, at all socioeconomic levels and all levels of intelligence, and the effect is not limited to children who are already disposed to being aggressive.*
>
> —COMMISSION ON VIOLENCE AND YOUTH OF THE AMERICAN PSYCHOLOGICAL ASSOCIATION

## Terrorism Stressors

Terrorism stressors come in many forms, from distant violent acts to electronic attacks on computers. These stressors become what might be called a type of trepidation stressor, since it leads to a fear or uneasiness about the future or a future event. Even if we are personally safe and secure, we may feel the stress of terrorism through our exposure to the loss of friends or loved ones, and a heightened awareness of vulnerability through media reports about the "war on terrorism."

## Stressors That Are Better Reduced Than Managed

This book will help you to learn effective ways to live more successfully with many of the stressors we have just defined. Some stressors, however, are better approached in direct ways to help reduce or eliminate them rather than learning ways to cope more effectively with them. If drinking too much coffee makes you jittery or irritable, it is more efficient to reduce this chemical stressor by substituting water or caffeine-free drinks than to use the techniques in this book to attempt to be less irritable or shaky.

> *Even if I knew certainly the world would end tomorrow, I would plant an apple tree today.*
>
> —Martin Luther King Jr.

The majority of environmental stressors can be managed most efficiently by making environmental changes. For example, if you work in an excessively noisy environment or live next to noisy neighbors, some of the techniques you can learn from this book would help to reduce the muscle tension you experience in response to the noise. A more direct approach might be to use earplugs. Other techniques in the book might help you if you were afraid to ask your boss or neighbors for a change in the level of noise. Thus some of the relaxation or assertiveness techniques presented here could help you indirectly to make an environmental change; but making the change would be your real goal.

To help you make such changes, think of yourself as an environmental engineer or architect. Some of your ideas and blueprints may come from the chapter on time management. To avoid expressway traffic jams, for example, a growing number of the workforce are changing the times they arrive at and leave their offices. Others van-pool and enjoy reading a newspaper or talking with friends on the way to work.

> *Life is like a game of cards. The hand that is dealt you represents determinism; the way you play it is free will.*
>
> —Jawaharlal Nehru

Still others listen to prerecorded books on tape. Thus they change the drudgery of commuting to the enjoyment of recreational "reading." Take a good look at your work and play. If you are creative, the rewards are many.

**FOUR**

## Beginning to Manage Your Stress

*Life is not accountable to us, we are accountable to life.*
—Viktor Frankl

YOU NOW KNOW SOMETHING ABOUT THE STRESSORS IN YOUR LIFE, the stress responses of your body, and the long-term effects of chronic stress. With this knowledge, you may want to eliminate stress from your life. This goal seems worthwhile, but it brings to mind two thought-provoking cartoons. The first shows a man in flowing robes who is sitting cross-legged on an isolated mountain-top. Three physicians are standing in front of the man. They are dressed in white coats and hold stethoscopes in their hands. One doctor says to the others, "Well, at least we know it's not stress-related!" The second pictures a glassy-eyed beggar in a gutter calling out to a well-dressed man carrying a black bag. "Don't you remember me, doc? I'm the man you told to slow down and let my business take care of itself!"

Let us assure you that we are not going to teach you how to escape to mountaintops or eliminate all stressors in your life. Nor are we suggesting a stress *reduction* program. Rather, we are offering you a stress *management* program. Stress can be stimulating and can make your life exciting. Our goal is to help you learn how to live with your stressors without letting them interfere with the quality of your life. We want you to reduce the wear and tear on your body, but we also want you to enjoy life.

The stress in most of our twenty-first-century lives will not decrease. Just as animals evolve and adapt to new environments, the survivors of our generation will be the individuals who learn to adjust to and enjoy the "future shocks" of our changing world. We cannot change all the future stressors that we will probably face, but we can change our responses to them.

We would like to suggest you find a partner to train with. This is particularly important if you are not working with a professional. Once you have decided to start, it may be helpful to discuss your plans for practice with a family member or close friend. Such people can offer valuable suggestions and encouragement. In addition, a public commitment to practice is often more difficult to break and a better source of motivation than a private one.

> Shall we gather strength by irresolution and inaction? Shall we acquire the means of effectual resistance by lying supinely on our backs and hugging the delusive phantom of hope . . . ?
>
> —Patrick Henry

Research has shown that most behavior change involves seven stages, many of which are repeated after relapse and before achieving the final stage. The stages are precontemplative, contemplative, planning, change, maintenance, relapse, and permanent change. We hope these first chapters have prepared you for the next stages in your journey of learning to manage your stress effectively.

## PROFESSIONAL HELP

More and more psychotherapists are learning how to conduct stress management training and adding it to the services they provide. Psychotherapists can be psychologists, psychiatrists, social workers, nurses, or counselors. These professionals can also help you assess the appropriateness of stress management training for your problems.

Some of the long-term psychological effects of chronic stress, such as depression and personality changes, may require other forms of treatment. As we've noted, intense and recurrent fears of things that are not dangerous are called phobias. Many phobias, such as fear of airplane travel or public speaking, respond well to the stress management training described in this book. Others may require treatment that only a psychotherapist can provide. A professional can help you decide on the best treatment for you.

If you have a stress-related disorder but always seem to find reasons why you cannot slow down and practice stress management, read the time management chapter and the last chapter in this book. If you are still having difficulty, a psychotherapist may help you to understand it and decide if you want to change your lifestyle. If you want or need additional guidance, information in the last chapter will help you choose one of these professionals.

## WARNINGS AND PRECAUTIONS

*If there is any possibility that the problems you are experiencing relate to a physical illness, read no further—see your physician.* Poor diet, hormonal imbalances, and other physical problems can wear the masks of stress or anxiety symptoms. If you have not had a physical examination recently, we recommend that you have one.

If you are currently under a physician's care for diabetes, asthma, an ulcer, hypertension, a thyroid disorder, or serious depression, consult with your physician before starting this stress management training program. The dosages of the medications your physician prescribes for these conditions may need to be monitored as your skills in stress management increase. Finally, if you have heart disease or severe headaches, your stress management training should be conducted under professional supervision.

## RELAXATION TRAINING

Section 2 emphasizes relaxation training. Relaxation is a very important part of stress management. The ability to relax quickly in any situation will serve two purposes. First, as soon as you begin using it, it will help you reduce daily wear and tear on your body. Next, it will give you the self-control to decide how you want to handle stressful situations so as to decrease anxiety, anger, or other fight-or-flight responses and enjoy the experience. Being able to stay calm, relaxed, and in control is an important part of being able to change stressful situations in positive ways. Without this ability, you can be at the mercy of your stressors and you may react to them rather than acting on them.

You may want to use the detailed relaxation instructions in this book to make your own relaxation recordings. Appendix I lists musical and environmental selections that are compatible with relaxation practice. If you record your own relaxation instructions, you may want to use some of these selections. Many of the selections have a calming effect on mood, as well as heart rate and respiration. Select the musical or environmental background that you find especially relaxing.

## RECOMMENDED BOOKS AND RECORDINGS

In Appendix III, we have listed prerecorded relaxation recordings and other recommended listening materials for many of the chapters in this book. The recorded materials can help you to practice new techniques or learn related information.

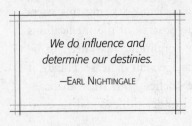

*We do influence and determine our destinies.*

—EARL NIGHTINGALE

We have also included recommended books in Appendix III to accompany most chapters. These readings can also help to expand and deepen your knowledge of the topics covered in this book.

# SECTION II

## Relaxing Ways for a Stressful World

*Go placidly amid the noise and the haste,*
*and remember what peace there may be in silence.*
—Max Ehrmann

**FIVE**

# Progressive, Deep Muscle, and Scanning Relaxation:
*When You Can't Fight or Flee, Flow*

*There is more to life than increasing its speed.*
—Mahatma Gandhi

How often, when we are stressed and worried, do we hear someone say, "Just relax"? Perhaps a friend makes this suggestion when you are feeling uptight about job frustrations or other demands. Maybe your dentist says, "Just relax," when the drill begins to hum. When patients complain of nervousness, headaches, backaches, or just plain exhaustion, physicians often tell them to relax. Many people tell us to relax but never tell us how.

For most people, relaxation is the best skill to learn at the beginning of stress management training. Progressive relaxation is a technique for muscle relaxation, which was developed by Dr. Edmund Jacobson. As a medical student in the 1920s, Dr. Jacobson realized that even when he was relaxed, his muscles were still somewhat tense. He became aware that this muscle tension might reflect the increasing pace of life. Even then, almost every individual was facing ever-growing demands that were almost unknown to earlier generations. The average businessman was striving for greater and greater achievements in hopes of security. Businessmen often fought off fatigue until they were nearly exhausted. Social events were becoming more complex, and recreational activities often failed to provide the needed relaxation and diversion.

Dr. Jacobson realized that he, as well as his patients, needed more than just encouragement to relax. Through his long and distinguished career, he developed a systematic program for training people to relax their muscles completely.

He studied the effectiveness of his techniques by measuring the amount of electrical activity produced in the muscle fibers. The results suggested that many people report feeling totally relaxed when asked simply to sit and relax. But, Dr. Jacobson discovered that most people had what he called "residual tension," of which they are unaware. His later studies demonstrated that people could produce greater relaxation by practicing progressive relaxation than by simply trying to sit and relax.

Over the years, Dr. Jacobson and other scientists have carefully studied and refined progressive relaxation. It now offers a proven, systematic way to control muscle tension. In addition to helping people learn how to relax, the techniques have been used for many disorders, including anxiety, insomnia, headaches, backaches, and hypertension. Physiological research has demonstrated that the procedures produce a profound relaxation. When measured with sensitive electromyographic instruments, major muscle groups can be trained to what is called zero firing threshold. This is total muscle relaxation.

The physical relaxation produced is pleasant and tends to leave the individual with a sense of refreshment. Dr. Jacobson believed that tense muscles had a lot to do with tense minds and that mental relaxation would follow physical relaxation.

Many people use progressive relaxation techniques as a form of recreation. More and more of the techniques are being incorporated into physical fitness programs and exercise classes. Some people find that after vigorous exercise it is helpful to bring their bodies back into a resting state by using these relaxation procedures.

If you have diabetes, progressive relaxation training may be of particular benefit to you. In *The Mind-Body Diabetes Revolution,* Richard Surwit, Ph.D., explains in a serious but colorful way that stress is just like eating candy for the diabetic. Relaxation training can help you control the blood sugar levels that are raised to provide energy during the fight-or-flight stress response. In fact, Dr. Surwit's research, conducted at Duke University, shows that controlling stress can lower average blood glucose levels as much as some diabetes drugs and decrease the risk of some diabetic complications.

## WHY LEARN RELAXATION?

Many people question the need to learn how to relax. Some individuals see muscle tension as a sign of strength. For others, tension equals fitness rather than flabbiness. In the rush of everyday living, however, men and women have forgotten how to live without unnecessary discomfort. Muscle tension is not always a sign of strength. It can be a sign that energy is being wasted.

To have various muscles constantly tense as we wrinkle our forehead, squint our eyes, tap our fingers or feet, and shift our positions is not a sign of strength. When we nervously make a path to the coffee machine or automatically light up a cigarette, we are often looking for ways to release pent-up tensions.

Learning and practicing relaxation can be a sign of quiet

strength in knowing how to be selectively tense when a particular task must be performed. You also learn how to avoid wasting energies needlessly and conserve them for important accomplishments.

A football player may get up slowly and walk back to the huddle, as if he were dead tired. Yet a minute later, the same football player is pulling would-be tacklers down the field. He does not run to the huddle and jump up and down waiting for the next play to be called. He saves his energies for those things he truly wants to do.

It is important to know that people who learn to relax do not lose motivation. An executive who complained of neck and shoulder pain came to us but insisted that he was not tense and did not need to become more relaxed. He was a successful man in a large oil company and feared that if he learned how to relax, he would become less productive. It was only after several weeks of encouragement and practice that this high-level executive realized that he had been chronically carrying tension in his shoulder and neck muscles throughout the day and during the commute home. He was surprised that he was able to learn to relax these muscles without a decrease in his job performance. Consequently, he felt more energetic and productive. This energy was directed into more productive work and recreational activities.

It is important to remember that when we talk of teaching you to relax, we do not mean we will teach you how to become lazy, bored, or tired. A medical student in one of our classes reported that his father learned progressive relaxation as a bomber pilot during World War II. By using progressive relaxation, the pilots could remain alert and avoid fatigue.

## WHERE TO FIND MUSCLE TENSION

To relax muscles progressively, you begin by tensing and relaxing the major muscle groups of the body. In this way, you become aware of exactly where your muscles are located. Tensing and relaxing muscles helps you to increase your awareness of your body's muscular response to stress. As one becomes more aware of the location and feeling of muscle tension, the absence of tension becomes clear. In essence, you begin to recognize muscle tension and the difference between being tense and being relaxed.

The muscle groups around the head, face, neck, and shoulders are particularly important areas of stress. A great deal of tension may accumulate in these muscles. Every person is different. Other muscle groups should also be explored, including the arms, hands, chest, back, stomach, hips, legs, and feet.

It is also important to know which muscles seem to stay tense. Take a moment to look in the mirror and think about being angry or anxious. Are your legs in a defensive stance? Is your jaw tight? Do your eyes seem intense? During the next few days, observe how you sit and stand in different places and at different times. Try to find out which of your muscles seem to remain tense.

## TESTING YOUR MUSCLE RELAXATION

It is important to know that after tensing, a muscle will automatically relax more deeply when released. Experiencing the difference between muscle tension and muscle relaxation increases the feeling of relaxation further.

Relaxation simply means doing nothing with your muscles. One way to test a person's depth of relaxation is to have someone lift or bend a relaxed arm at the elbow. If the arm is resisting or assisting the movement, it is not relaxed. The arm should be as easy to move as any other object of the same weight.

## WHY START WITH PROGRESSIVE RELAXATION?

Progressive relaxation is an excellent starting point for stress management training. It increases general bodily awareness and the recognition of specific muscles where tension is troublesome.

As you may recall, the oil company executive discovered that he had been living with excessive tension in his shoulders and neck. He had insisted relaxation in-sion and relax-dlessly tight did axation helped g before he ex-

their very first ion techniques cular nor diffi-stress manage-sequences, the egular practice ie way of life.

## DIFFERENTIAL RELAXATION

Another use of progressive relaxation is differential relaxation. Differential relaxation involves relaxing the parts of the body not needed for a certain task while tensing the necessary muscles that are in use. For example, when driving a car, it is not necessary to tense every muscle in your body. Often people find that their jaws or shoulders are tense while driving.

After practicing with progressive relaxation, you will find it eas-ier to relax the muscles that are not needed to perform a task. At the same time you learn how to keep only a moderate amount of tension in the needed muscles. This is very helpful in situations such as typing a report, preparing a meal, standing in line, and discussing business on the phone.

## Reaching Deeper Levels of Relaxation

Deep muscle relaxation is a form of progressive relaxation. It makes use of your new skills but does not include the tensing part of the progressive relaxation exercises. Deep muscle relaxation directs suggestions of relaxation to each muscle group in turn. The step-by-step nature of these exercises is similar to progressive relaxation, but now you learn to rely on mental awareness, deep breathing, and calming words or phrases.

> *He who is hurried cannot walk gracefully.*
>
> —Chinese proverb

## Building Relaxation into Everyday Living

It is useful to leave reminders in the office and at home to help you remember to observe your tension and to relax differentially. Small pieces of colored tape or yellow sticky notes may be attached to your watch, the telephone, or the rearview mirror. These will help remind you to scan your body for signs of tension every time you look to see what time it is, receive a telephone call, or prepare to change lanes.

Looking at your watch or a clock is often associated with nervousness and excessive tension. Converting "What time is it?" tension habits to the habit of responding with creative relaxation helps to build a sense of control over your body's tensions.

It may also be useful to put a sign on the bathroom mirror, your desk, or the dashboard of the car. Something like "Am I relaxed?" or simply "Relax" will work. Even the letter *R* can represent a cue to relax. A vacation snapshot in the office can provide a pleasant reminder of relaxation.

## RELAXATION FOR HEADACHES

Remember to continue practicing relaxation until it is as automatic as breathing. One of our patients suffered from daily tension headaches at work in the afternoons. Occasionally the pain was so intense that it forced her to leave work early. This only added to the stress she had to face the next day. As a secretary, she already had enough work stressors. Before she was referred by her physician for stress management training, she was unaware of the muscle tension in her neck and shoulders that preceded the onset of her headaches.

When she began learning progressive relaxation, she discovered that her tension had been increasing over the course of each day. She placed reminders to relax in the typing paper drawer and on the corner of the desk. In addition, she brought a travel alarm clock to work and set it under a pillow to ring quietly each hour. This helped her to remember to check her tension level and practice progressive relaxation. She also began to use her morning and afternoon coffee breaks as additional opportunities for practice.

Over the course of several weeks, her headaches decreased in frequency and intensity. As with many of our patients who discover the joy of managing stress, she had more energy for her personal life.

About a month later, she felt cured of her headaches and began skipping her relaxation at work. Her headaches returned. This is the relapse stage mentioned in a previous chapter. As one would expect, she experienced relief when she once again began to practice regularly. We hope her experience will help you prevent a relapse so you can maintain your change until you achieve permanence.

## CREATIVE CUING

Be creative with relaxation cues and use spare time to practice progressive and deep muscle relaxation. There are many times during the day when most of us have a few seconds to practice. Practice while waiting for an elevator, sitting in an office, holding on the telephone, or stopping at a red light. These situations can become cues to scan the body for tension. If you find unnecessary tension, use the time to relax and let go.

You may occasionally need to tense and release certain muscles that are difficult to keep relaxed. Briefly tensing all the muscles at once and then letting all of them go is helpful. Additional tensing and releasing may be especially helpful when first beginning stress management training.

Daily practice will help you become aware of which muscles are most troublesome. You may want to tense and release these muscles several times throughout the day. After practicing progressive relaxation several times, relaxing even the most difficult muscles becomes easy. Just take a deep breath and silently say, "Relax and let go" as the breath slips out. This routine can become automatic.

When you stop for a red light, scan your body for tension, take a deep breath, and say, "Relax and let go." Do the same when the phone rings or when any other frequent event occurs. In this way, you can teach yourself to relax your body automatically and quickly.

## How to Find Time for Cue-Controlled Relaxation

Cue-controlled scanning and relaxation are very important techniques that you will want to use for the rest of your life. To find time for these "six-second tranquilizers," think of all the time you spend waiting. According to one study, the average American spends about forty minutes a day waiting. This adds up to more than two years over a lifetime! Make use of the time you spend waiting in lines, stopping for lights, and standing at the checkout counter. Use the time to recuperate from stress, lower your blood pressure, and enhance your feelings of well-being.

## MEDITATION

Many people are exploring meditation as a form of stress management. Meditation is often associated with Eastern religions, but it can be practiced with or without a religious emphasis. Herbert Benson, M.D., a Harvard professor specializing in cardiovascular diseases and internal medicine, studied Transcendental Meditation scientifically and wrote about a meditative technique that he called the relaxation response. The relaxation response has been shown to be of significant value in the treatment of hypertension and psychosomatic illnesses.

The basic elements of the relaxation response and of most meditation techniques include finding a quiet place free from distraction, assuming a passive attitude, getting into a comfortable position, and focusing attention on one sensory input, such as a word, sound, thought, feeling, or symbol. The repetition of cue words in deep muscle relaxation training can be considered a form of meditation.

If you are interested in meditation, we encourage you to explore different forms such as yoga, Zen, or Transcendental Meditation. For this purpose, we have recommended several books, including Dr. Benson's *The Relaxation Response*, in Appendix III. Some of the unique benefits of meditation, in addition to relaxation training, are the insights that can be gained into our inner world and outer reality. Zen, a Buddhist sect, envisions an ideal personality, which we feel is worth striving for, that is capable not only of quiet meditation but also of life-affirming action.

We emphasize cue-controlled forms of relaxation for stress management, however, because people may have trouble setting aside time for daily meditation for the rest of their lives. In addition, our goal is to help you manage stress effectively throughout your day wherever you are, rather than in special places or at special times.

# Beginning Progressive and Deep Muscle Relaxation Practice

*Scheduling Formal Relaxation Practice*   We recommend practicing progressive and deep muscle relaxation at the same time once or twice each day for twenty to thirty minutes. Practice may be scheduled in the mornings and afternoons. Try to wait at least an hour after eating to practice relaxation or you may tend to fall asleep. During the workweek, use the morning coffee break or lunch hour, and then practice in the afternoon before or after going home. Some individuals prefer to practice after returning home from work and then later in the evening.

Relaxation practice is especially important at work if your job is even mildly stressful. Practicing at work may be necessary if you do not have a quiet place at home. If work is noisy, arrange quiet times at home.

If your home and work settings are not appropriate, find a quiet park, recreational center, or library. But be aware that the harder it is to get to your place of practice, the more difficult it is to maintain regular practice.

*Scheduling Brief Relaxation Practice*   Many people feel good in the morning but become more and more tense as the day wears on. They may finish work only to find themselves unable to enjoy their leisure time because of headaches, heartburn, fatigue, or other discomfort. The minor but constant problems encountered during the day generate tension and anxiety. This stress may grow as they wonder if there will be more problems and how long they can cope. The stress spirals upward.

Brief relaxation practice throughout the day can help break the dangerous stress spiral. These practice periods may last less than five minutes, but they can bring great benefit by helping you keep tension below critical levels. If you are unable to schedule formal relaxation practice in your working day, at least take brief breaks to relax.

Remember your first experience with the alphabet. You may have repeated each letter after someone, but you really learned it by practicing over and over, saying, "A, B, C . . ." until you could also say, ". . . X, Y, Z." This may sound dull, but it does not have to be. Remember the colorful pictures in your alphabet book? Some people use colorful anatomy books or images to increase their understanding of which muscles they are learning to relax. Others find friends to practice with. Learning the alphabet was the first step to reading your favorite books. Relaxation training is just the beginning of alleviating your symptoms of stress and finding more life satisfaction through stress management.

**Hospital and Other Programs**     If you are learning stress management training through a hospital, clinic, or health resort program, you may practice as often as the program recommends, ensuring that you gain maximum benefits in the shortest possible time. After you have completed the formal program, you may want to go back to each of the recommended steps of stress management training. In this way, you can increase your ability to apply all of the skills to your daily life.

**Keeping Good Progress Records**     Each time you practice, record the technique you used and how long you practice on a copy of the Home Practice Chart in Appendix IV. In addition, before and after each practice session, record your overall pre- and postpractice ratings. A score of 100 means total tension and a score of 0 means complete relaxation. If you have a frequent symptom such as headaches, you want to put marks for each occurrence next to the appropriate day. In a few weeks, you can count the marks and see your progress.

**Preparing**
**for Muscle**
**Relaxation**
**Practice**

For the most successful beginning, it is best to find a place where all outside noise is reduced to the lowest possible level. Practice the exercises in a quiet room and keep the lights dim. Tell others what you are about to do or put a Do Not Disturb sign on your door. Turn the phone off. The room temperature should be comfortable. If needed, have a blanket available to cover yourself. The exercises may be practiced while reclining on a sofa, lying on a bed, or sitting in a comfortable chair. We recommend using a lounge chair that reclines.

Lying on one side or with the chest down may strain parts of your body. This is not to say that it is impossible to benefit from relaxation in this or other positions, but it is easier to learn the exercises the first time while reclining on your back. Later, it will be beneficial to practice while sitting up and standing.

Clothing should always be comfortable and loose when practicing relaxation. Belts can be loosened in preparation for the exercises. It is often best to remove ties, jewelry, shoes, and eyeglasses or contact lenses, and not to have any gum or candy in the mouth.

**Problem**
**Solving:**
**Cramps and**
**Falling**
**Asleep**

If the room is very cold and your muscles are tired, do not tense the muscles too tightly or they may develop mild cramps. If a cramp occurs, knead the muscle and stretch it out. The most frequent cramp occurs in the calf muscle. If this occurs, pulling the toes toward your face and kneading the calf muscle will usually relieve the cramp. Using a room with a comfortable temperature and being sure that your muscles are not tired should eliminate cramping.

Never overstrain a muscle when you tense it. Tighten your muscles, but not to the point of quivering. If you have had any physical problems that may be affected by tensing various muscle groups, seek your physician's advice before practicing.

Some individuals have difficulty staying awake and will need to practice in a sitting position. It may be necessary to rest your elbow on the arm of the chair or surface of the bed while holding your hand up. In this position, if you start to fall asleep the hand should drop to the side and wake you up. Others have found it helpful to sit in a chair and hold an unbreakable object in one hand in such a way that the object will fall to the floor when released. When it falls, the sound arouses them.

Remember, the major advantage in learning relaxation comes from being able to relax when you are awake. If you wish to use the exercises to help you fall asleep at night, practice when you go to bed. Studies with insomnia have shown that sleep onset time can be decreased by an average of about twenty minutes. If you use the exercise to go to sleep, be sure to continue your daily relaxation practice. There is no substitute for regular daytime practice.

One of our patients who suffered from insomnia described his use of progressive relaxation in the following way. He was tensing and releasing each muscle group and adding the words, "Legs, relax and sleep; feet, relax and sleep; toes, relax and sleep." One night at this point in his practice, his wife came into the bedroom dressed in a sexy nightgown. The patient smiled and said, "OK, everybody up!" The joy of stress management is knowing you can raise or lower your stress response, depending on whether you are facing distress or healthy stress. Drugs and external chemicals cannot make this important distinction for you.

**Prescriptions for Intruding Thoughts** If you experience problems with intruding thoughts, you may want to try some of the following techniques. First, be gentle with yourself and do not get angry when you realize you have lost your concentration. Allow your thoughts to leave your mind as quickly as they came, and bring your attention back to the exercises or muscle group you were focusing on.

If your thoughts are persistent, you may want to command

yourself very firmly to stop the distracting thoughts and return to the relaxation. At first, it may be necessary to say "Stop!" out loud. With practice you can say it in a whisper, and finally you can say it silently to yourself. A similar approach is to repeat the silent "Stop!" or "No!" several times and then return to the relaxation exercises. These techniques are called "thought stopping." They can be used in many situations when you want to control unwanted thoughts.

It is also helpful to make the relaxation very brief. You might set an alarm (a kitchen timer works well) for five minutes to see if you can concentrate that long. If not, then set it for fewer minutes. When you succeed, gradually increase the time until you can do all of the exercises.

Another technique involves attempting to relax just a few groups of muscles without losing your concentration. Decide that you will first try to relax just the face and neck. Congratulate yourself on your success and then move to your arms and hands. In this fashion, go through the other muscles briefly. Try the chest and stomach, the hips and thighs, and then the calves and feet.

If you are unable to complete a small group of muscles, try again, but this time make the group even smaller. For example, relax only your forehead and eyes. When your concentration improves, you may go through larger muscle groups until you can progress throughout the body without stopping.

## How To Do Muscle Relaxation

*Using* *Relaxation* *Recordings*   If you are using recorded relaxation exercises, schedule times now and begin listening to the recordings of progressive and deep muscle relaxation. Review the relaxation programs suggested in Appendix III to help select an appropriate practice recording. Remember to list for each practice session your overall relaxation levels on the Home Practice Chart in Appendix IV.

**Guiding**     If you will be guiding yourself through the relaxa-
**Yourself**    tion exercises, review the directions below. You may
                find it helpful to read the directions several times.
You may also want to ask someone to read the relaxation instructions slowly to you. If possible, you may want to record these
instructions to help your practice.

The following written exercises recommend a particular sequence of relaxing your body. The sequence begins with your
head and ends with your feet. We have found that most people
prefer to relax their facial and head areas first. After relaxing the
rest of the body, it may be annoying to tense and relax facial muscles. Some individuals, however, prefer to start with their hands or
feet and finish with their head. If you find this to be your preference, modify the sequence or return to the head area after completing the progression through the rest of the body.

Some people find certain muscles more difficult to relax than
others. For example, relaxing the neck or shoulders frequently requires extra practice. Return to difficult muscle groups and repeat
the relaxation for these muscles after progressing through all the
other exercises. The time it takes for you to become deeply relaxed
will become briefer as you refine your relaxation skills. Eventually,
relaxation can become as automatic as breathing.

## OUTLINE FOR PROGRESSIVE RELAXATION

### I. Basic Technique
   A. Separately tense your individual muscle groups.
   B. Hold the tension about five seconds.
   C. Release the tension slowly, and at the same time
      silently say, "Relax and let go."
   D. Take a deep breath.
   E. As you breathe slowly out, silently say, "Relax and let go."

### II. Muscle Groups and Exercises
   A. Head

    1. Wrinkle your forehead.

    2. Squint your eyes tightly.

    3. Open your mouth wide.

    4. Push your tongue against the roof of your mouth.

    5. Clench your jaw tightly.

B. Neck

    1. Push your head back into the pillow.

    2. Bring your head forward to touch your chest.

    3. Roll your head to your right shoulder.

    4. Roll your head to your left shoulder.

C. Shoulders

    1 Shrug your shoulders up as if to touch your ears.

    2. Shrug your right shoulder up as if to touch your ear.

    3. Shrug your left shoulder up as if to touch your ear.

D. Arms and hands

    1. Hold your arms out and make a fist with each hand.

    2. One side at a time: Push your hands down into the
       surface where you are practicing.

    3. One side at a time: Make a fist, bend your arm at
       the elbow, and tighten up your arm while holding
       the fist.

E. Chest and lungs

    1. Take a deep breath.

    2. Tighten your chest muscles.

F. Arch your back

G. Abdomen

    1. Tighten your abdomen.

    2. Push your abdomen out.

    3. Pull your abdomen in.

H. Hips, legs, and feet

    1. Tighten your hips.

    2. Push the heels of your feet into the surface where
       you are practicing.

    3. Tighten your leg muscles below the knee.

4. Curl your toes under as if to touch the bottom of your feet.

5. Bring your toes up as if to touch your knees.

Complete word-by-word scripts to record relaxation (autogenic or visual imagery) exercises and available recordings can be found on the Internet at www.stresscontrol.com.

## OUTLINE FOR DEEP MUSCLE RELAXATION

### I. Deep breathing
A. Breathe deeply and slowly.
B. Silently say, "Relax and let go" each time you breathe out.

### II. Body scanning
A. Focus on relaxing each muscle.
B. Feel the tension slip out each time you breathe out.
C. Progress from your forehead and the top of your head to your feet and toes.

### III. Examine the feelings of relaxation

### IV. Massaging relaxation
A. Imagine a gently massaging relaxation flowing through your body.
B. Feel the massaging relaxation move slowly from forehead to toes.
C. Move to another muscle or muscle group each time you breathe out.

### V. Cue words
A. Silently say, "Peaceful and calm" while continuing to relax.
B. Silently say, "I am at peace" while continuing to relax.

### VI. Return to Activity
A. Count forward from one to three. Open your eyes at three and feel relaxed but alert.

## OUTLINE FOR BRIEF SCANNING RELAXATION

Practice this brief scanning exercise while you are waiting for an elevator or a red light or standing in a line. In the time it takes to breathe in and out three times, you can become aware of any tension and release it.

1. As you breathe in, scan your face, neck, shoulders, and arms.
2. As you breathe out, feel any tension slip away.
3. As you breathe in, scan your chest, lungs, and abdomen.
4. As you breathe out, feel any tension slip away.
5. As you breathe in, scan your hips, legs, and feet.
6. As you breathe out, feel any tension slip away.

## MUSCLE RELAXATION SUMMARY

We recommend daily practice of your muscle relaxation skills, once or twice a day if possible. Be sure to mark your practice on the Home Practice Chart in Appendix IV. We usually recommend that a person continue to practice progressive and deep muscle relaxation exercises once or twice daily for at least a week. Scanning relaxation may be practiced many times daily.

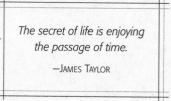

*The secret of life is enjoying the passage of time.*

—JAMES TAYLOR

If you are under the guidance of a psychologist or other professional, follow his or her instructions. If you are overviewing the book first, practice progressive and deep muscle relaxation once and continue reading the book.

After a few sessions, you will be able to relax unneeded muscles differentially while you perform tasks with needed muscles. For example, you do not need a tight jaw or clenched fist while writing a memo at your desk. Be sure to use brief relaxation whenever you see the cues that you have set up in your home or office to help you relax.

If you drive to work, you may want to use stopping at a red light as a cue to scan your body mentally. Whatever your cue, ask yourself different questions: "Is my forehead wrinkled? Are my jaw muscles tight? Is my stomach knotted up?" Then let your breathing become smooth and rhythmic. Allow the relaxation to replace tension, and a wave of calm to come over your body. Try to be creative and find more places where you can practice your new skills.

# SIX

## Autogenic Phrases and Images:
### How to Relax from the Inside

*Quiet minds cannot be perplexed or frightened,*
*but go on in fortune or misfortune at their own private pace,*
*like a clock in a thunderstorm.*
—R. L. STEVENSON

"AUTOGENIC" MEANS SELF-REGULATION OR SELF-GENERATION. This relaxation technique was developed by Johannes Schultz, M.D., and Wolfgang Luthe, M.D. It uses and builds on the passive, receptive attitude you learned in deep muscle relaxation training. The power of the trained mind to influence the body in a healthy fashion is the cornerstone of this technique.

Autogenic training is thought to help balance the body's self-regulating systems—its homeostatic mechanism. Just as a thermostat regulates temperature inside a room, the homeostatic mechanism regulates what goes on inside of our bodies.

Our internal, self-regulating systems automatically help to control heart rate, blood circulation, breathing, and many other functions we need to survive. If we lacked such an automatically regulated system, we would have to spend our time consciously commanding our heart muscles to pump and our diaphragms to pull air into our lungs.

These functions are also a part of the fight-or-flight system we described earlier. The sympathetic nervous system can automatically increase arousal to help us prepare for confronting or retreating from a potential danger. This reaction is adaptive when the threat requires such action; but for modern man, most threats are psychological or philosophical. For these threats, it is not adaptive to increase heart rate and breathing, or to constrict peripheral blood vessels to help redirect blood flow to vital organs.

## REPROGRAMMING INNER CALM

Autogenic training helps you control stress by training the autonomic nervous system to be more relaxed when you are not faced with a real need to fight or run. This technique follows in a natural progression after you have learned to control tension in your major muscle groups. It would be difficult to learn autogenic training before learning to produce a general state of relaxation in your muscles because autonomic nervous system responses are more difficult to recognize.

Autogenic relaxation is accomplished by passively paying attention to verbal cues for relaxation. It can be thought of as helping to reprogram the subconscious mind to create a state of internal calm. In contrast to progressive and deep muscle relaxation, autogenic training involves no direct muscle relaxation exercises. Instead, the body is conditioned to respond to particular verbal cues that generally reduce physical arousal and tension. Autogenic training emphasizes smooth and rhythmic breathing, a regular and calm heartbeat, and pleasant warmth with relaxing heaviness throughout the extremities of the body.

## PASSIVE CONCENTRATION AND THE RECEPTIVE MODE

You will need to assume a passive, receptive attitude even more than you did in deep muscle relaxation training. In autogenic training this is called "passive concentration." In some ways being passive and concentrating seem to be contradictory, and this is one of the reasons that the work of Drs. Schultz and Luthe was a breakthrough in modern science. An example may explain the technique of passive concentration better than a definition can.

Recall an occasion when your eyes began to fill with tears or you began to cry. You may remember a relationship breaking up or a loved one dying and the sadness you experienced thinking of the person you were losing. You may also associate crying with dirt or onion juice in your eyes. For a few seconds, close your eyes and imagine a personal memory or any of the above examples. If you take the time to recall the experience vividly, you will notice that when you open your eyes they are wetter than before you closed them.

Now, if you do the same thing but actively tell yourself that you must cry, and try to force yourself to cry, you will probably find that you are unsuccessful. Crying is an automatic function. Without practice, most of us cannot do it on command. We all probably know someone who has practiced this automatic response and seems to be able to produce "crocodile tears" at will. This person may have learned to focus on sad events and thoughts and conditioned the tear ducts to flood the eyes.

Autogenic training involves conditioning positive and relaxing responses. The originators of the process, Drs. Schultz and Luthe, maintain that by concentrating passively, a person can lapse into an unstructured, free-floating state of mind, which is relaxing in itself. The key is to focus on a relaxing phrase or image that will help to "mediate" or passively cue the automatic responses you desire.

Focusing on the words "My breathing is smooth and rhyth-

mic" or on an image of gentle waves rolling out can trigger a relaxed respiration rate. But although the process of focusing must
be deliberate, it does not involve the usual rules for human
achievement. If you were to focus on "I want my breathing to
be smooth and rhythmic" or "I am going to make my breathing
smooth and rhythmic, or else!" you probably would not be successful.

Learning to accomplish something worthwhile by learning not
to work actively at it is unusual for most people. Passive concentration skills and autogenic training require careful practice, but if
you have been successful learning progressive and deep muscle relaxation, this technique will seem much easier.

## BIOFEEDBACK: THE MACHINES SAY YOU CAN

At first, many of the people we train do not believe that they
can control automatic functions. Biofeedback machines, however,
show them that they can produce changes. The instruments
also show them the amount of change they have produced.

The word "biofeedback" can be divided into three parts to
make it more understandable. "Bio" refers to living organisms or
tissues. "Feed" means to give or, in this case, display. "Back" refers
to the direction in which this information is provided. Thus
"biofeedback" is simply a term for the modern technology of measuring a person's internal (bio) response and giving the person immediate knowledge (feedback) about that response.

An early form of biofeedback was taking your own pulse for a
minute. Now, machines can tell you second by second exactly
how many beats per minute occur and whether the rate is increasing or decreasing.

It is known that one of the common automatic responses that
accompanies relaxation is vasodilation or widening of the arteries
in the arms, hands, legs, and feet. A pleasant, warm, and heavy
sensation occurs as the blood flow increases into these areas. With

a biofeedback machine, the temperature of the hands or feet can be measured while this internal relaxation takes place.

## BLOOD CIRCULATION, TEMPERATURE, AND BIOFEEDBACK

Autogenic exercises help train the arteries and circulatory system to remain in a more relaxed state. A way of thinking about this form of internal tension is to consider that all the blood vessels are made out of muscle—a special form of muscle. Thus blood vessels can tighten up (constrict) or relax and widen (dilate). If the balance between this action is "disregulated," a person may experience physical stress responses.

Let's consider some of the disorders that can be influenced by the disregulation of this balance. If the peripheral vascular system is constricted, for example, there is less space for the blood to flow, and a person's blood pressure may increase. Constantly cold feet or hands may also reflect constriction and poor circulation. In addition, migraine headaches are influenced by overdilation of the arteries of the brain after a period of constriction.

The use of autogenic training and temperature biofeedback has been helpful in regulating blood flow. This method has even been successful when vasoconstriction was complicated by blocked arteries. One of the authors worked for six months teaching a patient with severe arterial blockage how to increase blood flow to his legs and arms. The patient was afflicted with what is known as Buerger's disease. His arteries were so extensively blocked and his circulation so poor that both of his legs had been amputated below the knees. Lack of circulation to the fingers contributed to constant pain and frequent infections.

At the time, biofeedback was a relatively new treatment, and there were still many skeptics. We may have been the first to attempt to use biofeedback with Buerger's disease.

When the patient began autogenic training and biofeedback the temperature at the tips of his fingers was below 70 degrees F—

lower than the surrounding room temperature. As the training progressed, he would come into the session with an average finger temperature of 85 degrees and could increase it to as high as 94 degrees while receiving the temperature feedback.

Although autogenic training and biofeedback could not remove the blockage from his arteries, it did appear to help increase the blood flow, probably by dilating the smaller accessory arteries that were not blocked. As you can imagine, when biofeedback helped to keep him from further surgery, he almost became the hospital's biofeedback salesman.

Exactly how autogenic training works is not completely known. The technique works for many people, and we now know that the heavy and warm feeling of relaxation in the arms, hands, legs, and feet is a real phenomenon. Not only have temperature changes been reported, but Dr. Luthe's early research showed that the increase in blood to an area also contributed to an increase in weight.

## The Little Girl in a Swing Who Calmed an Irregular Heart

Tachycardia is a condition with symptoms of rapid and irregular heartbeats. A patient had experienced tachycardia for three years before she was seen by one of the authors. She was twenty-one years old and worked as a secretary. She aspired to become an executive secretary, took college courses at night, and always received excellent ratings from her supervisors.

This patient complained that when her boss said he needed a letter or report typed immediately, her heart rate would increase and become irregular, and her heart would feel as if it were pounding. She usually was able to finish the work, but over a period of years she became more and more distressed. The tachycardia became more frequent as she accepted more responsibility.

She began autogenic training after learning to use muscle relaxation. When she practiced autogenic training, she was able to produce a calm and regular heart rate. With encouragement, she began practicing in front of a keyboard at home, and discovered that she could control her heart rate by imagining a small girl swinging rhythmically under a tree while the wind gently blew through her blond hair. She began practicing autogenic training and using this imagery.

Eventually, she was able to imagine the little girl swinging while she was typing at work. This helped her to remain calm. Her tachycardia became less and less of a problem, as she was able to regulate her heartbeat by imagining the girl swinging to and fro.

When describing her success at work, she also reported that if she quickly developed this image and held it in the back of her mind while she typed, her typing seemed to have a smoother rhythm. She felt that this practice contributed to greater speed and fewer errors.

## SELF-REGULATION AND SYMBOLIC IMAGERY

The use of imagery to help regulate various bodily responses is not new. A symbol is one thing that stands for or suggests something else. The little girl swinging under the tree represented the more rhythmic beating of the heart. This sort of symbolic imagery has been used in hypnosis since the time it was discovered; more recently, it has been incorporated into both relaxation and biofeedback.

Why does symbolic imagery work? Why does it seem very important in trying to regulate the automatic bodily systems? One theory suggests that different parts of our brain think in different ways. The left side of the brain is very logical and verbal. "Talking" yourself through a problem or telling yourself to lift a glass of water and drink from it may originate there. The right side of the brain seems to think more in pictures and is less logical.

This phenomenon may explain why people have counted sheep to go to sleep through the ages. The technique probably survives because verbal counting tends to bore the left side of the brain to sleep, while the picture of the sheep jumping over the fence tends to bore the right side of the brain to sleep. With both sides of the brain occupied, we have a hard time worrying about something that might arouse us and keep us from falling asleep.

According to a related theory, the right side of the brain may control the autonomic nervous system and our automatic functions. If this theory is correct, it would help us understand why we must both passively concentrate and use images to help regulate blood flow or heart rate. If we actively and logically concentrated, we would engage our left brain. This part of the brain may not be where the control for circulation originates. In addition, the left brain may critically evaluate a suggestion for your heartbeat to become regular and decide, "I don't have control over my heartbeat. It just happens automatically."

The autogenic training exercises will introduce you to symbolic imagery and help you to regulate your respiration and circulation. You may discover after practicing that other symbols work for you. Experiment and discover the symbols you use to imagine changes occurring in your body.

One of the authors worked with more than sixty hypertensive individuals and found their symbolic imagery to be highly creative. Some of these people would imagine the complete vascular system and see the vessels relaxing as blood flowed through. One man saw muscles "tight as rocks" pushing against the vessels and watched the rocks slowly dissolve. A person who worked in gas transmission saw a pipeline system and was able to open up valves and decrease pressure or redirect flow. Others saw the heart connected to a system of flexible hoses. Another person imagined a clear plastic model of the human body and placed a thermometer at the tips of the fingers. She visualized the blood flow increasing to the hands and also watched the temperature rising.

What are your symbols for how your body works? As you practice autogenic training, be creative with the images you use to help your breathing become smooth and rhythmic, your heartbeat calm and regular, and the blood flow to your extremities heavy and warm.

## WAYS TO USE YOUR NEW SKILLS

Many people find they are able to practice autogenic phrases or visualize relaxing scenes briefly throughout their day to promote a calming response. The secretary imagined the little girl swinging as she began to type. Several people we know relax their breathing as they go into stressful situations by thinking of the ocean waves rolling in and out. Others allow the image of a slowly ticking metronome to pace their breathing or heart rate.

We recommend that people with high blood pressure check their blood pressure at work. You may bring your own blood pressure cuff and stethoscope or stop by the medical clinic at lunch. This helps you get exact feedback about your blood pressure, and you may decide you need to spend less time eating during your lunch break and use the time to practice autogenic exercises.

Often individuals suffering from migraine headaches prefer autogenic training to other relaxation techniques. Focusing on the continued relaxing warmth of the hands and feet seems to help prevent the onset of headaches. Currently, research is being done to help us better understand how this works.

Certain individuals may experience cold hands or feet and can warm them by imagining the sun shining brightly on them as they work. Discover what responses you need to work with and, after practicing the autogenic exercises, begin incorporating your new skills into your daily activities.

## SCHEDULING AND RECORDING AUTOGENIC PRACTICE

Autogenic training should be practiced during the same times you previously practiced muscle relaxation exercises. Again, we recommend that you use the same times twice daily. During the work-week, use the morning coffee break or lunch hour and then practice in the afternoon after arriving home.

Occasionally, we recommend that a person practice a muscle relaxation exercise during one practice session and autogenic training during the other. This alternation is done when a person is relatively confident of his ability to relax his muscles but still has some difficulty maintaining his muscle relaxation levels throughout the day. Some individuals also like to use muscle relaxation exercises or autogenic exercises to help them sleep at night. This should be done in addition to the other scheduled exercise periods.

Record your practice on the Home Practice Chart in Appendix IV. Remember to record the technique used, how long you practiced, and your relaxation levels.

## PREPARING FOR AUTOGENIC TRAINING

Once again, as with muscle relaxation, plan on practicing autogenic training in a place that is private, quiet, comfortable, and free from distractions. Be sure family, friends, and coworkers will not interrupt you.

As before, the first thing to do is to get comfortable. You may wish to practice in the same place that you have been practicing your muscle relaxation exercises. We have already mentioned that it is beneficial to become conditioned to relaxing in a special place. You may already be in a habit of relaxing immediately when you sit in your favorite chair.

Be sure that all of your body is supported so that further relaxation will not cause your arms or legs to fall from the force of gravity. This is sometimes a problem with autogenic training. When the arms begin to feel heavy and warm, they may slip off the sides of the chair if they are not properly positioned.

Your hands should be open, your legs uncrossed, and your clothes loose. Be sure your neck is supported in a high-backed chair or on pillows. If you cannot find something to support your head, you can let your head hang forward or balance it comfortably in an upright position.

## COMMON PROBLEMS AND THEIR SOLUTIONS

When you first start autogenic training, it is best to allow yourself enough time to experience changes in respiration, heart rate, and circulation. Often a person can calm breathing and heart rate quickly, but it takes longer to experience heavy and warm relaxation in the arms, hands, legs, and feet. If you have a brief period of time to practice, concentrate only on your breathing and heart rate.

Let us say, for example, that you are able to relax your whole body in five minutes during your morning coffee break. When you first start autogenic training, you will probably find it difficult to produce heavy and warm feelings in such a short time.

It will be better if you schedule adequate time when you come home than to discourage yourself by not producing the feelings at work. You may decide, however, to calm just your breathing or heart rate during a brief period at work. After you are able to produce relaxing heaviness and warmth at home, you may also want to begin briefer practice at work.

Some people find it hard to assume a truly passive attitude. Even when they are repeating the autogenic phrases, other thoughts come to mind. Combining the autogenic phrases with images will usually help. If thoughts still intrude, do not dwell on them or criticize yourself for having them—just gently bring your mind back to the phrases and images.

## OUTLINE FOR AUTOGENIC PHRASES AND IMAGES

I. **Deep breathing exercises**
   A. Imagine ocean waves rolling in and out.
   B. Silently say, "Breathing, smooth and rhythmic."

II. **Heartbeat regulation exercises**
   A. Imagine slow ocean waves.
   B. Silently say, "My heartbeat is calm and regular."

III. **Blood flow**
   A. Right arm and hand
      1. Silently say, "My right arm and hand are heavy and warm."
      2. Imagine the warm sun.
   B. Left arm and hand
      1. Silently say, "My left arm and hand are heavy and warm."
      2. Imagine the warm sun.
   C. Legs and feet
      1. Silently say, "My legs and feet are heavy and warm."
      2. Imagine the warmth flowing down from the arms and hands.

IV. **Summing-up phrases: "I am calm."**

V. **Return to activity**
   A. Count forward from one to three.

> *Nothing can bring you peace but yourself.*
>
> —RALPH WALDO EMERSON

## Imagery Training:
### *The Windows of Your Mind*

*"It's all inside your head," she said to me.*
—PAUL SIMON

OUR THOUGHTS, IMAGES, AND OTHER MENTAL ACTIVITIES CAN BE harmful when they are upsetting to us. What does "upsetting" mean? You could say that you are pushing up the setting of your arousal. This adds to stress.

Most of us have struggled with unwanted thoughts only to find ourselves upset. Maybe something at work is extremely pressing, or perhaps a personal problem is troubling us. Thoughts about the problems keep spinning in our minds, almost as if they were being rolled around in a clothes dryer. One idea leads to another, and soon we find ourselves totally worked up and in a frazzle. We keep rehashing the problem without finding a solution. We may find that we are unable to pay attention to anything else during the day, or we become so aroused that we cannot sleep at night.

## I Think, Therefore I Am

When introducing progressive relaxation, deep muscle relaxation, and autogenic relaxation, we made the point that these relaxation techniques work because it is almost impossible to be physically relaxed and tense at the same time. You simply cannot do both simultaneously—at least not very well! Relaxing your mind is based on the same principle. You cannot be thinking relaxed, peaceful, and calming thoughts while your mind is racing wildly up and down the stairways of your life.

## Picture Yourself in a Boat on a River

You have read how to relax muscles that are under your voluntary control and how to calm systems of your body that are usually regulated automatically, such as heart rate and blood flow. You are now about to learn how to produce relaxing images and thoughts. These images and thoughts can be used to block out intruding and upsetting ideas. You can learn how to do this with imagery training. The goals of imagery training are to reduce and control mental anxiety.

Anxiety usually involves both physical and mental parts, but at times one of these may be stronger than the other. For example, one may be physically tired and yet be unable to sleep because of upsetting thoughts. This is mental anxiety.

By using pleasant visual images, we can control upsetting thoughts and enjoy a deep state of physical relaxation. Learning to control your thoughts takes knowing what you need to think about, practicing those thoughts, and then using them when you want to relax.

Once you have developed your ability to create pleasant mental images, you will be able to begin to visualize yourself being successful and meeting the goals to which you aspire. There are additional ways of learning to control and enjoy what you think and feel. Some of the additional ways will be presented in later chapters.

## IMAGERY, MUSIC, AND YOUR MIND

Mental imagery is a little like a daydream. You may want to start by trying to visualize, in your mind's eye, a pleasant scene you have seen many times. Try to reexperience the scene in every way you can.

The technique should use both sight and sound. We could use the term "audiovisual imagery" to describe the procedure.

Many people listen to music to calm themselves. It is hard to be calm, to whistle a tune, and think anxious thoughts at the same time.

The music on visual imagery recordings helps you produce a state of calm. When you practice visual imagery without using a prerecorded imagery tape, we invite you to add your favorite music. You may also want to use pleasant environmental sounds, such as gentle ocean waves rolling in and out. Appendix I lists different musical and environmental selections that you may find helpful.

## IMAGERY AND THE FIVE SENSES

As you learn imagery, you will also want to add your other senses: taste, touch, and smell. Maybe mental imagery really means sensory imagery.

When you practice the imagery exercises, try to include all five of your senses. Make believe you can see the lush green of a tropical rain forest with your eyes, hear the sound of the birds at sunrise with your ears, smell the scent of the many multicolored flowers with your nose, taste the salt from the sea breeze with your tongue, and feel the soft grass beneath your feet.

## COMMON PROBLEMS WITH IMAGERY TRAINING: INTRUDING THOUGHTS

Be patient with yourself as you begin to learn mental relaxation. Complete concentration, even on pleasant images, requires a great deal of practice. Do not get upset if unwanted thoughts come to your mind. This happens even to the most practiced masters of other mental techniques such as yoga and meditation.

Being forewarned is being forearmed. Knowing that unwanted thoughts may come to your mind will help you treat these thoughts calmly. Tell yourself that the thoughts will soon pass if you do not pay attention to them and if you return to your pleasant image. Do not fight them. Let them gently pass. This is where the practice comes in. If you get upset about all these thoughts racing by, you will be increasing your stress rather than decreasing it. Allow the thoughts to leave your mind as easily as they came into your mind. Simply refocus on the imagery once again. Every time you find yourself distracted, gently refocus on the imagery.

If you continue to have difficulty with intruding thoughts, you may want to begin using the thought-stopping technique that was mentioned briefly in the muscle relaxation chapter. Now, after saying, "Stop!" quickly refocus on the imagery you were trying to visualize. This two-step technique can be used whenever you find yourself preoccupied and unable to shake a thought and return to the task at hand.

## HELPFUL HINTS

Make your images your own. Only you can experience and know what images are relaxing to you. Also, only you can know what images and scenes are upsetting and should not be used. Work on having at least one personally relaxing scene that you use for relaxation.

Practice letting your personally relaxing image come rapidly into your mind. Take a deep breath and imagine breathing in the clean air from your special image. As you breathe out, feel the relaxation spread over your body, and allow yourself to be in that comfortable place for a brief moment. When you return to whatever you were doing, bring with you the feelings of relaxation from your personally relaxing scene.

## Using Relaxation Recordings

If you are using recorded relaxation exercises, schedule times now and begin listening to the recordings on visual imagery. Before and after each practice session, remember to list your overall relaxation levels on the Home Practice Chart in Appendix IV.

## Guiding Yourself

If you will be guiding yourself through the relaxation exercise, review the directions below. You may find it helpful to read the directions several times. You may also want to ask someone to read the visual imagery instructions to you. If possible, you may want to record these instructions and then use the recording to practice. In either case, the instructions should be read slowly and calmly.

## More Helpful Hints

Continue using progressive, deep muscle, and autogenic relaxation whenever you can. Be sure to keep checking and decreasing your muscle tension and autonomic arousal by using the cues and signs you have made for yourself. These methods not only will help you enjoy the health benefits of the relaxation response but also will increase your receptivity to the wondrous world around you.

### OUTLINE FOR IMAGERY TRAINING

I. **Basic technique**
  A. Form a clear image of a pleasant scene.
  B. Try to include images from other senses.
    a. Smell: smell the scent of flowers.
    b. Touch: feel the grass beneath your feet.
    c. Sound: hear the birds singing in the trees.
    d. Taste: taste the salt air on your lips.

II. **Suggested images**
  A. Tropical island
    1. You are on a mountaintop.
    2. Below is a tropical rain forest.
    3. The morning rains are ending.
    4. In the distance is a white, sandy beach and palm trees.
  B. Cloud
    1. A cloud gently floats down.
    2. It surrounds your body and supports you completely.
    3. You are in the cloud and gently float off in a gentle breeze.
  C. Valley
    1. The cloud floats down to a green valley.
    2. Water laps against the shore of a small lake.
    3. You get into a small boat and begin to float gently.
    4. You drift until the boat washes up against a shore.
  D. Willow tree
    1. You recline next to a willow tree.
    2. You begin to sleep and dream of other images.

a. Sunny beach

b. Field of wildflowers

c. Cool forest

d. Log cabin

e. Clear stream

f. Sloping hill

**III. Return to activity by counting forward from one to three.**

## PERSISTENCE AND VISUAL IMAGERY TRAINING

Visual imagery training is difficult for some adults, and sometimes children can have a much more powerful command of the use of imagination. We have often learned to shut down our mind's eye and think about problems and stressors. Sometimes our intruding thoughts make it difficult to quiet our minds with relaxing images. Be patient and persistent with imagery practice. Use thought stopping to block interrupting thoughts. Alternate the imagery training with the other forms of relaxation training. Once you begin to master imagery training, it can be a powerful ally for using images of success and metaphors of achievement to overcome fears and stressors in your daily life. **Complete word-by-word scripts to record relaxation (autogenic or visual imagery) exercises and available recordings can be found on the Internet at www.stresscontrol.com.**

> *When nothing seems to go right, think of a stonecutter hammering away at his rock. He strikes perhaps 100 times without making a dent and yet on the next blow, the rock splits in two. It wasn't the last blow that did it, but all that went before.*
>
> —HARVEY MACKAY

# EIGHT

# Mind-Body Physical Therapies
# for Relaxation and Stress Management

*Stiff and unbending is the principle of death.*
*Gentle and yielding is the principle of life.*
*Thus an army without flexibility never wins a battle.*
*A tree that is unbending is easily broken.*
*The hard and strong will fall.*
*The soft and weak will overcome.*
—Tao Te Ching

WHEN CHRONIC STRESS LEADS TO MUSCLE TENSION AND SPASM, relaxation training alone may not be sufficient to smooth out the contracted muscle. This is when therapies such as biofeedback, massage, and other exercises classified as mind-body may be helpful. The benefits come not only from stretching and smoothing tight muscles, but also from promoting a lifestyle change where regular attention is directed toward healthy exercises and time is taken away from chronic rushing to smooth the effects of stressful living.

To achieve the mind-body connection, various traditional and innovative bodywork exercise programs have gained popularity, including Pilates, yoga, tai chi, and other movement methods. The mind-body harmony achieved through physical practices can help with physical conditioning and mental relaxation to promote a powerful form of stress management.

The mind-body emphasis can be added to any regular physical fitness activity. Aerobic classes can begin and end with mental exercises of imagery, relaxation, stretching, or spiritual focus. When we exercise we can focus on music to lift our mood and transcend our worldly trials. But some methods of exercise have the mental focus built in as an integral component, and one of the main goals is often stress management and the release of tension and distress caused by modern lifestyles.

## THE PILATES METHOD

Pilates is a popular mind-body conditioning method that can increase flexibility. Pilates is about moving in a graceful, flowing way. The exercises, which mostly address the full range of motion, can be done with or without special equipment. Each movement is executed according to six basic principles: control, concentration, centering, focus, precision, and breathing. The participant is encouraged to master the mind in order to gain complete control over the body.

## YOGA

Today, yoga is believed to be one of the most effective and most gentle forms of exercise, not only for the body, but also for the mind. Most modern yoga practices include physical postures, controlled breathing exercises, and various forms of meditation. There are many techniques of yoga, and each has a particular emphasis, such as breath and movement, mental focus and meditation, postures held for extended periods of time, or a flow from one pose to another.

## Tai Chi

There is a long history of movement and exercise systems associated with tai chi. The slow, graceful movements of tai chi increase strength and flexibility and improve balance and circulation. It emphasizes stretching and turning in each of the movements to gain these and other benefits. Tai chi has been described as "meditation in motion," where the continuity of its movements, combined with the devotion of one's undivided attention, heals and revitalizes both the body and the mind.

The physical component of tai chi consists of basic principles and over a hundred movements. Some of the principles reflected in the movements are relaxation, balance, lining up the body, correcting angles, squaring the hips, controlling the step and the transfer of weight, and stretching and relaxing the spine. The movements are gentle, continuous, and circular. A relaxed state of mind is an important part of the practice of tai chi.

In Taoism, physical health is inseparable from attitudes, emotions, and perspectives. Tai chi emphasizes an attitude of calmness and compassion, both during practice and in daily life. This not only allows students to deal with stress more effectively but can promote physical health as well.

## Movement Classes

Movement classes teach awareness of habits in everyday movement, including harmful habits and how to stop repeating them. The goal is a more natural, easy and pleasant way of moving, at work and play. This is especially helpful in relieving and preventing neck and back strain and stress syndromes.

Movement classes reeducate the mind and body and help a person discover a new balance in the body by releasing unnecessary tension. The techniques can be applied to sitting, lying down, standing, walking, lifting, and other daily activities.

A mind-body learning method developed by Moshe Feldenkrais focuses on learning new movement skills to be integrated into daily life. Unlike conventional exercise, the Feldenkrais Method is not directed at the muscles or body as such, but rather focuses on increased neuromuscular body awareness. It combines movement education, gentle touching, and verbal feedback to create more efficient movement.

A method developed by Matthias Alexander, an actor who created it for his personal use after discovering that his poor posture was responsible for his chronic voice loss onstage, uses gentle touch and verbal guidance to teach movements for balance, posture, and coordination. The Alexander Technique also helps to relieve tension and pain.

A methodology called Gyrokinesis systematically and gently works the joints and muscles through rhythmic and undulating exercises. The exerciser does choreographed sets of spiral movements of the arms and legs. This work mobilizes the spine through a series of arching, curling, bending, twisting, and spiraling movements. As with Pilates, a multitalented performing artist developed this system in Europe. Both methods utilize special equipment and result in lengthening and strengthening of core muscle, increased flexibility, and a leaner physique.

## Martial Arts

These disciplines are often better known as methods of self-defense or combat. However, they are also beneficial in the development of physical fitness, as well as the promotion of mental and spiritual development. These highly disciplined activities aim to unite body and mind, and bring balance to the participant's life. Some disciplines, such as karate, usually emphasize muscular strength, power, agility, and endurance, while other methods, such as aikido, are aimed at coordination, breath control, relaxation, and mental focus.

## SUMMING IT ALL UP

Mind-body movement therapies have experienced phenomenal growth in the past decade, but with more than a hundred thou-

*There is nothing stronger in the world than gentleness.*

—HAN SUYIN

sand practitioners and dozens of methods available in the United States alone, it is difficult to know what is best for each of us. The brief descriptions we have offered are meant to help direct your interest. The resources we provide in Appendix III will help you learn more. We recommend you try several different techniques to decide which therapy may be the most beneficial in helping you manage your stress effectively.

# SECTION III

## Overcoming Your Special Stressors

*Just for today, I will let go of anger.*
*Just for today, I will let go of worry.*
*Just for today, I will give thanks for my many blessings.*
*Just for today, I will do my work honestly.*
*Just for today, I will be kind to my neighbor and every living thing.*
—THE FIVE SPIRITUAL PRINCIPLES OF REIKI

NINE

# Image Rehearsal

*I saw that all the things I feared, and which feared me,*
*had nothing good or bad in them save insofar as the mind*
*was affected by them.*
—SPINOZA

YOU HAVE NOW LEARNED PROGRESSIVE, DEEP MUSCLE, AND SCAN-ning relaxation to relax muscles over which you have voluntary control. You have also learned autogenic training to help you relax and regulate those parts of your body that are usually not under your voluntary control. In addition, you know how to relax by using visual images of pleasant scenes. You have learned to massage and stretch the muscles through mind-body exercises. Now you are ready to apply these skills in new ways to deal with some of the major stressors in your life.

## Choosing a Target Stressor

Most of us have some areas of our lives that are particularly stressful. Make a chart or a list of your current stressors. You may find Chapter 3 helpful in listing the stressors you are currently experiencing. Try to become more and more aware of your stressors. As you do, your list should grow.

> It isn't the burdens of today that drive men mad. Rather, it is regret over yesterday or fear of tomorrow. Regret and fear are twin thieves who would rob us of today.
>
> —Robert J. Hastings

To quantify the stress you currently experience, assess where it falls on a scale of 0 (no stress) to 10 (the maximum you could imagine). Take account of all factors that may be sources of stress—for example, you may not find noise or pregnancy distressful, but list such stressors anyway to help you understand all areas of stress in your life. Consider whether relaxation and controlling your body's stress response would help you feel calm, in control, or in less pain. Update your list frequently by adding, removing, or changing stressors. These will be called your target stressors. Choose one of these to work on.

Some people choose talking in front of a group or with a person of the opposite sex. Many people select a work stressor. If you have a phobia, such as fear of heights, air travel, crowds, or closed spaces, you may choose this as your target stressor. If you are reducing your weight, you may want to focus on your eating behavior in difficult situations. If you are trying to stop smoking, you may want to work on scenes where the urge to smoke is strong. It is often stressful to resist urges when you are modifying harmful habits.

All of us have our own particular stressors. Pick one that is not the most difficult for you but still gives you a good deal of trouble.

It is best to pick a mild to moderate stressor so as to increase the likelihood of success before you tackle your most upsetting stressors. But you should pick one that is important enough to you to make your efforts worthwhile and keep your level of motivation high.

Research and clinical work have shown that if we imagine stressors while feeling calm and relaxed, we can gain control and mastery over them. In this way, the techniques of relaxation that you have learned can be transferred to any situation you find upsetting.

## MENTAL SIMULATION AND REHEARSAL

Most athletes use imagery to rehearse winning performances in their sport. In fact, a study involving college students demonstrated that image rehearsal could be almost as effective as real practice. A number of students were tested for accuracy in basketball shooting and divided into three groups. One group was told to come back in twenty days but not to practice. Another group was asked to practice shooting baskets twenty minutes per day. The last group was asked to rehearse in their minds shooting the baskets for twenty minutes per day. They were told to watch the ball go through the hoop and hear the swish of the net. After twenty days, the group that did nothing was retested and showed no improvement. When the image-rehearsal group was retested, the improvement was about the same (23 percent) as for the group that had actually practiced (24 percent)! This is a good example of how rehearsing success helps people become winners. You will not find successful athletes rehearsing failures. In fact, if they do not play well, they often will immediately rehearse doing better the next time.

You may also want to use your imagination to rehearse acting in a skillful and relaxed manner in the face of your life challenges.

Not only will you become less anxious, but you will build up your confidence and your ability to handle the situation. The winners in life practice, so make it your goal to experience your stressors in a calm fashion.

To strengthen your stress management skills, you may also wish to practice stress reduction while watching a movie or a show on television. When you are in the middle of a tense scene, use your training to relax. You may be surprised at how calm you can become after a while. This is very good practice for the stress reduction you will want to use in your everyday life.

The most common mistake people make in applying what they have learned is to try their most difficult stressor first. Practice relaxing and being calm first with your easier target stressors. With practice, you will be surprised how easily you handle your stressors, and your self-confidence will grow.

### IMAGE REHEARSAL

| | |
|---|---|
| **I. Getting Relaxed** | *Practice progressive and deep muscle relaxation to become as completely relaxed as possible.* |
| **II. Practice Visual Imagery Relaxation** | *You might want to imagine that you are lying in a beautiful meadow or other calm scene. Continue to stay in a peaceful, safe, imaginary meadow, and try to keep the feelings of peace and calm as we now imagine some scenes that may be slightly stressful (anxiety-producing or anger-provoking). Try to see these scenes as clearly as you can, but know in your mind that if at any time the scene makes you uncomfortable, you can immediately return to the pleasant image of yourself lying peacefully in your meadow.* |

**III. Successful
Rehearsal of
Stressful Scenes**

*See yourself very much in control, confident,
and the master of your target stressor. See
yourself very successfully meeting the problems
head-on, with confidence and control. Visualize yourself coping successfully with your
target stressor. Continue to rehearse being
calm and in control while seeing yourself facing your target stressor for thirty seconds.*

**IV. Return to the
Meadow and
Relaxation**

*Now, leave that scene behind and return
to your peaceful meadow. Think to yourself "Face relax. Neck relax. Shoulders relax.
Arms relax. Chest relax. Abdomen relax.
Hips, legs, and feet relax." Remember the relaxation you have felt before and let it flow
back into your body. You are safe and comfortable, deeply relaxed. Practice your relaxation until you have returned to a very
relaxed state.*

**V. Repeat Successful
Rehearsal of
Stressful Scenes**

*Once again begin to imagine the stressful
scene. (You can go on to another stressor if
the last one did not trigger a lot of stress or
tension.) Picture yourself in total command
of the situation. Pause thirty seconds and visualize the stressful scene in your mind. Then
return to your relaxing scene. Repeat three or
four times the rehearsal of target stressors followed by relaxation.*

**VI. Return to
the Meadow
and Relaxation**

*Now, leave all stressful scenes behind and
return to your peaceful meadow. (You may
wish to go through more scenes. If so, return
to your peaceful meadow each time. If not,*

*then complete the following exercises.) Each time you breathe out, say to yourself, "I am calm." You are alert and awake but fully at ease. Focus on feelings of deep, deep relaxation. As you practice thinking of stressful life areas (anxiety or anger scenes) and seeing yourself in command and relaxed, you will continue to gain more and more control. Soon you will be able to face real-life situations with greater confidence. You will control these situations, rather than allowing them to control you. You will have the power to imagine yourself in your relaxing place. You will be able to do this quickly and easily, getting control of yourself and then facing life's challenges.*

**VII. Awakening Safely**    *Now, see yourself safe and secure, exactly where you started these exercises. Remove yourself from the meadow. Count forward from one to five. One, still profoundly relaxed. Two, very relaxed. Three, relaxed, but more alert. Four, eyes open. Five, wide awake. Before getting up, stretch your muscles. Take a deep breath, and you will feel confident, alert, and refreshed.*

> *Genius, that power which dazzles mortal eyes, is oft but perseverance in disguise.*
>
> —HENRY WILLARD AUSTIN

The next chapters may help you identify other sources of stress on which to practice your relaxation and image rehearsal skills. Do you have job or money stress? Have there been traumas or life changes that would become target stressors to conquer?

# TEN

# It's My Job

*To have a great purpose to work for, a purpose larger than
ourselves, is one of the secrets of making life significant.*
—WILL DURANT

MORE THAN HALF OF ALL AMERICAN WORKERS REPORTED BEING
at least somewhat stressed at work, and 40 percent are very
stressed by their jobs. One-quarter of these employees either often
or extremely often feel burned out by their work and view their
jobs as the number one stressor in their lives. Three-quarters of
the employees believe the worker has more on-the-job stress than
a generation ago.

High levels of stress can have a huge impact on the way employees do their jobs. A study on workplace stress by the National
Institute for Occupational Safety and Health, a federal agency responsible for conducting research and making recommendations

for the prevention of work-related illness and injury, found that health care expenditures are nearly 50 percent greater for workers who report high levels of stress. These workers are more likely to develop cardiovascular disease and psychological disorders, to have increased absenteeism and tardiness, and to develop an increase in stress-related illness, such as colds, headaches, and stomach problems. An amazing 132 million workdays a year are lost because of stress-related absenteeism and lost productivity.

Companies have downsized, either through attrition or layoffs, to cope with a bad economy, and the leading cause of workplace stress is worry about the economy. Other workplace stressors include worry about the specific job, low morale at the workplace, and difficult job responsibilities. Problems at work are more strongly associated with health complaints than are any other life stressor—more so than even financial problems or family problems.

## WHAT IS JOB STRESS?

Job stress is the harmful physical, behavioral, cognitive, and emotional responses that occur when the requirements of the job do not match the capabilities, resources, or needs of the worker. Job stress can lead to poor health, absenteeism, and even injury.

The concept of job stress is often confused with challenge, but challenge energizes us psychologically and physically. As you will learn later in the chapter about stress and personality, challenge balanced with mastery can motivate us to learn new skills and master our jobs. When a challenge is met, we feel relaxed and satisfied. Challenge is actually an important ingredient for healthy and productive work, and is most likely what people are referring to when they say, "A little bit of stress is good for you."

## WHAT ARE THE CAUSES OF JOB STRESS?

The causes of job stress involve both worker characteristics and working conditions. Individual characteristics such as personality and coping style lead to strategies that focus on how to help workers cope with demanding job conditions. In addition to the stress caused by work, many employees bring personal concerns and stresses over a variety of things, including money and family, into the workplace.

Besides worker personality, certain working conditions are stressful to most people and can have a direct influence on worker safety and health. Such factors include excessive workload demands and conflicting expectations. These conditions suggest that a job redesign may be the best job stress strategy.

Individual and situational factors can intervene to strengthen or weaken the effects of job stress. The need to care for an ill or aging parent is an example of a factor that may intensify the effects of stressful working conditions.

Certain job conditions may lead to more or less stress. These include the design of tasks such as workload, infrequent rest breaks, long work hours, shift work, and hectic or routine tasks that have little inherent meaning, do not utilize workers' skills, and provide little sense of control. Management style can also contribute to stress when there is a lack of participation by workers in decision making, poor communication in the organization, and a lack of family-friendly policies. A poor social environment and lack of support or help from coworkers and supervisors will also contribute to job stress. Conflicting or uncertain job expectations, too much responsibility, and too many hats to wear can lead to a sense of overload. Job insecurity, lack of opportunity for growth, advancement, or promotion, and rapid changes for which workers are unprepared can all contribute to job stress. Other job stress factors include unpleasant or dangerous physical conditions such as crowding, noise, air pollution, or ergonomic problems.

## Job Stress and Health

In the past twenty years, many studies have looked at the relationship between job stress and a variety of ailments. Mood and sleep disturbances, upset stomach and headache, and disturbed relationships with family and friends are examples of stress-related problems that are quick to develop and are commonly seen in these studies. These early signs of job stress are usually easy to recognize. But the effects of job stress on chronic diseases are more difficult to see because chronic diseases take a long time to develop and can be influenced by many factors other than stress. Nonetheless, evidence is rapidly accumulating to suggest that stress plays an important role in several types of chronic health problems—especially cardiovascular disease, musculoskeletal disorders, and psychological disorders. Some studies suggest a relationship between stressful working conditions and suicide, cancer, ulcers, and impaired immune function.

## Stress, Health, and Productivity

Some employers assume that stressful working conditions are a necessary evil—that companies must turn up the pressure on workers and set aside health concerns to remain productive and profitable in today's economy. But research findings challenge this belief.

Recent studies of so-called healthy organizations suggest that policies benefiting worker health also benefit the bottom line. A healthy organization is defined as one that has low rates of illness, injury, and disability in its workforce and is also competitive in the marketplace. National Institute of Occupational Health and Safety research has identified organizational characteristics associated with both healthy, low-stress work and high levels of productivity. Examples of these characteristics include the following:

- Recognition of employees for good work performance

- Opportunities for career development

- An organizational culture that values the individual worker

- Management actions that are consistent with organizational values

## STRESS PREVENTION AND JOB PERFORMANCE

In the *Journal of Applied Psychology,* an insurance company reported several studies on the effects of stress prevention programs in hospital settings. In one study, the frequency of medication errors declined by 50 percent after stress management activities were implemented in a seven-hundred-bed hospital. In a second study, there was a 70 percent reduction in malpractice claims in twenty-two hospitals that implemented stress prevention activities. In contrast, there was no reduction in claims in a matched group of twenty-two hospitals that did not implement stress management training.

## WHAT CAN BE DONE ABOUT JOB STRESS?

Nearly half of large companies in the United States provide some type of stress management training for their workforces. Stress management programs teach workers about the nature and sources of stress, the effects of stress on health, and personal skills to reduce stress—for example, time management or relaxation exercises. Stress management training may rapidly reduce stress symptoms such as anxiety and sleep disturbances; it also has the advantage of being inexpensive and easy to implement.

However, in work settings in need of organizational change,

the beneficial effects of stress management programs may be short-lived. If the root causes of stress are the job environment and not the worker, then system changes may be needed. The identification of stressful aspects of work (e.g., excessive workload, conflicting expectations) and the design of strategies to reduce or eliminate the identified stressors may be necessary.

Low morale, health and job complaints, and employee turnover often provide the first signs of job stress. But sometimes there are no clues, especially if employees are fearful of losing their jobs.

Certain problems, such as a hostile work environment, may be pervasive in the organization and require company-wide interventions. Other problems such as excessive workload may exist only in some departments and thus require narrower solutions such as redesign of the way a job is performed. Still other problems may be specific to certain employees and resistant to any kind of organizational change, calling instead for stress management or employee assistance interventions. If you are in a position to help your place of employment take positive action to address the job and organizational aspects of stress, then see the additional resources in Appendix III.

If you feel that you will do better learning how to cope with the demands of your career and job, then use this book as a guide to building the skills that you need. Certain factors can help the individual to reduce the effects of stressful working conditions. A good grasp of the stress management techniques in this book can minimize job stress by promoting:

- Physical self-control to reduce the body's harmful reaction to stress

- Positive self-talk to minimize self-defeating thoughts that make the job more stressful

- Life-change management to deal with changing careers and workforce demands

- Assertive communication skills to help clarify unclear job expectations and express job-related needs

- Time management skills to help gain control over aspects of your job by helping to pick deadlines and prioritize tasks

- Balance between work, family, and personal life

- Physical exercise to provide an outlet for job stress and to enhance physical health

- Good nutrition to fuel your body to face job demands

- A support network of family, friends, and coworkers

- A relaxed and positive outlook

> *Choose a job you love, and you will never have to work a day in your life.*
>
> —CONFUCIUS

# ELEVEN

# Mind Over Money:
## *Managing Financial Stress*

*We are prone to judge success by the index of our salaries or the size of our automobiles rather than by the quality of our service and relationship to humanity.*
—MARTIN LUTHER KING JR.

WE DECIDED TO DEDICATE A CHAPTER TO FINANCIAL STRESS SINCE this has been such a major source of stress for most Americans. When couples rate their sources of stress in a marriage, men and women typically rate sources of stress differently. There is one exception. Both the man and the woman most often rate money as the number one source of stress in the marriage. Dr. Charlesworth wrote a book with financial advisor Wayne Nance called *Mind Over Money: How to get Control of your Finances and Revitalize your Emotional and Physical Well-being.* In this book he explored the idea that financial pressure is often related to stress and attempts at coping. Much like food and drugs, spending money and consumerism have become American addictions, often masking sources of stress and masquerading as a cure. We are exposed to the lifestyles of the "rich and famous" through television and tabloids, and made to feel that if we had this or that then we would be happy and our lives would be free of stress.

We search for the American dream, but perhaps long ago we became confused as to what this American dream really means. We have become a country full of two-income families and latchkey kids, but we still cannot keep up with our spending appetites. The media bombard us with new products and "must-have" items. We strive for the latest fashions, big-screen televisions, computers, and cars. But through this process we are slipping farther and farther from true happiness, and we find ourselves "living to work" and "working to live" while losing touch with what is truly important in our stress and life management plans.

> *The American consumer: someone who knows the cost of everything, but the value of nothing.*

## FINANCIAL WELLNESS

Taking charge of your financial stress means exploring the area of money with an emphasis not just on having more but on what financial wellness may mean in your life. We have become a deficit-spending society, and deferring our debts to future generations may compound money stress beyond what could have been imagined a few decades ago. If money is a major source of stress in your life,

> *Men measure by the false standards that everyone seeks power, success, riches for himself and admires others who attain them while undervaluing the truly precious things in life.*
>
> —SIGMUND FREUD

> *Failure seems to be regarded as the one unpardonable crime, success as the all-redeeming virtue, the acquisition of wealth as the single worthy aim of life.*
>
> —CHARLES FRANCIS ADAMS

then we encourage you to read through this chapter to gain a perspective on financial wellness, and then follow up with other resources we recommend to acquire financial wellness. Sometimes financial wellness is not accomplished by earning more, but by changing values and managing your relationship with money. Some religious practices promote an inner peacefulness about living that is accomplished through behaviors based on the premise "It's a gift to be simple and a gift to be free." Use this chapter to explore whether the stress of pursuing money has robbed you of all the pleasures of enjoying each day.

## THE NEW FRUGALITY

As individuals and a country, we have shackled ourselves with debt from our consumption addiction. We will have to go through a vicious withdrawal period, and just like a junkie climbing walls while sitting in a chair, it will not be easy. The underlying psychology of the last quarter of the twentieth century was "Charge it" and "I deserve to have as many things as he does." The underlying psychology of the new millennium may have more to do with "Live within your means" and "Neither he nor I deserve to have so much, to indenture future generations, or to be ecologically irresponsible."

> *A man in debt is so far a slave.*
>
> —RALPH WALDO EMERSON

The live-for-today policies and politics violate basic moral values and traditions that could provide our children's children with a better world. Perhaps it is time to begin the slow process of change that will bring the economic part of our stress management plan back into balance with our true traditions and real needs.

## MIND OVER MONEY

The book *Mind Over Money* offered very practical and detailed guidelines for taking charge of your financial world. It discussed how to get out of credit card debt and how to prepay your mortgage, how to budget and understand cash flow. It also explored issues related to insurance, investments, wills, and retirement planning. If the area of financial wellness is important for your stress management plan, then we encourage you to get *Mind Over Money* and not only read it but work your way through it. The guidelines in this chapter are meant more as a way of raising your consciousness about the role that the relationship of stress and money play in your life. When that is done, you will be better-equipped to decide whether this is one of the areas in which you need to begin your more concentrated life management study. Taking charge of your financial life means neither burying your money in the ground nor spending it for quick gratification. It is a lifestyle change that allows you to put money to work for your goals of having a positive and fully functional lifestyle, no matter how much or how little you have.

> *Beware of little expenses;*
> *a small leak will sink*
> *a great ship.*
>
> —BENJAMIN FRANKLIN

## DON'T EVALUATE YOUR SUCCESS BY MONEY

Who are the truly successful people? Perhaps they are the people who have found peace of mind and reached their greatest individual potential. These people seem to have lived lives where their actions and behaviors were in balance with their beliefs and values. And many such people may die with few material possessions. Mahatma Gandhi died possessing a pair of sandals, a staff, a spinning wheel, and glasses to read his prayer book. Yet we may all see him as a very successful person.

> *The measure of a man's life is the well spending of it, and not the length.*
>
> —PLUTARCH

In a speech by trial attorney Rick King, past president of Rotary International, he told a story about a trip he took to India for a Rotary Health, Hunger, and Humanity project. He described visiting a very small, very poor village where the homes were huts with walls made largely of cow dung. In this village it was the custom to give a gift to a guest in your house. Knowing this custom prompted one of the members of the project to secretly give a gift to the guide, to be given to the chief. Then the chief would have a gift to give away, and no one would have to know where it came from. But the chief refused the gift. When the guests arrived at the chief's hut, they saw the chief, his wife, who was holding a newborn baby, and their many children. The chief spoke through the interpreter and said, "A guest in your home is a god." He then looked around the barren hut and picked up and gave to the guests a banged-up milk pail that was used to feed the children. Rick King reflected that the real gift that day was the handshake of a man of integrity and ethics.

> *It's a wise person who has enough and is happy with it.*
>
> —AESOP

## LIVE WITHIN YOUR MEANS

Alvin Toffler wrote a book called *Future Shock* that talked about mankind reaching the limits of changes that it could tolerate. Dr. Charlesworth took the liberty of reworking Toffler's words about change to fit the current world in terms of financial stress: "There are discernible limits to the amount of charging that normal credit can absorb. . . . By endlessly accelerating $charges$ without first determining their limits, we may submit our recreational consumerism to demands they simply cannot tolerate."

## UNDERSTAND WHAT YOU REALLY WANT FROM YOUR SYMBOLS OF SUCCESS

Often we really want the feelings we experience from having our symbols of success. These feelings are contained in words such as

> The way to stop financial joy-riding is to arrest the chauffeur, not the automobile.
>
> —WOODROW WILSON

"freedom," "security," "power," "happiness," "self-worth," "success," "satisfaction," "respect," "peace of mind," "adventure," and "love."

The possessions we acquire to get these feelings are simply symbols of the real thing. These symbols include money, job or career, clothes, cars, house, marriage, family, sex, a lover, education, degree, and travel.

There's absolutely nothing wrong with wanting symbols. However, it helps to know that the house, car, better body, career, or money we want is simply a method or behavior to get something else, something inner, something experiential: security, fun, energy, satisfaction, love, knowledge of God, or inner peace.

If you know the experience you are looking for, you can make lists of things that might provide it. Knowing what you really want dramatically improves the chance of finding the methods and behaviors to fulfill what you seek. If you know you want adventure and think a red sports car is the way to get it, you also know the sports car is part of the methods and behaviors that will bring you adventure. If the car does it, fine. But if the payments on the car, high insurance premiums, and exorbitant repair bills leave you little time for adventure, then you may need to explore other methods or behaviors to gain adventure.

A song titled "The Power of Love," sung by Billy Falcon, describes a man in his Mercedes, with another one just like it in his garage, with power steering, power seats, and power windows. He goes home to his empty house with the swimming pool. His wife

> *Loneliness and the feeling of being unwanted is the most terrible poverty.*
>
> —MOTHER TERESA

is playing tennis and his son goes to boarding school. He sits and cries. His symbols have not led to what he truly desires. Billy Falcon says, "He ain't got the power of love." Next he describes Louis, who drives a beat-up old car with "no power nothing," but a big smile on his face while he holds his girlfriend, Grace. His possessions may be few, but "he's got the power of love."

## LET YOUR SELF-ESTEEM BE BASED ON WHO YOU ARE, NOT WHAT YOU HAVE

Sometimes finding our values amid our confusion and conflicts is the catalyst to turn our lives around. Darrel Teel was a drifter with no home or job; what money he did get was used to buy alcohol. He found a handbag bulging with $29,200 cash in a field while he was looking for cigarette butts. The money was the lost life savings of an elderly lady who just did not trust banks.

> *You are what you are when nobody's looking.*
>
> —ANN LANDERS

Darrel's initial excitement and feeling of greed changed into soul-searching, and he turned the money in to the sheriff's department after thinking, "I don't steal. I'd like to earn this kind of money, but I don't steal."

This one act of honesty seems to have turned Darrel's life around. He received a citizen's award, the community raised $3,000 to help him start his life anew, and he had several job offers to select from. He quit drinking. With this one act of honesty, Darrel regained his self-respect, pride, and dignity.

## Pursue with Vigor What You Truly Value

Within each of us is the potential to live great and fulfilling lives. We have the power to shape the course of our life and destiny.

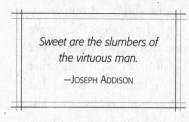

*Sweet are the slumbers of the virtuous man.*

—Joseph Addison

Every day we are given twenty-four more hours to spend, and those can be spent vigorously pursuing our true goals and values, or they can be spent unwisely. Once spent, they are gone forever. When you examine truly great people, you find that they follow the dictates of their conscience, are in harmony with their values, and often dedicate a part of their life to serving their fellow man. By contrast, often the stress of pursuing money leads us to a life of suffering.

## Spend Your Time Wisely

When we work with stress management clients, we try to emphasize that today they have twenty-four hours, and how they spend those twenty-four hours is a choice, conscious or unconscious. We hope to die at a hundred or older, and we intend to live our life according to that plan. But we could be wrong and die today. Either way we try to spend the time we have been given doing those things that fit our val-

*How earnestly I must exert myself in order to give in return as much as I have received.*

—Albert Einstein

ues. Live your life both as if today were the last day of your life and as if you are going to live to be a hundred years old! In a later section on time management we will encourage you to further explore your goals and how you spend the days and years of your life.

The founder of American psychology, William James, said, "The great use of life is to spend it for something that will outlast it."

> *I want to be a happy idiot and struggle for the legal tender.*
> —JACKSON BROWNE

We outlast life through our children, our ideas, and our deeds, and as Jackson Browne said, "Nothing survives, except the way we live our lives." Part of our value system that helps us survive the stress, suffering, and tragedies that befall us all is the belief that things may happen for a reason and that it is our task to find that reason and make it meaningful. We do not always live in a just world. Rabbi Harold Kushner clarified this beautifully in his book *When Bad Things Happen to Good People.* We do not have that answer, but we believe that it all balances out in the end. Drought, flood, or insects may destroy the seeds we sow. But we keep planting if we believe that some of the seeds will grow. If the only seeds you sow are related to money and the stress to get it, then what will you do if life disrupts this pursuit in some way?

> *And there are those who have little and give it all. These are the believers in life and the bounty of life, and their coffer is never empty.*
> —KAHLIL GIBRAN

## SUMMARY OF MONEY AND STRESS

We hope that you have what you need, and have the ability to "sharpen your axe" and get the skills you need to acquire a life free from the stress of worries about money and material possessions. If you are struggling with cash flow and making good financial decisions, then please explore the resources in Appendix III, read *Mind over Money*, take classes at a community college and learn about finances, but also take charge of the stress created by a consumer society driven by deficit spending. Find the value of your life outside the decimal points and dollar signs!

> Do not equate money with success. There are many successful money makers who are miserable failures as human beings.
>
> —LLOYD SHEARER

## TWELVE

# Acute and Post-traumatic Stress Disorders

*Where were you when the world stopped turning?*
—ALAN JACKSON

MOST OF US WILL SURVIVE A TRAUMATIC, LIFE-THREATENING EXPE-
rience sometime during our lives. We will respond with intense
fear, helplessness, and horror. Within a couple of days, depending
on the traumatic event, up to 50 percent of us will develop the
symptoms of an acute stress disorder. We will feel detached, as
though we are in a fog, and we may forget important aspects of
the trauma, yet we will reexperience it in nightmares or flashbacks
and want to avoid anything that reminds us of the trauma. In addition, the stress will make us jittery, irritable, and sleepless.

Beyond acute stress disorder is the more prolonged post-
traumatic stress disorder (PTSD)—a condition that has been

known for over a hundred years under different names. During World War I and II it was called "shell shock" or "combat fatigue." Post-traumatic stress disorder is defined in terms of the trauma and the response to the trauma. Strong reactions to trauma are normal. The events of September 11, 2001, caused grief and sadness throughout our nation. Some of this grief was temporary, and some has become longer in duration and reflective of PTSD. The scope of the PTSD problem is substantial—the condition is found in 15 percent of Vietnam veterans and 18 percent of women who were victims of physical assault. Ten percent of the population will suffer from PTSD at some time in their lives.

The acute symptoms associated with trauma are very distressing and can impair our social and occupational lives for up to four weeks. Fortunately, there are many things we can do to ease the suffering and recover from an acute condition well before the more prolonged post-traumatic stress disorder sets in. Understanding the stress response, knowing what to expect, and finding ways to get what we need most will make a big difference.

## What Are Acute and Post-traumatic Stress Disorders?

Acute stress disorder is one of the newest psychiatric diagnoses. It was created in 1994 to recognize symptoms that almost anyone can experience during the first month after a traumatic, life-threatening event. Events can include rape, criminal assault, kidnapping, car accidents, shootings, explosions, torture, war, hurricanes, floods, and fires. Even the news that a loved one has faced such an event can be traumatic and can cause an acute stress disorder.

Any traumatic event is extremely upsetting and may leave us frightened, helpless, and horrified, but the features of acute stress disorder also include some symptoms that change the way we experience our feelings, our world, and ourselves. We may even have problems remembering important aspects of the event. These are called dissociative symptoms and can be understood as protective ways of distancing ourselves from the horrible associations that we have with the traumatic event.

Some dissociative symptoms involve strange, surreal feelings that we are somehow not truly ourselves or that our world is only vaguely familiar and not quite normal or real. We may end up in a daze and become less aware of our surroundings or feel numb, detached, and/or cut off from our emotions. We may be unable to remember something important about the traumatic event. Someone with acute stress disorder will have three or more of these dissociative symptoms for at least two days.

In addition to dissociative symptoms, people with acute stress disorder will relive the event in thoughts, images, dreams, flashbacks, or distress when exposed to things that remind them of the event. For these and other reasons, people with the disorder will avoid thinking about the event, talking about it, going to where it occurred, or doing anything else that might remind them of it.

Someone with the disorder will also have trouble calming down. They may startle at sounds that are like those of the event, find it difficult to concentrate, become irritable, feel jumpy, or have a great deal of trouble sleeping.

Experts estimate that 70 to 90 percent of Americans will face a traumatic event sometime in their lives. The more intense, dangerous, and long-lasting the event, the more likely it is that the victim will develop an acute stress disorder. For example, women who feared for their lives during a rape had two and a half times the incidence of acute stress disorder than those who did not. People who have been traumatized in the past are more likely to suffer from the disorder, as are those with prior emotional problems. In addition, those who faced a man-made trauma rather than a natural disaster may be more likely to have an acute stress disorder. It is believed that there are very few people who would truly be immune to acute stress disorder if a trauma were extreme enough.

People with acute stress disorder find it very difficult to carry out many activities of daily living. Those who have used or abused alcohol as a way to anesthetize their feelings in the past may begin drinking again or drink more heavily. Those who have lost their friends or family in a disaster may suffer survivor guilt. Others may struggle with guilt over what they had to do in order to survive. Some may consider or even commit suicide. Others may become impulsive and tempt fate with risk-taking activities. Those caring for people with acute stress disorder must be alert to these problems.

Risk factors for the disorder include living in a war-torn country or a place where tornadoes and hurricanes are common. Dangerous occupations such as firefighting, police work, the military, and emergency room work increase the odds of having an acute stress disorder. Surprisingly, among people who are grieving the loss of a spouse, those with higher incomes and self-esteem have more difficulty adjusting to the loss than those with fewer resources. Race and age were also factors. This may also be true of other traumatic losses and is attributed to the way the event shatters their view of the world as more controllable, predictable, and secure than those with fewer resources. In these studies, the strength of the person's social network made little difference in how well he or she adjusted to the loss.

Understandably, those with acute stress disorder have serious difficulties at home and work or find it impossible to do things that should be done as a result of the trauma, such as getting help from authorities or talking to relatives who could help. If these and other symptoms continue or surface a month after the initial trauma, the person may be suffering from post-traumatic stress disorder or PTSD. The diagnosis was officially recognized in 1980 after the symptoms of PTSD were found among many soldiers returning from the Vietnam War.

Some recent research suggests that the traumatized people who are most likely to develop PTSD may be those who have certain biological responses immediately after the trauma. According to one study, these include a very rapid heart rate and high levels of cortisol, a stress chemical.

## How Do I Know?

If you have faced a traumatic event during the last month, you are at risk for acute stress disorder. Was your life threatened? Did you suffer a serious injury that disabled you? Did you witness a murder or someone's death? Or were you told that a close friend or family member died or suffered? Were you or your family in a natural disaster? If so, you may have experienced a trauma. For children, inappropriate sexual events do not have to involve threatened or actual violence or injury to be considered traumatic.

What was your response to the trauma? Did you experience intense fear, helplessness, or horror? If you are a parent, did your child have one of these responses or did your child's behavior become disorganized or agitated? If so, you and/or your child are at risk for acute stress disorder.

Among those people who have faced a trauma and responded in one or more of these ways, not everyone has an acute stress disorder. For example, research has shown that among victims of a natural disaster, 4 percent will be diagnosed as having acute stress disorder; among victims of physical attack, 19 percent; among car accident survivors, 13 percent; among bystanders to a mass shooting, 33 percent; among survivors of firestorms and serious earthquakes, between 25 and 33 percent; and among prisoners of war and concentration camp survivors, 50 percent.

Some events that are traumatic enough to be followed by an acute stress disorder may surprise you. British psychologists found that up to 3 percent of mothers may suffer acute stress disorder after labor and childbirth. As many as 10 percent of women have the disorder after a spontaneous abortion. So if you feel intense fear, helplessness, or horror after an event, the event may have been traumatic enough to be followed by an acute stress disorder.

If you have an acute stress disorder, you will probably feel very strange and distant from yourself and the world you knew before the trauma. For example, you may feel as if you are in a fog. You can hear what people are saying, but their voices may sound very far away, and the words may seem lifeless. Things are less colorful and vivid; your surroundings are like props and backdrops in a play rather than the real world. Food may be bland and tasteless. Odors and fragrances are barely smelled and seem flat. You may touch things but really not feel them the way you did before the trauma. It's as if being in a daze.

The acute stress may leave you feeling as if you are just going through the motions of living. It is as if you are in someone else's body even though you know it is your own. In this condition you just don't feel as if you are the same person you were before the trauma.

You may forget an important aspect of the traumatic event. For example, when you retell what happened, parts of the story are missing. If someone fills in some details, they may seem strangely familiar, but you just can't recall them.

Another common feature of acute stress disorder is the lack of strong feelings. You may feel numb, almost anesthetized to your feelings. Rather than hot with anger toward the person who threatened your life, you may feel apathetic and cold. Your feelings may seem a thousand miles away, or you may feel nothing at all. This lack of emotional responsiveness is not only a reaction to the perpetrator if you were a victim, but to those you care about as well. It is hard for you to laugh or cry, love or hate.

Still another way that you may reexperience the trauma is what is called a flashback. A sound or scene may trigger a flashback episode during which you actually feel as if you are reliving part of the event. Finally, when you sleep, you may have the same nightmare of the event several times each night, awakening with your teeth clenched and your body drenched in sweat.

Understandably, if you have an acute stress disorder, you try to avoid or escape anything that arouses recollections of the trauma. If you were in an automobile accident, for example, you might stay at home or stop driving. You might start taking buses and keep your eyes closed while riding so that you don't have to look at the traffic.

Much of your time might be spent avoiding thoughts, feelings, conversations, activities, places, and people associated with the trauma. When people ask about the accident, you would change the topic of conversation. You might stop seeing or calling a friend who was in the car with you. It might become hard to watch television, or you might channel-surf for programs like sports or westerns, which won't remind you of the accident.

The impact of an acute stress disorder on a person's life should not be underestimated. It can disrupt your work, your home life, or both. You would probably feel distressed much of the time, and it would be hard to get important things done in one or more areas of your life. On the other hand, many victims of rape or other trauma can drag themselves through life, but they may not be able to take care of some necessary task such as seeking legal recourse, applying for financial aid, or even telling family members about the trauma.

A traumatic event may bring you to the attention of professionals for a variety of reasons. You may be injured and rushed by ambulance to the emergency room of a hospital. You may be called to the hospital when a loved one is in the intensive care unit. If you faced a natural disaster, emergency personnel may come to your assistance at your home or office. On the other hand, you may need to seek professional help when the symptoms of acute stress interfere with your work at home or on the job.

## What Is a Normal Response to an Abnormal Event?

What is a normal response to an abnormal, traumatic event? Here the lines get very fuzzy, and professionals struggle with the difference between a normal adjustment and an acute stress disorder. After a tragedy, a crisis, or a major loss, most people go into a protective state of shock. There are typically two stages of shock: denial and numbness.

At first, people struggle with the event by denying it. Then, in small doses, as they tell others about the tragedy, people stop denying the event and go into the second stage of shock, that of emotional numbness. Then, as they stop denying their intense emotions and talk about them, they begin to reconnect to their feelings and to other people.

The normal experience of shock can take hours or days. How long is too long? There are no clear answers, but when the anxiety, avoidance, and distress impair the person's ability to function at home and work, an acute stress disorder may be present.

Children usually take longer to come out of shock than adults. They will withdraw or, conversely, chatter about everything except the event until they feel safe enough to talk about the trauma. They may take even longer if there is no one whom they trust to reach out to them with sensitivity and patience to get them to talk about the event or to act it out in play or artwork. Here, a professional is needed to assess the length, depth, and breadth of the response to see if a disorder is present.

Research has shown that parents underestimate the traumatic nature of the physical injuries that hospitalize more than six hundred thousand children each year. One study found that over 90 percent of children hospitalized for injury felt the experience was traumatic, while less than two-thirds of parents assessed the event as traumatic.

## What Can I Do?

If you are experiencing an acute stress disorder, there are many
things you can do to recover, and help is available in a variety
of forms. One of the most important ways to help yourself
is to talk about the trauma with
family, friends, clergy, rescue personnel, and almost anyone you
trust who will listen. You must
hear yourself tell others what happened until you know that it
happened and you know how you
feel about it. This takes a great
deal of time and patience. You will

> *Because I remember, I
> despair. Because I
> remember, I have the duty
> to reject despair.*
>
> —Elie Wiesel

need to repeat your story many times. If family and friends don't
know what to say, tell them that you need them to listen, not
to talk. Writing about the event and your responses can also be
beneficial.

It helps to understand something about stress to understand
why this is so important. As we explained in Chapter 1, when
faced with anything we perceive as dangerous, our bodies go
through what is called the fight-or-flight response. This is a survival response. Breathing quickens, heart races, blood pressure
rises, perspiration covers the skin, and our muscles tense up to
prepare to run or attack the danger. Once the threat is over, our
bodies slowly return to normal.

When we face a traumatic event, it takes longer to switch out of
the survival mode. Unless we are convinced that the threat has
passed, our bodies continue to prepare to fight or flee from it. The
high levels of anxiety and avoidance we described earlier are evidence of the flight response. We can't sleep, feel restless, startle easily, and remain on alert while trying to get away from anything that
reminds us of the traumatic event. The dissociative symptoms of
emotional numbing, depersonalization, diminished awareness, and

amnesia are evidence of an inward flight. The irritability and anger we feel are evidence of the fight response.

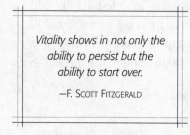

*Vitality shows in not only the ability to persist but the ability to start over.*

—F. SCOTT FITZGERALD

Talking about the trauma helps us to recognize that the danger has passed and that we are safe again. For this reason emergency room doctors learn to repeat, "It is over, you are safe now." When loved ones and friends hold us in their arms, this also helps us know we are safe and that the danger has passed. We also need to get as much information about the traumatic event as we can get. Information about our medical condition, the status of others, and details of the event decreases our tension and keeps us from forming dangerous conclusions that might perpetuate our fight-or-flight response. In addition, those who listen to us need to know the normal responses to trauma so that they can reassure us that we are not out of control or going crazy.

## STRESS, DEPRESSION, AND DRUG ABUSE: FALLOUT OF SEPTEMBER 11

A survey of New York City residents in the wake of the September 11, 2001, terrorist attacks found high levels of both depression and post-traumatic stress disorder among respondents and documented an increase in substance abuse. People who experience major trauma and those with PTSD or depression may self-medicate with drugs or alcohol to relax, cope with stress, or relieve symptoms. Postattack rates of depression and PTSD were approximately twice baseline levels previously documented in a 1999 study. Dr. David Vlahov and his colleagues at the New York Academy of Medicine estimated that of the approximately 911,000 people in the area of New York, the trauma resulted in approximately 67,000 PTSD and 87,000 depression diagnoses. He esti-

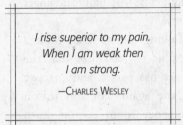

*I rise superior to my pain.
When I am weak then
I am strong.*

—CHARLES WESLEY

mated that 265,000 people increased their use of any of the substances in question: 89,000 smoked more cigarettes, 226,000 consumed more alcohol, and 29,000 used more marijuana.

## PROFESSIONAL HELP

If you find that you still have the symptoms of acute stress disorder, it is best to seek help from community agencies, self-help groups, your physician, and/or a mental health professional. A physician may prescribe medications to help reduce the anxiety so you can sleep and overcome the avoidance that keeps you in the emergency flight response. Recent research by Gelpin and colleagues has shown that continuous utilization of benzodiazepine medications to reduce post-traumatic symptoms, even when initiated close to the time of trauma exposure, did not reduce such symptoms at follow-up. There is evidence that dreaming helps to emotionally integrate distressing memories. In terms of medications, all types of PTSD symptoms except sleep disturbance will respond to the selective serotonin reuptake inhibitors (SSRIs) and other related drugs.

*To build may have to be
the slow and laborious task
of years. To destroy can
be the thoughtless act
of a single day.*

—SIR WINSTON CHURCHILL

**Mental Health Referrals**    Let's assume you have decided that you could benefit from psychotherapy. Your therapist will probably use a number of the psychotherapy approaches. If your anxiety is intense and you are not on medication, your therapist may encourage you to see your primary-care physician or a psychiatrist to discuss the possibility of medication.

**Cognitive Restructuring**  Cognitive restructuring is a major psychotherapeutic approach used to treat acute stress disorder. Whenever we exaggerate our thinking (our cognitions) we evoke exaggerated emotional responses. Most traumatic events are extreme events, but how you think about them, once they have occurred, does not have to be extreme.

> *Courage is not the absence of fear, but rather the judgment that something else is more important than fear.*
>
> —AMBROSE REDMOON

**Relaxation Training**  Another major psychotherapeutic approach to acute stress is relaxation training. You may benefit from several approaches to relaxation to help release tension in muscle groups and calm your mind.

**Systematic Desensitization and Exposure Therapy**  If you develop an excessive and self-defeating fear or phobia about aspects of the traumatic event, systematic desensitization and exposure therapy will use what you learned in relaxation training to recondition your mind and body to respond with confidence rather than fear to images of the distressing experiences. Once you have been desensitized to the feared situation in your imagination, the therapist will then encourage you to gradually expose yourself to it in real life.

**Holistic Approaches**  Your psychotherapist may also help you use your spiritual resources in dealing with an acute stress disorder. Most religious and wisdom traditions have addressed the age-old question of why bad things happen to good people. Rabbi Harold Kushner wrote a very inspiring and helpful book by that title (see Appendix III).

> *I must not fear. Fear is the mind-killer. Fear is the little-death that brings total obliteration. I will face my fear. I will permit it to pass over me and through me. And when it has gone past I will turn the inner eye to see its path. Where the fear has gone there will be nothing. Only I will remain.*
>
> —FRANK HERBERT

## LIKE A BRIDGE OVER TROUBLED WATER, I'LL BE THERE

Probably the most important thing you can do to help someone who is suffering from an acute stress disorder is to listen and then listen again. Someone with an acute stress disorder needs to tell his story over and over again to get past the denial and the emotional numbness that we all use to protect ourselves from overwhelming events and feelings. There are no magic words, and clichés will backfire. Beware of "It could be a lot worse," "She's better off now," or "Don't talk like that. You'll lick this in no time." You may desperately want to find some comforting words, but often there are none. When these traumatic emotions surface, remind yourself to listen, to stay with the person and to be a big ear and not a big mouth. Your quiet presence is what the person needs most.

## INFORMATION-PROCESSING INTERVENTIONS— EMDR AND TAPPING

When we are overwhelmed and cannot fully process distressing or traumatic experiences, we may store the immediate emotions and distorted thoughts very close to the way we initially experienced them. When we remember the trauma or encounter similar situations, we may reexperience the stressful emotions and physical sensations. This inadequate information processing of disturbing emotions may also be true of relatively minor but stressful events. This is why it is so important for us to review traumatic events by talking about them repeatedly, discharging emotions while awake, and getting enough sleep to process the event through dreams. Derailed or incomplete information processing is the target of some relatively new and effective interventions for PTSD and phobias.

Eye movement desensitization and reprocessing (EMDR) was developed by Dr. Francine Shapiro to alleviate the distress associated with traumatic memories. During EMDR, the client attends to emotionally disturbing material in brief sequential doses while simultaneously focusing on an external stimulus. The therapist usually directs lateral eye movements as the external stimulus but may also use other stimuli, including hand-tapping and audio stimulation. In this way, new associations are forged between the traumatic memory and more adaptive memories. Dr. Roger Callahan developed a similar technique for dealing with trauma and phobias called "tapping." He believes that the flow of energy is blocked by traumatic events. By tapping on select acupuncture meridian points while the patient attends to traumatic or phobic memories, the flow of energy is restored.

> *You gain strength, courage and confidence by every experience in which you really stop to look fear in the face. You are able to say to yourself, "I have lived through this horror. I can take the next thing that comes along." You must do the thing you think you cannot do.*
>
> —ELEANOR ROOSEVELT

## MUSIC AS THERAPY

It is no accident that the tragic events of September 11 spawned an outpouring of meaningful songs and dedicated concerts. Music

> *Did you open your eyes in hope it never happened? Close your eyes and not go to sleep?*
>
> —ALAN JACKSON

has the power to heal by keeping the traumatic event in the fore-front of our mind while we work through the tangle of emotions. Alan Jackson's "Where Were You (When the World Stopped Turning)" spoke not just to country music fans but to all Americans. He was able to identify many of the feelings associated with acute stress, and helped us to feel normal despite these abnormal emotions. Songs to our heroes spoke volumes about our losses. Ellis Paul sang about how "New York City looked just like the gates of hell," but his pain was segued into a determination "to laugh, believe, dream, roll up my sleeves, and give everything until there is nothing left to give." Ray Stevens used his classic humor to lighten our pain when he sang about "Osama—Yo'Mama," and on the same album stirred the emotions with the anthem "United We Stand." Lee Greenwood helped heal America with his "Proud to Be an American."

When our patients have a trauma they are working through, we encourage them to find music to fit their personal situation and work through their emotions. There are many songs of loss, death, disease, and tragedy. Appendix I can help you explore the use of music to cope more effectively.

> *We who lived in concentration camps can remember the men who walked through the huts comforting others, giving away their last piece of bread. They may have been few in number, but they offer sufficient proof that everything can be taken from a man but one thing: the last of human freedoms—to choose one's attitude in any given set of circumstances—to choose one's own way.*
>
> —VICTOR FRANKL

## Acute and Post-traumatic Stress at a Glance

Some events that happen to us are so overwhelming and frightening that they cause temporary or permanent changes in our physical and psychological sensitivity to stress. When there is a significant traumatic event, everyone can expect to develop at least some of the symptoms of anxiety and stress. Some people may be more biologically vulnerable, have a history of more traumas, or be more directly affected by the trauma. Most symptoms of acute or post-traumatic stress disorder can be managed and treated effectively. The treatment includes early and supportive stress debriefing, group and peer support, psychotherapy (including relaxation training, anxiety reduction, and cognitive therapy), and medications.

### THIRTEEN

# Life-Change Management

*May you have a strong foundation when
the winds of changes shift.*
—BOB DYLAN

MANY OF THE STRESSORS WE HAVE BEEN LEARNING TO RECOGNIZE and manage are day-to-day, week-to-week stressors. These might be called the stressors of the prevailing winds—the stressors that prevail in our daily lives.

In Chapter 3, we asked you to consider some stressors under a category called "change stressors." It is said that about the only thing that we can count on in life, besides death and taxes, is change. For better or for worse, nothing ever stands still. Modern life presents us with more change than ever before. Alvin Toffler wrote a popular book about the acceleration in the rate of change called *Future Shock*. We change everything rapidly:

where we live, where we work, our friends, and even our intimate relationships.

Change of any sort can be scary or exciting, and it usually triggers our stress response. Some people make a change in lifestyle to reduce stress, but it backfires. During his first interview, one of our patients described why he had moved to Texas. He had gone to a counselor in Florida, who had listened to his problems and suggested that his anxiety might be the result of difficulties in his marriage, his job, or his friendships, so he had filed for divorce, gotten fired, and moved out of state. His decision may have shown poor judgment, but many of us make other decisions that inadvertently add up to just as much stress.

In this chapter you will have the chance to chart the challenges in your life. In the last part of this chapter, you will learn ways to manage these life changes better.

## From the Laboratory

Drs. Thomas Holmes and Richard Rahe, at the University of Washington School of Medicine, have made major breakthroughs in our understanding of the effects of life changes on health and disease. Convinced by their own experiences as physicians, and following up on the earlier work of Drs. Adolf Meyer at Johns Hopkins and Harold Wolff at Cornell University, Drs. Holmes and Rahe set out to measure the life changes that seem to precede illnesses.

From case histories of five thousand patients, they gathered a long list of life events that seemed to precede major illnesses. They then asked about four hundred people to compare the amount, intensity, and length of time they needed to adjust to each life event on the list. The people were asked to assume that marriage had a certain numerical value, use it as a standard of comparison, and assign a numerical value to each of the other life events on the list.

Scientists began using this scaling system to understand and predict susceptibility to illness. Thousands of individuals reported the number of times they had experienced the events. Holmes, Rahe, and others multiplied the number of times an event was experienced by the readjustment value given to the event and summed these products to find a life-change score for each person. Those who had high life-change scores were much more likely to contract an illness following the events. The illnesses ranged widely, from accidents to alcoholism, cancer to psychiatric disorders, and flu to the common cold.

## THE SOCIAL READJUSMENT RATING SCALE

**Directions:** *Read each life event and indicate in the space provided the number of times you have experienced the event in the last year. Multiply the number of times you experienced the event by the points next to it and total up the products.*

| LIFE EVENT | Stress Value | Number of times you experienced the event in the last year | Your total life change scores |
|---|---|---|---|
| 1. Death of spouse | 100 × | _____ | = _____ |
| 2. Divorce | 73 × | _____ | = _____ |
| 3. Marital separation from mate | 65 × | _____ | = _____ |
| 4. Detention in jail or other institution | 63 × | _____ | = _____ |
| 5. Death of a close family member | 63 × | _____ | = _____ |
| 6. Major personal injury or illness | 53 × | _____ | = _____ |

| LIFE EVENT | Stress Value | Number of times you experienced the event in the last year | Your total life change scores |
|---|---|---|---|
| 7. Marriage | 50 × | _____ | = _____ |
| 8. Being fired from work | 47 × | _____ | = _____ |
| 9. Marital reconciliation with mate | 45 × | _____ | = _____ |
| 10. Retirement from work | 45 × | _____ | = _____ |
| 11. Major change in health or behavior of a family member | 45 × | _____ | = _____ |
| 12. Pregnancy | 40 × | _____ | = _____ |
| 13. Sexual difficulties | 39 × | _____ | = _____ |
| 14. Gaining a new family member (e.g., through birth, adoption, oldster moving in, etc.) | 39 × | _____ | = _____ |
| 15. Major business readjustment (e.g., merger, reorganization, bankruptcy, etc.) | 39 × | _____ | = _____ |
| 16. Major change in financial state (e.g., a lot worse off or better off than usual) | 38 × | _____ | = _____ |
| 17. Death of a close friend | 37 × | _____ | = _____ |

| LIFE EVENT | Stress Value | Number of times you experienced the event in the last year | Your total life change scores |
|---|---|---|---|
| 18. Changing to a different line of work | 36 × | _____ | = _____ |
| 19. Major change in the number of arguments with spouse (e.g., either a lot more or a lot less than usual regarding childbearing, personal habits, etc.) | 35 × | _____ | = _____ |
| 20. Taking on a mortgage greater than $10,000 (e.g., purchasing a home, business, etc.) | 31 × | _____ | = _____ |
| 21. Foreclosure on a mortgage or loan | 30 × | _____ | = _____ |
| 22. Major change in responsibility at work (e.g., promotion, demotion, lateral transfer) | 29 × | _____ | = _____ |
| 23. Son or daughter leaving home (e.g., marriage, attending college, etc.) | 29 × | _____ | = _____ |
| 24. In-law troubles | 29 × | _____ | = _____ |
| 25. Outstanding personal achievement | 28 × | _____ | = _____ |
| 26. Spouse beginning or ceasing work outside the home | 26 × | _____ | = _____ |

| LIFE EVENT | Stress Value | Number of times you experienced the event in the last year | Your total life change scores |
|---|---|---|---|
| 27. Beginning or ceasing formal schooling | 26 × | _____ | = _____ |
| 28. Major change in living conditions (e.g., building a new home, remodeling, deterioration of home or neighborhood) | 25 × | _____ | = _____ |
| 29. Revision of personal habits (e.g., dress, manners, associations, etc.) | 24 × | _____ | = _____ |
| 30. Troubles with the boss | 23 × | _____ | = _____ |
| 31. Major change in working hours or conditions | 20 × | _____ | = _____ |
| 32. Changes in residence | 20 × | _____ | = _____ |
| 33. Changing to a new school | 20 × | _____ | = _____ |
| 34. Major change in usual type and/or amount of recreation | 19 × | _____ | = _____ |
| 35. Major change in church activities (e.g., a lot more or a lot less than usual) | 19 × | _____ | = _____ |

| LIFE EVENT | Stress Value | Number of times you experienced the event in the last year | Your total life change scores |
|---|---|---|---|
| 36. Major change in social activities (e.g., clubs, dancing, movies, visiting, etc.) | 19 × | _____ = | _____ |
| 37. Taking on a loan less than $10,000 | 17 × | _____ = | _____ |
| 38. Major change in sleeping habits (e.g., a lot more or a lot less sleep, or change in part of day when asleep) | 16 × | _____ = | _____ |
| 39. Major change in number of family get-togethers (e.g., a lot more or a lot less than usual) | 15 × | _____ = | _____ |
| 40. Major change in eating habits (e.g., a lot more or a lot less food intake, or very different meal hours or surroundings) | 15 × | _____ = | _____ |
| 41. Vacation | 13 × | _____ = | _____ |
| 42. Christmas | 12 × | _____ = | _____ |
| 43. Minor violations of the law (e.g., traffic tickets, jaywalking, disturbing the peace, etc.) | 11 × | _____ = | _____ |
| | | **GRAND TOTAL** | _____ |

## CHARTING THE WINDS OF CHANGE

Carefully follow the directions on the Social Readjustment Rating Scale. Take your time and try to include any event that is similar to the one given in the scale. Sometimes a friend or a family member can help you. When you are finished, total up your life-change units for the past year.

The studies that Drs. Holmes, Rahe, and other scientists have conducted provide us with a way of looking at our life changes. In general, a score of 150 to 300 is considered moderate, while a score above 300 is considered high. High scores have been correlated with susceptibility to illness and accidents in large group studies. High life-change scores have even been associated with injury among college football players. But if you scored above 300, it does not mean you are going to get sick or have an accident.

People seem to respond on an individual basis depending upon how much hassle each life event creates for a particular person. In fact, Drs. A. D. Kanner, Richard Lazarus, and colleagues developed a Hassles Scale to better understand the predictive power of the day-to-day, smaller events in our lives. Other research suggests that people who have clear and meaningful goals or tend to be stimulus-seekers seem to be able to withstand more change. A high score for someone in distress on the Social Readjustment Rating Scale, however, means that it might be wise for that person to learn how to manage life change more effectively. Regardless of your score, you may find the following techniques helpful.

## HOW TO MANAGE LIFE-CHANGE STRESSORS

The first step that Dr. Holmes suggests is that we all become familiar with the life events discussed in the Social Readjustment Rating Scale and become aware of the amount of change they require. Discussing with a friend the number of points given to each life event can help you do this. You could also simply review your life and think about the changes that you have experienced.

To familiarize yourself with the values, see if you agree or disagree with the ratings that were given by hundreds of people. Obviously, some events are easier for you to adjust to than they would be for other people. Likewise, some events are more difficult for you to cope with than they would be for other people. The points given are averages, but in general, they apply to all of us.

Dr. Holmes suggests putting the scale where you and your family can see it frequently. We often suggest to our patients that they reassess their current life changes at the end of every month, when they pay the bills and reassess their financial changes. It is helpful to keep the rating scale with the folder where you place the bills. This will help to remind you to take a good look at your current life conditions every month. At the very least, consider an annual review around New Year's or when you receive your W-2 or other tax statements early in the year.

## Anticipating Life Changes

Dr. Holmes also suggests anticipating life changes, planning for them in advance, and pacing yourself. Just as weather conditions change on a seasonal basis, many life changes can be predicted. Some events follow the seasons of life. For example, retirement from work, children leaving home to get married or attend college, and beginning or ending formal schooling are all stressful changes.

Still other life events can be planned well in advance, so that we don't have to face too many life changes in too short a time. For example, we can choose the date for our marriage, we can apply for a new job now or later, and we can delay buying a home or moving. If some of the things we have less control over occur, such as being fired from work, we can put off making the changes over which we do have control. It is similar to taking our temperature. If we are living life at a near feverish pace, recording our change score can remind us to cool off and put the freeze on other big changes.

Reading or hearing the predictions of scientists and others who use the trends and events in our current situation to project future developments can help you anticipate other changes in our society. We have recommended several books and audio programs listed in Appendix III for this purpose.

## SEASONS OF LIFE

Several books have appeared that shed light on the predictable crises that people go through in life. This genre of books began with Daniel Levinson, Ph.D., who wrote *Seasons of a Man's Life*, and Gail Sheehy, who wrote *Passages*. Several of these books that deal with the different predictable crises we are faced with as we go from birth to death are referenced in Appendix III.

An important part of your stress management training is to realize that some life crises are predictable. The evolution of our lives is not determined by chance alone. We all go through a series of stable periods alternating with transitional periods. During stable periods, we make certain crucial choices and seek to attain particular goals and values. During transitional periods, we work toward terminating previous patterns and begin to work toward initiating new patterns. Realizing that certain patterns of living occur in a predictable fashion gives us the opportunity to cope with these life changes in a more adaptive and healthy manner.

## EARLY ADULTHOOD

The first major transition period that adults go through begins at the end of adolescence. This transition may start around the age of seventeen and last until around the age of twenty-two. During this transition, we begin to modify existing relationships with important individuals, groups, and institutions. We make a preliminary step into the adult world. We begin to explore the possibilities of the adult world and to imagine ourselves as a participant in it.

Transition periods do not affect everyone equally. Many individuals will remain in a student/learning capacity throughout the chronological years of seventeen to twenty-two, which may postpone the transition crises of early adulthood.

## ENTERING THE ADULT WORLD

Typically, an individual will begin to enter the adult world between the ages of twenty-two and twenty-eight. There is a shift from a position of being a child in a family to the position of being a novice adult. Choices are made regarding occupation, relationships, values, and lifestyles.

During the transition into the adult world, a person tends to explore the possibilities of adult living but also avoids making strong commitments. At the same time, and almost paradoxically, a person begins to create a stable life structure. A person tries to avoid making strong commitments and attempts to view all the alternatives but also tries to settle down and become more responsible.

During the crisis period, some individuals may capriciously change jobs, relationships, and places of residence. Others find that they make a strong commitment in one sector of life, such as work, but do not make that commitment to other sectors, such as their personal life. Still other individuals will not suffer a great deal from crises during this period and may postpone exploring and questioning their values and goals.

As individuals begin to approach their late twenties, they may begin to question the commitments they have previously made. They may also begin to question whether they want to keep life forever the way they have established it.

## Turning Thirty

Around the age of thirty, a major transition period occurs. During this transition period, a person becomes more serious, more restrictive, and more "for real." People feel a strong need to move forward and to produce the elements that they may feel are missing from their lives. There is a feeling that perhaps too soon it will be too late. During this period, some people will build upon the past without making fundamental changes, while for others this will be a stressful crisis.

During the transition period, around age thirty, marital problems and divorces peak. It is often a time for changes in occupation or for settling down after a period of transient jobs. During the early thirties, many people enter psychotherapy as they experience the strong emotions that often accompany crises.

## Settling or Settling Down?

After going through this period of transition, a person reaches a settling-down point that may last from the age of about thirty-two until thirty-nine or forty. During this period, the major tasks include establishing a place in society and "making it" in a vocation. Great efforts are made to build a better life and to attain certain goals.

Toward the end of the thirties, a dilemma is reached when an individual wants to be more independent and more true to his or her own wishes. The dilemma is that the person at this stage also wants to continue to retain the respect and reward that he or she has built in the world.

## Midlife Transition

The midlife transition, which occurs next, may last roughly from the ages of forty to forty-five. At this time, people may begin to question what they have done with their lives. They try to discover their real values. They look back on their earlier dreams and ask themselves if they still want those dreams.

According to one study of individuals going through midlife transition, approximately 80 percent of the people experience very severe struggles within themselves and the external world. The struggles involve questioning virtually every aspect of the life they have created. The person may, at this time, test a variety of new choices out of a need to explore as well as out of confusion.

It is important to realize as you learn how to manage stress that these life changes and crises are very normal parts of development. A transition is often a crisis. But a crisis involves both danger and opportunity. The danger is of losing some security, but the opportunity is of discovering new and untapped inner resources.

People during their midlife crisis often recognize that certain long-held assumptions and beliefs about themselves and the world are not true. They will have gone through a period of seeking to accomplish various goals and fulfilling various dreams. But they may find that the dreams they have sought are not the true goals that they want to pursue in life.

Albert Ellis, a prominent psychologist, once said that experience is the only thing that we are guaranteed in life. If we set up other ultimate goals, we can find ourselves racing toward them, only to be dissatisfied when we reach them. We must also recognize the precariousness and uncertainty of life. It can be taken from us and our loved ones at any time. Perhaps the best goal to strive for in life is to experience fully the richness of living.

This paradox may explain the words of the song "A Satisfied Mind": "It's so hard to find one rich man in ten with a satisfied mind." As we seek to race toward various goals and needs that have been artificially created and may be somewhat illusory, we may find that we grow stressed because we have set up something other than the experiencing of life as an ultimate goal. For example, we may race toward getting certain designer blue jeans only to find out that a new designer is in favor this month. What needs are we trying to fill with designer jeans?

We personally believe it is necessary to think seriously about our goals and the importance we place on achieving them. We hope that the time management and spiritual stress management chapters will help you establish your true goals. The knowledge of predictable life crises and the identification of valuable goals can help you through the changing seasons of your life.

## BOREDOM

Earlier, we spoke about the stress of boredom. This is also a change stressor because the lack of change often brings on boredom. When we are not excited about what we are doing, we often become depressed, irritated, and uptight. Variety is the spice of life, and without it our senses become dull or we become jumpy. It is during times of boredom that we may wish to consider making some of the changes we can control on the Social Readjustment Rating Scale.

If your score on the Social Readjustment Rating Scale is below 50, it might be a healthy decision to take action to increase your change score. A low score does not mean you are a boring person or that you are not necessarily under a lot of stress. But if you have a low score and you feel stressed, you could be experiencing boredom.

You may consider changes such as finding a more rewarding job, changing the number of arguments with a spouse (preferably decreasing them), altering your responsibilities at work, changing your living conditions, revising your personal habits, or changing the type or amount of recreation, church activities, or social activities.

## WORKING HARD AT STAYING WELL

Another way of managing a high level of change stress is to work harder at staying well. You do this by applying the skills that you will learn from this book and slowly adopting healthier living habits. The time to be sure to apply the knowledge in the chapters on exercise and nutrition, for example, is when you are experiencing the greatest amount of stress from the variable winds or tropical storms of change.

Another healthy habit is to get the proper amount of sleep so that you are well rested to face the stress that change can bring. You should also be careful not to neglect your body. During times of change, you need to maintain good hygiene and exercise.

You certainly would not want to change your living habits radically because you would be adding stress. After all, a revision of personal habits adds 24 points, a major change in sleeping habits adds 16 points, a major change in eating habits adds 15 points, and so on. Nevertheless, it is possible to increase your healthy living habits slowly during times of major social readjustment.

## A Volunteer, Mrs. Jackson

Mrs. Jackson, who was taking stress management training as part of preparation for volunteer work with patients, counted up her points on the rating scale and had a total of 25. Mrs. Jackson had experienced a vacation and Christmas during the last year but had not had any other life changes.

Mrs. Jackson's score is an example of possible understimulation. If Mrs. Jackson was not entering volunteer work and had come for stress management help, the authors might have asked her to consider seeking additional stimulation and making changes in her life to prevent boredom. Joining the volunteer group would add 26 points to her total because she would be beginning or seeking work outside the home. Her sense of excitement and interest in the new project was evident.

## An Executive, Mr. Cummings

Another student of stress management who came to us as part of a program for executives in a major industry was surprised to find that he had accumulated a great many potentially stressful life events. Mr. Cummings said that nothing could be better in his life.

During the last year he had married (53 points) the girl of his dreams, who had shortly thereafter become pregnant (40 points). He had decided to get married because he had gotten a raise at work (38 points) and a promotion (29 points). His promotion had come as a result of his selling more real estate than anyone else in the office (28 points). In addition, his change in status at the office had allowed them to buy the new home they dreamed of (31 points), and he had even more time away from work (20 points) to spend time enjoying his new son (39 points). Mr. Cummings saw little of his old friends at the bowling alley or the pub (18 points), but he enjoyed his honeymoon (13 points) and the family atmosphere of Christmas that year (12 points).

You can tell from this man's recent experiences that he had accumulated a great deal of change stress. In fact, Mr. Cummings's total was over 300 points, which suggested that he probably should slow down and make fewer major life changes during the next year and be sure he got enough good food, sleep, and rest so as to protect himself from the increased probability of illness. Becoming aware of life-change stress helped this man to anticipate life changes and plan for them in advance.

## Are You Sitting on a Two-Legged Stool?

Most of us are striving for a happy and meaningful life. Balance is needed to achieve and maintain such a life. Balance means that you avoid building your life around one person or one thing, no matter how wonderful it may seem. If you do, no matter who or what it is, losing it could be devastating.

> The history of man is a graveyard of great cultures that came to catastrophic ends because of their incapacity for planned, rational, voluntary reaction to challenge.
>
> —ERICH FROMM

Sigmund Freud considered work, play, and love to be three major parts of life. Other psychotherapists have called these by other names, but most agree that they are important building blocks for a balanced life. If we ignore any one of them, we ask too much of the other two. It is like sitting on a stool with only two legs—you may find yourself on the floor.

FOURTEEN

## The Help-Your-Heart Report Card

*People who fly into a rage always make a bad landing.*
—FORTUNE COOKIE

HEART DISEASE IS THE MAJOR CAUSE OF DEATH IN THE UNITED States. This has not always been the case in America, and it is not true of many other countries in the world. In the United States, the rate of death from heart disease has increased dramatically since the turn of the last century. A large percentage of these deaths occur between the ages of thirty-five and fifty and are classified as premature deaths. Unless causes and cures can be found, the World Health Organization predicts that coronary heart disease may well become the greatest epidemic mankind has ever faced.

Coronary heart disease results from damage to the arteries that supply blood to the heart muscle. The damage to the coronary arteries is called atherosclerosis. The heart is a muscle, and without oxygen and nutrients from the blood it cannot survive. Angina pectoris involves brief periodic attacks of chest pain caused by insufficient delivery of blood to the heart. A heart attack, or myocardial infarction, occurs if the lack of oxygen is extended and part of the heart muscle actually dies.

## PHYSICAL RISK FACTORS

Research suggests that many factors increase the risk of coronary heart disease. Men who are aging and have high levels of cholesterol, high blood pressure, diabetes, a family history of heart disease, and unusual heartbeat rhythms are at higher risk than other people. People who smoke, become obese, or fail to get sufficient exercise are also at risk. But physical risk factors cannot be found in nearly half of all new cases of coronary heart disease.

## PSYCHOLOGICAL RISK FACTORS

As early as 1892, physicians were aware of the distinct personality traits of coronary patients. In the late 1950s, Drs. Meyer Friedman and Ray Rosenman led the field of cardiology into a study of what they later called Type A behavior, a coronary-prone behavior pattern. Originally, these doctors were investigating the role of dietary cholesterol in heart disease. In the midst of reviewing the contradictory evidence for this risk factor, they found themselves listening to the then president of the San Francisco Junior League.

The evidence was not contradictory for this outspoken woman. "I told you right from the first," she said, "that you would find that we are eating exactly as our husbands do. If you really want to know what is giving our husbands heart attacks, I'll tell you. It's stress, the stress they receive in their work—that's what's doing it."

Drs. Friedman and Rosenman investigated the relationship between stress and coronary heart disease, as had other scientists; but they discovered a particular pattern of behavior with which they could explain a great deal of what was happening to men in this country. In the book *Type A Behavior and Your Heart,* Drs. Friedman and Rosenman introduced to the public this pattern, which they called Type A behavior. Type A individuals are often competitive, impatient, and hostile, while their counterpart, Type B's, are seldom angry and not preoccupied with achievement.

## FROM THEORY TO FACT

The strongest evidence for the importance of Type A behavior came from a well-controlled study known as the Western Collaborative Group Study. In 1961, Drs.

> *The lust for power is not rooted in strength, but in weakness.*
>
> —ERIC FROMM

Friedman and Rosenman examined through interviews three thousand healthy middle-aged men for certain behavior patterns. The men were also medically examined for coronary heart disease. About half of these men were classified as Type A.

Eight and a half years later, the Type A men had twice the coronary heart disease as the men who were originally judged as Type B. Other researchers have documented greater blockage of the coronary arteries among Type A individuals than Type B individuals. Of course, not all Type A men suffer coronary heart disease. But who wants to gamble when we have only one life? This seems to be one of the few situations in which a grade of B is better than a grade of A! Complete the following exercise to find out your grade.

## THE A/B LIFESTYLE QUESTIONNAIRE

**Directions:** *As you can see, each scale below is composed of a pair of adjectives or phrases. Each pair represents two kinds of contrasting behavior. Choose the number that most closely represents the type of person you are and put it under the column labeled "Your Score." Add your scores to get your total score.*

**RATING SCALE**

Your Score

| | | | |
|---|---|---|---|
| 1. | Work regular hours | Bring work home or work late | _____ |
| | | 0 1 2 3 4 5 6 7 8 9 10 | |
| 2. | Wait calmly | Wait impatiently | _____ |
| | | 0 1 2 3 4 5 6 7 8 9 10 | |
| 3. | Seldom judge in terms of numbers (how many, how much) | Place value in terms of numbers | _____ |
| | | 0 1 2 3 4 5 6 7 8 9 10 | |
| 4. | Not competitive | Very competitive | _____ |
| | | 0 1 2 3 4 5 6 7 8 9 10 | |
| 5. | Feel limited responsibility | Always feel responsible | _____ |
| | | 0 1 2 3 4 5 6 7 8 9 10 | |
| 6. | Unhurried about appointments | Frequently hurried for appointments | _____ |
| | | 0 1 2 3 4 5 6 7 8 9 10 | |
| 7. | Never in a hurry | Always in a hurry | _____ |
| | | 0 1 2 3 4 5 6 7 8 9 10 | |
| 8. | Many interests | Work is main interest | _____ |
| | | 0 1 2 3 4 5 6 7 8 9 10 | |
| 9. | Try to satisfy self | Want to be recognized by others | _____ |
| | | 0 1 2 3 4 5 6 7 8 9 10 | |

**RATING SCALE**
Your
Score

10. Not very precise      Careful about detail    _____
0 1 2 3 4 5 6 7 8 9 10

11. Can leave things temporarily unfinished    Must get things finished    _____
0 1 2 3 4 5 6 7 8 9 10

12. Satisfied with job    Striving on the job    _____
0 1 2 3 4 5 6 7 8 9 10

13. Listen well    Finish sentences for others    _____
0 1 2 3 4 5 6 7 8 9 10

14. Easygoing    Hard driving    _____
0 1 2 3 4 5 6 7 8 9 10

15. Do things slowly    Do things quickly    _____
0 1 2 3 4 5 6 7 8 9 10

16. Do one thing at a time    Think about what to do next    _____
0 1 2 3 4 5 6 7 8 9 10

17. Rarely angry    Easily angered    _____
0 1 2 3 4 5 6 7 8 9 10

18. Slow speech    Forceful speech    _____
0 1 2 3 4 5 6 7 8 9 10

19. Express feelings easily    Bottle up feelings    _____
0 1 2 3 4 5 6 7 8 9 10

20. Rarely set deadlines    Often set deadlines    _____
0 1 2 3 4 5 6 7 8 9 10

**YOUR TOTAL A/B SCORE**    _____

## What Your Total A/B Score Means

If your total score was 160–200, and especially if you are over forty and smoke, you may have a high risk of developing cardiac illness.

If your total score was 135–159, you are in the direction of being prone to cardiac disease. You should pay careful attention to the advice given to Type A's.

If your total score was 100–134, you are a mixture of A and B patterns. Beware of any potential for slipping into Type A behavior.

If your total score was less than 100, your behavior is generally relaxed and you express few of the reactions associated with cardiac disease. You probably have a Type B pattern.

Your score should give you some idea of where you stand in the discussion of Type A behavior. Even Type B persons occasionally slip into Type A behavior. It is important to remember that any of these patterns can change over time.

## Type A Behaviors

Friedman and Rosenman described Type A behavior as "an action-emotion complex that can be observed in any person who is *aggressively* involved in a chronic, incessant struggle to achieve more and more in less and less time, and, if required to do so, against the opposing efforts of other things or persons." It appears that the mechanism involved is related to what we have called the stress response.

In the course of struggling against time and other people, the fight-or-flight response is triggered repeatedly and chronically. As a result of the abnormal discharges of adrenaline and cortisol, most Type A people not only have an increase in the cholesterol and fat in their bloodstream, but have a more difficult time getting the cholesterol out of their bloodstream. As would be expected, they also have an increase in clotting within the arteries.

Friedman and Rosenman include the following behaviors in their description of the Type A, coronary-prone individual. Type A individuals always move, walk, eat, and talk rapidly. They tend to hurry to the end of their sentences. Type A individuals are impatient with the rate at which things happen. They tend to interrupt others and finish the sentences of people who are speaking slowly. They find it difficult to wait for others to do things they might be able to do faster. They hurry themselves in every activity they can.

Type A individuals try to do two or more things at once. They may think about business difficulties while they are driving to work or playing a game. They may try to eat and read at the same time. When others are saying something that does not relate to what they want to talk about, they always struggle to bring the conversation back to their interest. They have a difficult time relaxing or doing nothing, even if they are on vacation. They are often so preoccupied that they do not appreciate things around them that are unrelated to their main goals.

Type A's are more interested in getting things done than in getting enjoyment from doing them. They try to schedule more and more in less and less time. They often find themselves having scheduled more than can be accomplished and having allowed little time for unexpected interruptions or emergencies.

The Type A personality is extremely competitive, and these people try to achieve more than others. Their goals are more money, more possessions, more friends, more activities, more, more, more. They tend to judge themselves by the number of successes they have rather than the quality of their successes. In addition, they look upon their successes as the result of their ability to get things done faster than others, rather than as a result of their skills. They often exhibit gestures that suggest constant struggle, such as grinding their teeth or clenching their fists.

In summary, Type A individuals are hard-driving, competitive, impatient, and aggressive. They tend to be achievement-oriented, striving, and hostile. Another way to put it is to say that the Type A's slogan is an angry "We try harder."

In the scientific community, increasing emphasis is being placed on the relationship between hostility and heart disease. A Duke University follow-up study of 255 physicians conducted almost twenty-five years after they took a hostility test in medical school showed that those with scores above the midpoint on the scale had nearly five times as much coronary heart disease than those below the midpoint. The overall mortality for those with high scores was 6.4 times greater than for those with scores at or below the midpoint.

## TYPE B BEHAVIORS

Type B individuals, on the other hand, are free of all the habits described above. They seldom feel any sense of time urgency or impatience. Type B individuals are not preoccupied with their achievements or accomplishments and seldom become angry or irritable. They tend to enjoy their recreation, finding it fun and relaxing. They are free of guilt about relaxing, and they work calmly and smoothly.

## TAKE A SECOND LOOK AT YOURSELF

It is important to realize that these are descriptions of extremes. Nevertheless, remember that half of the three thousand healthy men whom Drs. Friedman and Rosenman studied were identified as Type A. If you were familiar with the Type A behavior pattern before you took the exercise, another way to guide yourself is to imagine which group your spouse, children, or friends would put you in if they had to choose between one or the other.

If you find that you are a Type A individual, you will want to decrease your risk for coronary heart disease by taking a good look at your lifestyle and making some of the changes we are about to suggest. If you are a Type B, read over these suggestions, use the ones that seem to apply to you, study the Type C characteristics listed at the end of this chapter, and continue your healthy behavior.

## But I'm Healthy

If you had no signs or symptoms of heart disease, you may wonder why you should try to change. According to Friedman and Rosenman, the Type A's are often the hardest to convince. As early as 1978, the National Heart, Lung, and Blood Institute reviewed the evidence and determined that Type A behavior was a risk factor for coronary heart disease of the same magnitude as serum cholesterol.

Every year two hundred thousand Americans die suddenly of heart disease, without having had any previous symptoms. In fact, heart disease and in particular hypertension are called the silent killers. This alone may be sufficient motive for you to decide to change your behavior. Another reason to decide to change is to become more efficient and more effective by setting clear priorities and using other stress management skills. Still another reason, perhaps one of the most important, is to improve the quality of your life.

## More Recreation?

Trying to change Type A behavior does not just mean taking more time for recreation. Gary Schwartz, a noted Yale University psychologist, pointed this out by recounting his observation of three fishermen. It was a beautiful spring day, with a blue sky and a calm lake. Two of the fishermen were drifting along quietly in a rowboat, sipping cold drinks and enjoying the scenery and the companionship. They hardly ever checked their lines to see if the bait had been taken. The third fisherman was alone in a boat with a high-powered motor. He had five different rods positioned off both sides of the boat. This third fisherman ran frantically back and forth checking the lines and yelling wildly downstream, "Did you catch anything?" He moved his boat with determination from spot to spot.

The first two fishermen are Type B, and the third is Type A. They were all fishing, but the very different effects on their bodies should be clear.

You might wonder if Type A's can change. The experience of hundreds suggests that they can. The gains are substantial, and the losses they feared seldom occur. You too can change!

## Now That I Know That I'm a Type A, How Can I Become a Type B Without Losing the Things I Want?

Part of the answer to this question is to decide whether what you are doing will bring you the things you want. Most Type A individuals are achievement-oriented and committed to job-related activities. It is not clear from some of the research conducted subsequent to the work of Drs. Friedman and Rosenman whether achievement-oriented activity is a critical element in Type A behavior. It is our opinion that many of the behaviors Friedman and Rosenman described can be engaged in without triggering the stress response.

You may wonder whether people who earn a great deal of money in high-status jobs are particularly likely to be Type A individuals. Many are, but an equally great number of people have succeeded without struggling against time or being angry and aggressive. There are Type A's and Type B's at every rung of our society's ladders. Impatience may not lead to success, and success is often found in spite of impatience!

When we try to do things too fast, we invite error and tend to adopt a rigid approach to what needs to be done. Repetitive thinking and acting tend to impede progress. When we are rushed, we are less likely to find creative and effective solutions to our problems. Thus it is not only possible but also more likely that we will succeed if we adopt some Type B behaviors. Type A's find they can be more successful than ever before after they start using stress management skills to achieve what they want.

## WHAT DO YOU WANT?

Most Type A individuals have desires that can be quantified. They want to acquire more objects or more money or to increase their production. The artist may want to produce more paintings in less time, the carpenter more homes, the researcher more publications, the broker more sales, the physician more cures, and so forth.

These quantitative accumulations may lead to outward success, but a preoccupation with them can create an inner void. When we die, all that is left is the way we have lived our lives. As the saying goes, you can't take it with you. Set aside some time to examine your goals and your abilities.

Much of the Type A's behavior is an attempt to store up accomplishments to overcome a general sense of insecurity and to control what is often not controllable. We need to take time to know who we are and where we are going. One way of doing this is to imagine yourself five, ten, and twenty years from now. Set aside time to use visual imagery to look at the goals you are striving for and the ways you are going about achieving them. It is helpful to remember that life is not a destination but a road to be enjoyed.

Although some research has not supported the importance of an achievement orientation in characterizing Type A behavior, three parts of the Type A pattern have been confirmed over and over. These are anger or hostility, time urgency, and aggressive competitiveness. Although it would not hurt to decrease the other behaviors described above, we will concentrate on these three.

## Humor and Hostility

Over the decades of research on Type A personality, it has become clear that one of the most important behavioral factors contributing to coronary heart disease is anger and hostility. Over twenty-five years ago, researchers observed that Type B individuals use humor to cope with stress and hostility. Hostile humor has also been found to be the main kind of humor enjoyed by Type A individuals, while Type B persons enjoy both hostile and nonhostile humor. This is consistent with the findings showing a close relationship between hostility and heart disease. Laughter at hostile humor may provide some benefits for heart-disease-prone individuals, but the benefits are clearly not enough to offset the bodily effects caused by the hostility. To counteract this effect, Type A individuals are encouraged to develop nonhostile aspects of their sense of humor.

## Time Urgency: Setting Priorities and Slowing Down

One of the best ways to decrease your sense of time urgency is to manage your time better and work more efficiently. We will devote a chapter to this later; but some of the suggestions that follow may be particularly helpful to the person with Type A behavior.

***Using a*** Most Type A's try to do too much in too little time.
***Calendar*** They find themselves fighting time. It is as though
***Instead of a*** they are using a stopwatch every minute of their
***Stopwatch*** day. One of the best ways to throw away an invisible stopwatch is to substitute a calendar as a timeline to success. Think in terms of years and months rather than minutes and seconds. For most people this also involves setting weekly priorities that are realistic and that will take them efficiently from where they are to where they want to be. Read the time management chapter to help establish your priorities.

**Slowing**
**Down**

Be sure to schedule time every day for the unexpected. Remember Murphy's Law: if something can go wrong, it will. By leaving yourself extra time for each task, you will be able to relax and enjoy the work. Schedule some time during the day between activities for relaxation. Avoid procrastination. It can lead to a rush just before the end of the day or a deadline.

When you start to feel impatient with someone or a task, use your impatience as a cue to relax. Type A individuals tend to interrupt conversations. When you feel the urge to interrupt or find yourself doing so, use that impulse as a signal to scan your body for tension and relax. Try not to assume that others are as impatient as you are. If you are late for a meeting, accept this human fallibility and avoid catastrophic thoughts about what the other person will do or say.

At the office, have someone screen your visitors and telephone calls. If you allow others to reach you at any time, even when you have someone in your office, you will probably try to hurry the caller or the person who believes he or she has your attention. This struggle will trigger the stress response. If no one is available to screen your calls, try to screen them yourself. Indicate that you are busy and will call back. This strategy is particularly important for homemakers. It is best if your communication shows that you have enough belief in your right to decide what you will do, and when to express your wishes assertively to the caller.

Try to clear your desk of reminders of things to do. Make a to-do list for the day and leave it inside a drawer or write it in an appointment book, so you can concentrate on the task at hand and have a sense of security.

We all have a limited amount of time in life. In the words of Kenneth Grooms, "There is more to life than increasing its speed." Rather than hurrying everything, try to choose the activities you will do and the people you will talk to. If someone is chewing off your ear, assert your right to end the conversation politely. Be firm and clear. You may want to read the chapters on assertiveness training to help you keep conversations from getting out of hand. When a telephone call is dragging out and you have things to do, tell the other person and, if necessary, hang up.

## PART OF THE UNCONTROLLABLE IS CONTROLLABLE

A number of researchers have determined that the most stressful situations, and those that are most likely to elicit or trigger Type A behavior, are those that are uncontrollable. Whenever you feel you cannot influence or change a situation, look carefully at your options and your goals. Assertiveness can often help you regain the control you will need so that the situation will not trigger your Type A behavior. In situations that cannot be controlled, remind yourself that, even though you cannot always control the world, you can control your body's response to the world.

When you find yourself rushing to get something done, ask yourself, "Has anything ever failed because it was done too well, too slowly?" If you sense that you are trying too hard to get closure, it may help to remember that only a corpse is completely finished! Perhaps this is part of the reason why we use the term "deadline."

In many jobs, the worker is the one who decides when the work is done. Too many Type A's never make that decision. Practice deciding when your work for the day is finished.

These changes are not easy to make, and you will need to remind yourself to slow down, stop consistently working late, and continue your job in the new day. The "hurry-up sickness" is a chronic illness. Be patient, even about making these changes. Leave yourself messages to slow down. When you do slow down, reward yourself. If you put a project aside at the end of a day rather than pushing yourself to complete it, congratulate yourself. Keep a record of these successes. You could be adding days and years to your life.

## Aggressive Competition or Calm Confidence

People with Type A behaviors tend to be hostile and competitive. Read the chapter on anger management, and when you start to get angry, remember to use that feeling as a cue to relax and strive for calm confidence. Use your thinking and your self-talk to work on the false perceptions you may have of threats, demands, and challenges. When you start to get angry because someone is not doing something quickly enough, check your beliefs. You may be thinking something like, "If I don't get this person to do this in time for the deadline, I will lose my job and look like a fool." Plan time for the unexpected, and remember the words of M. H. Alderson: "If at first you don't succeed, you're running about average."

Apply skills from the assertiveness chapters when you feel irritated or hostile. Be aware that some people may try to trigger your aggressive response. Recognize and avoid those who trigger your hostility, particularly other Type A individuals. If you get into an argument, ask yourself if winning the argument will really bring you what you want. Often you can simply agree to disagree.

## Developing Your Type B Behaviors

In the coming weeks, try to set aside time to expand your interests and your friendships. Take your lunch breaks if you usually work through them. Find people to share new experiences with you. Look for Type B individuals and increase the time you spend with these people. They will help you appreciate things you may have left behind in your rush toward accumulating numbers and accomplishments. Rather than rushing past things on your way through life, become more receptive to the world around you.

Delegate work. If you think no one else can do your job, imagine what would happen if you died. Most companies would find a substitute. If you own your company, think of delegation as life insurance for your family. Friedman and Rosenman point out the importance of rituals and traditions as ways of enjoying our lives and bringing new meaning to them. If you have moved away from traditions and have become preoccupied with work, you may find it enjoyable to create new family traditions or revive old ones.

One of the few things we are guaranteed in our travel through life is experience. You can expand and enrich your experience through hobbies, reading, the arts and humanities, and nature. You can avoid competing for these experiences because you are the only one who can have and enjoy them. If we move through life trying to get more done in less time, the days will pass all too quickly. We may end up having sold our right to experience and having received very little in return.

To begin enjoying new experiences, you may need to give yourself permission to use time for them. You may find yourself saying, "Tomorrow I'll let myself enjoy that." Remember, life is fragile and tomorrow may not be yours to count on. There is an old saying that can be applied to changing Type A to Type B behavior: "If not now, when?"

## Social Insecurity

A recent study of heart disease patients showed that it was possible to differentiate between those with more and less serious coronary atherosclerosis. The differentiation could be made not only by Type A behavior patterns but also by measures of social insecurity. Over 90 percent of the patients with both characteristics had severe atherosclerosis.

Social insecurity was indicated by patients reporting bashfulness, low self-confidence, sensitivity to criticism, difficulty being able to talk in groups, difficulty trusting people, and self-consciousness. They also tended to answer no when asked if they were good mixers or enjoyed many different kinds of play and recreation.

This study suggests that Type A behavior individuals who are also socially insecure may have a greater incidence of heart disease. Perhaps their striving for success and their striving to increase their attractiveness to others via accomplishments is a compensation for a lack of social security. If you are socially insecure, you may spend more time at work, and your hard-driving characteristics may be rewarded, but you may never have time to enjoy the social rewards for which you are striving.

> *It is when we all play it safe that we create a world of utmost insecurity.*
>
> —Dag Hammarskjöld

Think about your own social insecurity. If you find yourself anxious at parties and with other people, use the techniques in Chapter 9 to desensitize yourself. If you are less fearful of others, you will find it easier to spend more time engaged in Type B behaviors and enjoying the company of others.

## Develop the Characteristics of the Type C Stress-Resistant Personality

Research has now shown there may be another personality type that is stress-resistant even when maintaining what appears to be a Type A schedule of activities. The study at Duke University that demonstrated the link between hostility and heart disease by following 255 medical students twenty-five years later also found that some Type A personalities were healthier than the national average and seemed to thrive on the challenges and competition in their lives. Other Type A's were competitive and aggressive because they believed that most people around them were cheats and liars. In response, they felt compelled to connive and not tell the truth. Constantly at odds with everyone in their lives, they had high blood pressure and damaged arteries.

We call the healthy person who thrives on a challenging life the Type C personality. Who is this Type C person? Studies with ex-

> *Don't try to become
> well known. Try to
> become worth knowing.*
>
> —ROBERT FULGHUM

ecutives during the breakup of AT&T and an eight-year study in California suggest the following: Type C's are committed and confident; they feel a sense of control, and they have a balance between challenge and mastery. They do not worry about their competition catching up to them. Instead they look toward the future and feel what they do is worth doing and meaningful. They are not immune from "stuff happening," but they choose how they will react to what happens in life. They feel confident. They choose to do their homework, to learn new skills, to prepare their presentations, and to strive for success without increasing the risk of premature death.

## "IT'S EASY—I'VE WATCHED IT ON TV"

Several years ago we had the opportunity to discuss Type A behavior with a client who was a physician. Board-certified in both internal and orthopedic medicine, he had a history of over-achievement and Type A behavior within his family. One of his brothers has two degrees from a prestigious private school, one in mechanical engineering and the other in architecture. Another brother went to Yale, became an attorney, and wrote several books. Still another brother became a psychologist to try to make sense of it all, cure himself, and become a "Type A in remission." This physician had never skied before but agreed to meet his younger brother in Colorado to ski. His brother suggested he take three hours of ski lessons, but our client replied, "I don't need to. It's easy. I've watched it on TV."

One author has written that Type A's often live in the "panic zone" of too much challenge with too little mastery, too many commitments, and too much confidence. They are out of control. Our client experienced all of that on his first trip down the mountain. Fortunately, the tree that stopped him was only about eight feet tall. It flexed as he went over it, and tore only a small hole in his pants. The hole in his ego was much larger. After throwing his skis down the mountain, he discovered walking downhill in ski boots was no solution. That afternoon he took ski lessons. Today he skis very well. He can also laugh about that morning when he confronted some of his Type A characteristics and decided to work on becoming more of a Type C.

> *The future belongs to those who can blend vision, reason, and courage in a personal commitment.*
>
> —ROBERT KENNEDY

## BECOME THE CAPTAIN OF YOUR FATE

Two Emory University psychologists say the person most likely to succeed in life believes he has a measure of control over his own destiny. On the other hand, some individuals tend to feel that luck is the compelling factor and that they can do nothing about it. These researchers called the master-of-my-fate types "internals" and the luck-is-everything types "externals."

> *Out of the night that covers me, black as a pit from pole to pole, I thank whatever gods may be for my unconquerable soul.*
>
> —WILLIAM ERNEST HENLEY

Those who indicated they were "internals" almost invariably were the better students. The "externals" often drifted aimlessly, believing that they had no control over their fate. These findings have been replicated with people from all walks of life. If you feel you are drifting, develop more of the Type C personality. We will give you more examples and guidance in upcoming chapters, especially those that change what you think and what you eat, so you can take charge of your life in the healthy ways of the Type C personality.

# SECTION IV

## Attacking Your Stressful Behaviors, Thoughts, and Attitudes

*Change your words and you'll change your world.*
—ANON

*Victor Hugo's short story "Ninety-three" tells of a ship caught in a torrential squall. When the storm was at its height, the frightened crew heard a terrible crashing sound below. A cannon they were carrying had broken loose and was banging into the ship's side, tearing gaping holes with every smashing blow. Two men, at great risk to their lives, managed to secure the cannon. They knew that the cannon was more dangerous than the storm. The storm could toss them about, but the loose cannon within could sink them.*

*All the significant battles are waged within the self.*
—SHELDON KOPP

# FIFTEEN

## Taking the Stress Out of What You Tell Yourself

*I am an old man and have known a great many troubles—but*
*most of them never happened.*
—MARK TWAIN

ARE YOU READY TO LEARN SOMETHING ABOUT EMOTIONS THAT surprises many people? Feelings and emotions we experience are *not* caused by the events that precede them. For example, if someone calls us a name or if we lose money in the stock market, we might say that this made us angry or brought us disappointment. Our reasoning may seem to be true, but it is faulty.

The same events can cause very different feelings in different people. If you wanted to make someone angry at you and that person called you a name, you might be pleased. If you needed a stock market loss as a deduction for your income tax, such a loss might make you feel good. Feelings are not caused by events. If they were, everyone would have the same feelings after any given event.

Another example may help clarify these ideas. One of the authors was teaching an introductory course in psychology. About a week after the midterm exam, he gave a lecture on emotions. The author arrived with a stack of exams and told the class that the midterm grades could not be used because widespread cheating had been brought to his attention. He explained that he was giving the test again.

You can imagine what people felt. Think of yourself in this situation. What would you feel? Anxiety? Anger? Confusion? Most people felt these negative feelings. It might surprise you to learn that some people were very happy, some doubted the teacher, some felt guilty, and others claimed not to feel anything. Different people had very different reactions to the same event. It was clear that the event did not cause all these different feelings. If the author's wife had been sitting in the audience, she might have had another feeling. She might have feared for the life of the teacher! How could the same event cause so many different feelings?

## THE ABC's OF EMOTIONS

Albert Ellis, Ph.D., a renowned psychologist, developed a theory to explain the relationship between events and feelings. He reasoned that the true causes of feelings are not the events but the beliefs we have about these events. Dr. Ellis proposed a simple model to help us better understand emotions. Here are the ABC's of emotions:

- A's are the activating events. In the situation described above, the teacher's announcement was the activating event.

- B's are the beliefs. In this case, these were what each student believed about what the teacher said.

- C's are emotional consequences. In the example, these were all the different feelings that the students were having.

Most of the students who felt anger or anxiety had done well on the first exam and were afraid they would do poorly on the second exam. Most of those who were pleased had failed the exam and were happy to get a second chance. Others might have been pleased if they thought there had been widespread cheating and the cheaters were about to get their due. Most of those who claimed that they did not feel any strong emotions did not believe the author's announcement. The author's wife might have believed that someone would throw something at her husband!

This way of understanding our feelings is not new. As Ellis points out, the famous Stoic Epictetus wrote, "Men are disturbed not by things, but by the view which they take of them." As we noted in the preface, William Shakespeare rephrased this concept in *Hamlet:* "There is nothing either good or bad, but thinking makes it so." And Abraham Lincoln said, "People are about as happy as they make up their minds to be."

## The Boss and Your Beliefs

Take another example. If your boss calls you into his office, his intent may be to compliment your work. But before you go into his office, you wonder why he wants to see you. You may decide that he wants you to work late again, and you are irritated because you feel you are already doing too much work. By the time you get into his office, you may be angry in anticipation that he will ask more of you. In this example, A is the boss calling you into his office, B is the belief that he wants you to do more work, and C is the anger you feel boiling up inside of you.

You may have prejudiced your feelings, actions, and physiological reactions with your belief about the purpose for your being called into the boss's office. If you knew that the boss was going to compliment you, the activating event (A) would have been the same (boss calling you into his office), but your belief system (B) would have been different. In turn, the emotional consequence (C) would also have been different—perhaps pleasure or even excitement.

## Marriage and Your Beliefs

Each partner in marriage interprets the actions of the other person in terms of certain expectations or beliefs. These beliefs come from early experiences in our original families and the cultural norms of our society. The probability of misinterpretation is great. For example, when a husband does housework (A), his wife can see this as an appropriate contribution (B) or an indirect criticism (B) and thus feel gratitude (C) or anger (C). Another example would be when a wife is studying for a test and asks her husband to prepare the supper and take care of the children for the evening (A). The husband could feel anger (C) because he thinks a woman's place is in the home (B). Alternatively, the husband could feel pride (C) because he knows that her attending school is bringing them one step closer to their mutual goals (B). The potential for misinterpretations and unhealthy beliefs about a marital partner are some of the reasons why mind reading can be so dangerous and communication so important to strong relationships.

A final example involves a man whose fiancée was withdrawing and about to end their engagement. Both were single parents. Distraught, the man entered therapy. After much unfruitful discussion, the man agreed to ask his fiancée the key question "What is troubling you most about our relationship?" After repeated but gentle questioning, his fiancée explained that he must not love her because he never asked her to do anything for him. After all, he trusted his mother or sister but never her. The man hadn't asked her because he didn't want to burden her, given her other responsibilities. This was an unspoken but central belief that could now be addressed openly, and they could continue their engagement with greater confidence in their relationship. If beliefs cause the feelings we experience, we should be able to change our feelings or emotions by changing our beliefs. False and irrational beliefs may cause harmful, self-defeating, and unnecessary feelings. To change irrational beliefs, it is necessary to examine our beliefs and dispute them.

## Can't-stand-it-itis, Awfulizing, Musterbation, and Other Stressful Habits

Four irrational statements can be related to feelings of anger. These are the beliefs that may cause you to feel the stress response in many situations for which it is inappropriate. Do you think one or more of the following irrational thoughts when you are angry?

1. "I *can't stand* you treating me in such an unreasonable and unjust manner." These are the "can't stand it" beliefs that many of us suffer from. "Can't-stand-it-itis" is the pain that comes from not being able to stand something.

2. "How *awful* for you to have treated me so unfairly." This can be called "awfulizing." How often do you find yourself exploding an event out of proportion and making it "awful" instead of just unpleasant?

3. "You *should not, must not* behave that way toward me." This is sometimes called "musterbation." These unwritten laws and unnamed threats often lead to the stress response and to anger.

4. "Because you have acted in that manner toward me, I find you a terrible person who *deserves* nothing good in life, and you should be punished for treating me so." This

is sometimes called "undeservingness" or "damnation thinking."

All these statements tend to exaggerate our view of situations and upset us.

These same types of statements are sometimes used about situations that provoke anxiety in us. For example, if you have difficulty with public speaking, you may find yourself saying things like this:

1. "I *can't stand* talking in front of other people. Maybe I'll fall down! Maybe I'll faint!"

2. "How *awful* if I can't manage things." This is another form of awfulizing. It may be unfortunate if you can't manage something, but it is not awful.

3. "If I can't cope as well as I *must* cope, I am an inferior person, and I *deserve* what I get for not handling the situation." Perhaps you will have another chance. Are you really an inferior person, or do you simply lack skills in a particular area?

4. "I *should* have the ability to deal with the situation better." Who says you should? Do you have enough training to do it better? Where is it written that you should?

As you can see, anxiety statements can exaggerate the situation. Such statements tend to equate an evaluation of you as a whole being. Beware of labels: "I'm dumb," "I'm ugly," "I'm hopeless," and others. These are irrational and unhealthy beliefs. Such thinking is sometimes called "negative inner chatter" or "negative nonsense," and it is best avoided or replaced with healthier statements. The only way you can evaluate yourself or another person is to evaluate all of his or her actions over an entire lifetime. Few of us have the time to do so or the desire to take that responsibility!

## FINDING THE ENEMY BELIEFS

How can we attack and dispute these irrational beliefs so we can remain calm and avoid the anger or anxiety that can trigger the stress response? First, we must discover our main irrational beliefs. We can do this by looking for the "shoulds," "musts," and "have to's" in what we say and think. We can listen for words like "awful," "terrible," and "impossible." Finally, we can listen for phrases like "I can't stand that."

Sometimes irrational beliefs are hard to find. We may think the thoughts so quickly that they are almost automatic. In this case, you have to trace your thinking step by step, backward and forward, to figure out where the irrational beliefs are lurking.

Another way of uncovering the self-defeating beliefs from which you may suffer is to go through a list of beliefs that Albert Ellis and his colleague Robert Harper introduced in their book *A Guide to Rational Living*. Most irrational ideas concern either ourselves and our self-worth or the people and events around us. For this reason, we have divided the list into beliefs that seem to be primarily about ourselves and those that are primarily about other people and other things. As you go through these lists, check off those that seem to be causing you pain and problems in living, so you can return to them later.

### SELF-DIRECTED IRRATIONAL BELIEFS

1. I need everyone's love and approval for just about everything I do.
2. I should be able to do everything well.
3. If something bad happens, I should worry about it.
4. It is easier to avoid difficult things than to try them and risk failure.
5. I will enjoy life more if I avoid responsibilities and take what I can get now.

## OTHER-DIRECTED IRRATIONAL BELIEFS

1. Some people are bad and should be punished.
2. When things aren't going well in my life, it is terrible.
3. If things go wrong, I'm going to feel bad and there's very little I can do about those feelings.
4. What has happened to me and what I have done in the past determine the way I feel and what will happen to me now and in the future.
5. People and things should be different, and perfect solutions should be found for everything.

## Unhealthy Beliefs About Work

Another way to review these ten commonly held unhealthy beliefs is to consider the following problems that a secretary can get into if she holds these beliefs about her job.

One of the authors treated a secretary whom we will call Mrs. Williams. Mrs. Williams was referred by her gastroenterologist for a nervous stomach. She worked for two executives who were very demanding, yet they seldom spoke to her except to point out corrections she needed to make.

Mrs. Williams began to worry that she was incompetent and that she might lose her job. She began to type faster, making more mistakes, and avoided difficult tasks for fear of failing. At the same time, she was angry with her immediate bosses for not being more reasonable, and she felt their superior should call them on the carpet. Life seemed terrible. Mrs. Williams knew she would feel bad every day she went to work.

It became clear in our interviews that Mrs. Williams's central irrational belief was that without approval for her work, she "would just die." By slowly disputing this and other beliefs, she was able to accept the conditions at the office until she could apply for a transfer. For example, she came to realize that although gaining the approval of everyone she worked for would be very nice indeed, it was an unrealistic expectation and that she was more likely to get the approval of her friends and family than of her bosses.

Mrs. Williams also saw that by trying to be a faster typist and avoiding difficult tasks, she was making the problem worse. She began to reason that it would be great if her bosses were reprimanded, but they were, in fact, getting their work done satisfactorily. It was unlikely that they would either be reprimanded or change their ways. Then, through the assertiveness skills that she was learning in therapy, she learned how to express her feelings and her needs. She also realized that no matter what happened at work, part of her life might be unpleasant, but life itself was not terrible.

As a result, her stomach was upset less of the time. At follow-up, she stated that she had decided to get a new job. She also said that she was pleased that she could take the ups and downs better now because her happiness was less dependent on what happened in the office.

## ROLE-RELATED IRRATIONAL BELIEFS

Each of us has a variety of roles in life that can hook us into suffering the emotional consequences of irrational beliefs. One good example is the "supermom" who may believe that she has to be all things to all people in her family and at her job. Take some time to look at your roles and the irrational beliefs you may have about them.

## ATTACKING YOUR IRRATIONAL BELIEFS

Once you uncover the ABC's of your life, it's time to debate and dispute (D) your irrational beliefs actively and vigorously. Ask, "*What* makes it awful?" "*Why* can't I stand it?" "Why *must* they never do that?" "Where is it written that they must not do that or that I must do that?" Finally, ask, "Why should I judge the whole person or myself on the basis of one or even several acts?"

If your disputing (D) is successful, you will enjoy new and more effective emotions (E). You will have to attack your irrational beliefs vigorously and repeatedly to get the full benefit of thinking and feeling better.

## EXPOSING AND EXPELLING YOUR INNER ENEMIES

To help you detect and dispute your irrational beliefs, create a chart like the one below. First, identify the stressful emotions you are experiencing. Write those on the line next to emotional consequences. Then, fill in the activating event that seems to trigger your stress response next to A (the activating event).

Now, go back and try to figure out the beliefs you hold and fill those in next to B (beliefs). You may find it helpful to check the lists of beliefs just presented. Do this for most of the anger-arousing or anxiety-producing events that you encounter. Then begin to dispute the irrational beliefs by using the questions that we just reviewed. Write your rational arguments next to D (disputing). Finally, identify the new, healthier feelings that come with better thinking, and write them next to E (effective emotions).

### AN EXAMPLE OF A RATIONAL-EMOTIVE A TO E CHART

A. **Activating Event:**
   *Boss pointing out my errors.*

B. **Irrational Belief:**
   *I must be totally incompetent and I am sure I will lose my job.*

C. **Stressful Emotional Consequence:**
   *Anxiety, terror, worry, loss of sleep, overeating, etc.*

D. **Dispute Your Irrational Beliefs:**
   *It would be nice if I didn't make any mistakes, but I am not totally incompetent, just human.*

E. **New, Less Stressful, and More Effective Emotions:**
   *Some appropriate concern and motivation to get the job done correctly.*

## THE SHADOW OF A SABER-TOOTHED TIGER

We are focusing most of our attention on the emotional consequences (C's) of anger and anxiety because these are the primary emotions of the fight-or-flight response of stress. The ABC's also apply to other emotions, as we will show in the chapter about depression.

The belief that you are in danger is essential to the fight-or-flight response. Going back to the example of the cave dweller's stress response when the shadow of the saber-toothed tiger appeared, if the shadow was actually that of a tree in the moonlight, the entire fight-or-flight stress response was unnecessary wear and tear on the cave dweller's body. In the same way, it is best physically and emotionally to check our beliefs (B's) about the shadows of life (A's) if we want to have new and more effective responses (C's).

## COMMON PROBLEMS, UNCOMMON SENSE

For many people, becoming angry is related to doubting themselves, being unsure, or feeling intimidated by someone. It is important to remember that you are a fallible human being but nonetheless a worthy person with many good qualities. To be fallible means to be able to make mistakes. None of us was born goof-proof! We are sure you realize that you are bound to make mistakes, but many of us have the irrational belief that we should be perfect.

In addition, be sure that you understand you have worth for reasons other than your accomplishments or your appearance. These will fade in time, but you will always be worthwhile for being a person who is able to experience life and to share it with others. Finally, as Eleanor Roosevelt said, "No one can make you feel inferior without your consent. If you don't agree with their evaluation of you, they can't make you feel inferior. Your thought in life is your ultimate freedom, a birthright that no one can take away from you without your consent."

## Powerful Words to Wash Away Worries

It is said that overwork never killed anyone, but excessive worry can. When you are thinking a lot about something and it is distressing you, ask yourself, "Am I planning or am I worrying?" If you are worrying, stop and plan. If it is the wrong time or place to plan do something else, perhaps a relaxation technique.

Alternatively, ask yourself, "What's the worst thing that could happen?" Follow the events out to the very end, and you may find the worst is not so bad and may even have a silver lining. Some people who are dissatisfied with their jobs have done this and found their way to another job—a better one! If you dwell on world events or those you cannot control, remember the words of Ralph Waldo Emerson: "Can anybody remember when times were not hard and money was not scarce?"

## Two Rules for Stress Management

Robert Eliot, a cardiologist at the University of Nebraska, combined this cognitive approach with the relaxation response in the following way:

Rule No. 1: "Don't sweat the small stuff."
Rule No. 2: "It's all small stuff. And if you can't fight and you can't flee, flow."

## "They Who Laugh, Last"

We have been discussing the power of beliefs and how exaggerated thoughts (B's) lead to exaggerated emotional consequences (C's). Not all exaggerated thoughts are unhealthy. Often, if we further exaggerate an exaggerated thought, the absurdity of the exaggeration brings laughter. The benefits of humor are many. It breaks tension between people and brings them together as they relax and share in the laughter. It helps us gain a new perspective and take ourselves less seriously. Research has also shown physical benefits from the "internal jogging" of laughter. For more about this see our chapter on recreation and humor.

## The Three C's of the Stress-Resistant Personality

Suzanne Kobassa showed the power of beliefs in health and illness when she studied hundreds of employees during major changes such as the breakup of AT&T. Those employees who felt challenged rather than overwhelmed, in control rather than powerless, and committed rather than apathetic had half the illnesses as compared to the pool of coworkers. If you tend to feel overwhelmed, powerless, or apathetic, you don't need to feel that way about your stress resistance. Later research shows that you can learn to be more stress-resistant. We invite you to get your C's ready for change by building better B's about yourself and your world. See the chapters on Type A behavior and nutrition to help further develop your Type C characteristics to become more stress-resistant.

## UNCOMMON SENSE FOR ANGER

Sometimes we needlessly get angry because we take an unpleasant situation personally. When someone is directly offensive to you, you can control and contain your anger by refusing to be distracted from whatever you are doing. This is called being task-oriented. Stay focused and stick to what must be done in the situation to get the outcome you want. When you take insults personally, you get distracted from your tasks and caught up in unnecessary feelings. Recognize that the other person may be deliberately provoking you. By realizing what the other person is doing, you may find it easier to stay task-oriented.

Sometimes we get angry or anxious simply because that has always been our reaction to a certain situation. As you learn alternative ways of reaction to provocations or demanding situations, you will be less inclined to react with anger or anxiety. Try to catch yourself if you are saying self-defeating and irrational things like "I was born that way" and "You can't teach an old dog new tricks." These are irrational, self-defeating beliefs.

One of the most important ways you can control your anger is to recognize the signs of arousal or the stress response as soon as they occur. As you become more and more sharply attuned to the signs of tension and upset inside you, you will achieve greater ability to short-circuit the anger process and turn it off before it gets too strong. Intense anger can make you agitated and impulsive. As you learn to relax more easily and quickly dispute your irrational beliefs, your ability to regulate anger will improve.

## ANGER AS A USEFUL SIGNAL

Your anger can serve a very useful function. It can alert you about becoming upset and promote effective actions to handle the anger. Knowing that you can short-circuit your anger or anxiety, you will be less agitated and impulsive. When we are agitated or impulsive, we can make more mistakes, which lead to still more anxiety and anger. Stay task-oriented and instruct yourself to relax and dispute your irrational beliefs.

Sometimes we get angry because situations seem to be getting out of hand and we want to take charge. Sometimes we become concerned that things will not go the way we want them to, so we get angry trying to control them. We can learn ways of managing

> Men are not worried by things, but by their ideas about things. When we meet with difficulties, become anxious or troubled, let us not blame others, but rather ourselves, that is, our ideas about things.
>
> —EPICTETUS

our anger and gaining better control of situations. Dispute your belief that you "have to" get angry to change something. One of the best ways of taking charge of the situation is to remain calm when most people expect you, or even want you, to be upset.

Sometimes we get annoyed, upset, and angry because we have spent more time being conscious of our failures than of our successes. We sometimes forget or dismiss the good things that we do, and yet we never let ourselves forget our mistakes and shortcomings.

Now that you are learning to recognize and dispute irrational beliefs, be careful not to berate yourself when you have irrational beliefs and when you forget to dispute them. Remember, it's irrational to think you'll learn these skills overnight or become perfect. Beware of the belief that you should be able to relax and stay calm in all situations.

Try to remember to congratulate yourself whenever you accomplish something, particularly if you have been able to relax or manage your anger. Let yourself feel good about all of these successes. Enjoy each step in your journey toward your goals.

# SIXTEEN

# The Movies of Your Mind: Anxiety

*Your fears are like dragons guarding your
most precious treasures.*
—RAY WYLIE HUBBARD

IN THE LAST CHAPTER, WE DESCRIBED HOW OUR THINKING AF-
fects our feelings. You learned how irrational beliefs can lead to
self-defeating feelings and unhealthy stress. In this chapter, we will
replace irrational thinking with positive talking.

Many psychologists have proposed that our thoughts are best
understood as self-talk. These psychologists have helped us understand that what we silently say to ourselves about the events we experience influences us in many profound ways. What we say to
ourselves changes what we see and hear, what we feel, and what we
remember when we look back on our experiences. In this chapter,

we will concentrate on the ways in which the things you say to yourself can help you to prepare for and overcome anxiety. First, let's examine how we can create anxiety by what we say.

## What We Say Often Influences What We See, Hear, Feel, and Remember

When we go to a haunted house at a carnival, what we say to ourselves can influence what we will see, hear, feel, and remember about the experience. If we tell ourselves that we are alone in a spooky house, we will see it as threatening and scary. When things loom or leer at us, we will tell ourselves that we are in danger. Likewise, if we tell ourselves that the sounds that are played in the haunted house are real, we are likely to feel chills running up and down our spine.

On the other hand, if we constantly tell ourselves that all of the things in the haunted house are fake, and if we try to figure out how they were made to look real, we will probably not see ghosts or goblins but bedsheets and paint. Likewise, we will hear sheets of metal being rattled, rather than thunder. If we say that the frightening sights and sounds are caused by special effects, we probably will enjoy the spectacle and not feel anxious. We will remember it is an interesting and fun show, rather than a frightening experience.

Another example of a potentially frightening situation is preparing to interview for a job. If we are looking through the newspaper help-wanted ads and constantly say to ourselves that there is nothing there for us, we may be overlooking certain sections or jobs because self-talk is affecting the way we see what is in front of us. Should we finally make an appointment and walk in saying to ourselves that we do not have any skills and no one wants us, we may hear the interviewer's remarks somewhat differently from how she says them.

If we are critical of our skills, we may not hear the interviewer's encouragement to see an associate who might be of help in finding a job. We may hear questions as attempts to find out what we cannot do, rather than what we can do. When we start to think this way, we are likely to feel inadequate and anxious. If upon returning home from such an interview we say to ourselves that we will never get a job, we are likely to remember only the negative parts of the interview and not the positive ones.

All of these experiences are likely to give us what some of our patients have called the "screaming meemies." It is clear from these examples and from what we have learned about irrational beliefs in the last chapter that negative thinking and self-talking can upset us and interfere with what we are doing.

## WHISTLING A HAPPY TUNE

One way people deal with the anxiety of their self-talk is to whistle a happy tune, literally or figuratively. Any distraction can help break the connection between our negative talk and the "screaming meemies." Some people chew gum, smoke a cigarette, tap their fingers on a desk, or shuffle their feet on the floor. Most of these activities can lower anxiety, but they can be annoying, and there are other, more exciting options.

## THE POWER OF POSITIVE TALKING

The power of positive talking is very similar to the power of positive thinking that has been popularized by Norman Vincent Peale. In this chapter, we will provide you with things to tell yourself that have been shown to improve performance and decrease the "screaming meemies." The goal is to cope with anxious feelings so that you can concentrate on what you are doing and remain in a relaxed state of mind and body.

To manage a stressful situation, we need to take steps at four major time periods. These phases can overlap, but usually they follow one another.

We need (1) to prepare for the stressful situation, (2) to cope with feelings as they start to build, (3) to cope with feelings as they start to overwhelm us, and finally (4) to cope when the feelings have passed. Each step is important in helping you to enjoy coping. By breaking a potentially frightening experience into four parts and learning ways of coping with each, we can make the experience interesting and challenging, rather than overwhelming and unbearable.

One of the problems with positive talking occurs when we get stuck and don't know what to say to ourselves. Some of us have this problem in the early phases and others in the later phases of frightening or anxiety-invoking situations. This chapter will help you with each phase by providing clear, positive things to tell yourself each step of the way.

## The Talkies

Some of our patients have found it helpful to think of their anxiety-provoking events as part of a scary movie. In an earlier chapter, you learned how to use imagery for relaxing and rehearsing. Up until now, these have been silent movies. It is time to turn them into talkies.

In this chapter, you will concentrate on the horror movies of your life. In the next chapter, you will deal with the situations in which anger can get out of hand. So, when you are finished with the horror movies, you can turn to the war movies.

## Waiting in Line for a Ticket to a Horror Movie

Preparing for a stressful situation that evokes anxiety is the first phase in maintaining a relaxed state of mind and body. We need to rehearse what we plan to do, and we need to replace negative thinking with positive thinking. Imagine this rehearsal as what you say while waiting in line for a ticket to the horror movie.

If you are scheduled to give a speech in front of a business group in half an hour, what you say to yourself will affect what you will do and feel. Some of the ways of reducing anxiety while you wait for your turn to speak can be memorized or written on a piece of paper to review.

One of the most important things to ask yourself is "What is it that I have to do?" This question helps you to focus on the task at hand rather than all of your fears about doing it. You can tell yourself to think about what you will have to say so that you will have less time to upset yourself with thoughts of failure. You may review the outline of what you plan to say and even jot down a few notes about issues to address. Do not, however, make major changes in your presentation.

You have learned several ways of reducing your stress response, and you could say, "This may be difficult, but I know some ways to deal with it." You may want to tell yourself, "Time for a few deep breaths and relaxation. I feel more comfortable, relaxed, and at ease. I know this material very well and I have worked hard at preparing it." You can also say, "No putting myself down. I'll just think about what I need to do." If you start to worry, you can tell yourself, "Stop worrying, I *can* do it."

Concentrate on your past successes rather than your past failures. Thinking about your successes will lead to calming self-confidence. You may say that you have never succeeded. This is highly unlikely and usually comes from an irrational belief that what we do is either all good or all bad. In reality, almost everything we do involves some successful actions. Concentrate on these, and you will decrease your anxiety while you build your self-confidence.

The things you tell yourself are other self-fulfilling prophecies. Let's strive to make the prophecies those of calmness and coping rather than of gloom and doom.

## AS THE PLOT THICKENS

The next part to learn for coping with anxiety is what to say when the feelings start to build. In a film, this is the section created to build tension in the audience. Many of us hope that we will not feel any anxiety, and then we become even more anxious when we begin to feel scared. We start to tell ourselves that because we are feeling a little anxious, we will be overwhelmed before we know it. These pessimistic ideas only increase our anxiety. They are also self-fulfilling prophecies.

Many people are anxious when they know they will meet new people at a party. They may cope well on the way to the party but become very anxious as they walk toward a group of new people. This is when the plot thickens, and we need to know what to say to ourselves to cope with it.

You can tell yourself that the anxiety is a good reminder to begin using the relaxation skills you have mastered. You might say, "My muscles are starting to feel a little tight. Time to relax. Time to slow down." As the anxiety builds, you may want to say, "I *can* meet this challenge." As you are walking across the floor, each step seems longer than the next, and you don't know what you are going to do when you finally reach the new people. You can say, "One step at a time; I can handle the situation."

Of course, you also need to have a plan for approaching any situation. Much fun is made of standard or pat greetings, but they help open conversations. You may overcome the anxiety that prevents you from entering a conversation but still lack the social skills to carry on a conversation. The classic book *How to Win Friends and Influence People* by Dale Carnegie is a good guide for learning some of these skills.

As your anxiety rises, you can say, "I'll just think about what I have to do." This phrase is a reminder that it is best to concentrate on the task at hand. You may wish to observe the people you are meeting and notice what they are wearing and what they are doing so that you can ask appropriate questions and express interest in them. Next you might say, "Relax; I'm in control. I'll take a slow, deep breath." These positive statements should help you cope better and enjoy meeting people.

## ON THE EDGE OF YOUR SEAT

Being in the middle of an event and concerned that your anxiety might overwhelm you is similar to sitting on the edge of your seat during a scary movie. Knowing what to say to yourself can make a big difference. Some of us expect ourselves to be supercool and do the impossible. When our feelings start to overwhelm us, we are temped to give up, escape the situation, or try to avoid the next task.

An example is a student who is in the middle of an examination and begins to sweat, shake, and feel dizzy. Giving up, escaping, or avoiding will not help her to pass the exam. One of the best things the student can say is, "I'm not surprised I'm anxious. That's okay. I can handle it."

In many situations, such as examinations, it is possible to take a break and say to yourself, "I'll label my fear from 0 to 10. Five is motivating, but I'll pause and relax if it reaches 8." In addition, a person can say, "When fear comes, I'll just pause" or "It's okay to be anxious. I *can* handle it." The student may need to remind herself, "I won't try to eliminate the feeling totally. I'll just keep it manageable." Finally, the student may find it helpful to say, "I'll pay attention to the present. I'll answer one question at a time. I'll take a deep breath between questions."

All of these positive statements can help you when your feelings become overwhelming. You can see that they turn irrational beliefs around by helping us to accept our fallibility and to keep us task-oriented.

Somewhere in the middle between too little and too much is just the right amount of anxiety. This applies not only to examinations but also to most other activities in life. Many people find trying new activities scary. It is good to remember that some of this anxiety will help us to concentrate and to learn. In addition, in many sports an appropriate level of anxiety can help us excel. The positive thinking and talking we have just reviewed help us to keep our anxiety in the right ballpark for all of life's games.

## A SIGH OF RELIEF

One of the most important phases of anxiety management is the final phase, after the event has been concluded and the curtain goes down. We need to know how to optimize coping when it's all over and the feelings have passed. This is a unique opportunity for positive talk. It helps us to put things in perspective and to reward ourselves for our accomplishments. When we get a reward for something we have done, we are more likely to do it again. If we reward ourselves for positive talking, we are more likely to use the skill again in similar situations.

## COMMON PROBLEMS AND HELPFUL HINTS

Sometimes we are so scared that we cannot think positively. This is why it is important to memorize the coping statements for each phase of the event. If we are anxious, it is more difficult to remember. That is why we must master and overlearn the phrases so they will be available quickly when we are anxious.

Some people find that the phrases we have suggested are not right for their own problems. In this case, we suggest that you write down personal coping phrases. Be sure to include some phrases that will prepare you for the event, some to remind you to relax as the feelings begin to build, some to help you cope when the feelings become stronger, and some to keep perspective after the event and encourage yourself in the future.

It is very important that you put the techniques you have been reading about into practice. To do so, you will need to memorize the phrases and practice them systematically.

Many people think they are too busy to memorize these phrases. Try to use periods during the day when you are waiting for a bus or checking out in a supermarket or have other free times. These are good times to relax and review your new self-talk. Keep these phrases on a slip of paper in your wallet or daily planner for review during your free time. A good time to learn these statements is just before you go to sleep, and for this reason, we recommend that you leave the list on your nightstand.

When you practice, remember to avoid negative thinking. Negative thinking will only lead to avoidance or additional distress. Stay on guard against statements like "I always lose control" or "I just can't cope."

If you find that you are unable to remember the words in real life, decide what lines you have the most difficulty remembering. Then go over the statements again. Go slowly and use your skill of visual imagery, so that when you begin working on these techniques in real life, you will recall the statements and be able to cope more successfully. Make your "talkies" as clear and provoking as you can. It is helpful to exaggerate the anxiety-provoking events to test your skill. Continue doing this and you will find yourself better and better able to cope with your feelings in stressful situations.

Do not try to learn all the statements or visualize all the scenes at one time. It may be useful to review all of them in the beginning, but choose a few to memorize or work on each day. This is similar to taking a series of injections for inoculation against a disease. In fact, these techniques are sometimes called stress inoculation.

You may want to use a movie or a television show to practice these statements. Most shows have a beginning, a middle, a climax, and an ending. To practice, prepare for the excitement, lower your arousal as feelings start to build, cope when feelings start to overwhelm, and finally reward yourself when the show is nearly over. You may get caught off guard, but that is not bad preparation for the way stress sometimes catches us napping in real life.

You may find it easier to start practicing with reruns of your favorite adventure shows. Of course, you will not want to practice these skills all the time because part of the fun of watching a show is the excitement we experience. This is also true of life!

## THE POSITIVE SELF-TALK OF WINNERS

The winners in life can find something positive in every situation. There is an extremely successful executive who always says, "That's great!" when his employees bring him bad news. Then he and his employees find the silver linings. Eddie Cantor went broke during the Depression but turned bad into good by writing a best-selling joke book that helped millions laugh their way through those difficult times. Don't let others contribute negative self-talk that can interfere with your positive self-talk. If someone says how bad things look, either ignore the comment or turn it around. If you need help with this skill, work through the chapter on recreation and humor to develop your funny bone for effective coping.

When you practice your positive self-talk, be sure to emphasize your goals and what you want to achieve. Use the following guidelines to help you practice and enjoy positive goal-directed talking.

> *Worry is the interest paid before it is due.*
>
> —WILLIAM RALPH INGE

# TALKING CALMLY WORD-BY-WORD TO COPE WITH ANXIETY

## PREPARING FOR ANXIETY IN STRESSFUL SITUATIONS

| Effective Self-Talk | Less Effective Self-Talk |
| --- | --- |
| What is it I have to do? | There's so much to do. |
| If I do the thing I fear, the fear is sure to die. | This is always frightening, but I'll do it. |
| I am well organized and efficient. | I can't forget what I need to say. |
| I choose to do it. | I have to do it! |
| I know ways to deal with this. | I think I can handle it. |
| I have succeeded in situations like this one before. I am confident. | I won't worry anymore. |
| Time for a few deep breaths and relaxation. I am comfortable, relaxed, and at ease. | Usually the deep breathing lessens the anxiety. |

## COPING WHEN ANXIETY STARTS TO BUILD

| Effective Self-Talk | Less Effective Self-Talk |
| --- | --- |
| My muscles are partially relaxed. Time to relax even more. | My muscles are getting tense. I have to relax. |
| I *can* meet this challenge. Coping is my middle name. | This is frightening, but I think I'll be all right. |
| One step at a time. I can handle the situation. | I can't handle it unless I take one step at a time. |
| I'll just think about what I have to do. | Don't get distracted. Just do what you have to. |
| I'm in control. Relax and take a deep breath. | Don't get nervous. You are in control. |

**COPING WHEN ANXIETY STARTS TO OVERWHELM**

| Effective Self-Talk | Less Effective Self-Talk |
|---|---|
| Right now I feel nervous. But that's not like me. I'm also calm and confident. | Don't get nervous. You'll blow it. |
| If I do the thing I fear, the fear is sure to die. | I can't get afraid. I have to be cool. |
| I'll just pause. I *can* handle it. | Don't slow down. You've just got to beat this. |
| I'll label my relaxation level from 0 to 10 so that I keep it in a good range. | I'll label my fear from 0 to 10 so that I can watch it rise. |
| It's okay to feel some fear. It motivates me to do my best. | I shouldn't be afraid. |
| I'll pay attention to the present. | I shouldn't let my anxiety show. |
| I won't try to eliminate fear totally. I'll just keep it manageable. | I've got to stop being afraid. |

**COPING WHEN IT'S ALL OVER AND THE ANXIETY HAS PASSED**

| Effective Self-Talk | Less Effective Self-Talk |
|---|---|
| I didn't get everything I wanted. That's okay. I tried, and that's what really counts. | I didn't get everything I wanted. I should have done better. |
| I have succeeded in some ways, and I'll have these successes to draw on next time. | I wasn't a total success—maybe next time. |
| I did the right things for myself. The other person may be a little angry or sad, but that's okay. | I shouldn't have hurt the other person's feelings. |
| That wasn't as hard as I thought. Next time it will be even easier. | I didn't think I would make it. I hope next time it is easier. |
| I'm doing better at this. I'm making progress. | I'm not doing as well as I should. |

## DOING THE THING YOU FEAR MAKES THE FEAR DISAPPEAR

The key to success in learning to attack the irrational beliefs that control your anxiety is: practice, practice, and practice. There is no substitute. There is no shortcut. We learn to relax our bodies first, then our minds, but most of all we learn to face our fears and anxieties. With practice and a strong desire to overcome our anxieties we will be successful.

> Nothing in life is to be feared, it is only to be understood. Now is the time to understand more, so that we may fear less.
>
> —MARIE CURIE

# SEVENTEEN

# The Second Feature: Anger

*Little is improved by anger except the arch on a cat's back.*
—FORTUNE COOKIE

WE HAVE INTRODUCED SOME TECHNIQUES OF POSITIVE SELF-TALK for reducing anxiety. Positive self-talk can also help us manage the stress of other emotions. Anger is the "fight" in the fight-or-flight of stress.

Anger can lead to destruction of property, disruption of important interpersonal relationships, and termination of employment. There are many ways of dealing with anger, and in the next section we will help you learn some assertiveness skills. For many of us, however, it is first necessary to temper our aggression or violence so that we are able to put assertiveness skills to use. Changing our self-talk can help us temper our aggression.

## DON'T PUT UP, BUT DON'T SHUT UP EITHER

You have been learning new ways of dealing with anxiety by positive self-talk. Our goal for this chapter will be to help you learn sentences and statements that will help you avoid impulsive and negative responses to anger-provoking situations. We will show you ways to avoid putting up your dukes and fighting. At first, you will learn what to say to yourself. In the chapters on assertiveness training, you will learn what to say to others to help you feel more competent and meet more of your goals.

Some people do not have difficulty with the "shoot-'em-ups." Everyone experiences anger, but some people have been taught in childhood never to fight with either their fists or their words. There are some advantages to this style of life in that we avoid landing in jail, but suppressing anger has its hidden costs physically and socially. Unless we learn assertive ways of meeting our needs, we may experience frustration, tension, and psychosomatic disorders such as headaches, insomnia, and low back pain. Muscle tension disorders are so common and closely related that a primary-care doctor told us that low back pain is usually just a headache that slipped down the spine!

Suppressed anger can undermine our social relationships. It is often expressed in devious ways. "Sneaky" anger is called passive-aggressive behavior. The passive-aggressive person may consciously or unconsciously "forget" to do what he has agreed to do, or do it slowly or incorrectly. This passive behavior can be infuriating to the victims of covert anger, because it may be hard to confront and "prove" the perpetrator's behavior. Interestingly, passive-aggressive behavior occurs most in restrictive environments, and the victims may be overcontrolling out of their own suppressed fear or anger. Thus, anger acknowledgment and management is very important in relationships.

In the last chapter, you learned to talk to yourself through anxiety by breaking most events into four time phases. These include

(1) preparing for the feelings we may have, (2) coping when feelings of anxiety start to build, (3) coping when these feelings start to overwhelm, and (4) coping when the situation is over and the feelings have passed. These same phases are important in controlling our aggression.

In some situations anger is the appropriate signal, because fighting is necessary. As discussed in the early chapters of this book, however, we encounter very few situations in modern life that would make good use of our physical ability to overcome other people or objects.

## GETTING IN LINE FOR THE SHOOT-'EM-UPS

A good example of how talking to ourselves affects us involves a salesman who had a flat tire. He was in the country, far from any service stations. He had a spare tire, but he did not have a jack. The salesman walked until he came to a farmhouse. He began to talk to himself as he approached the farmhouse: "I bet the farmer won't want to help me. He probably has been plowing all day and is tired. Farmers don't like city folk anyway. He's going to think I'm really stupid for not having a jack. He'll probably laugh at me and tell me to go to town. Farmers can really be resentful."

The salesman got to the door of the farmhouse and knocked loudly. You can imagine the farmer's surprise when he came to the door and the man in front of him turned and yelled as he stomped away, "I didn't want your old jack anyway." There is a big difference between positive self-talk and negative self-talk.

To prepare for stressful situations that may provoke aggression, we need to rehearse what we will do and replace negative thinking with positive thinking. You can think of this phase as learning what to talk about while you get in line for the shoot-'em-ups. If you are going home and you know that the people in the apartment above you may play loud music and you have gotten into several fights in the past, your self-talk will affect what you do and feel. Some ways to reduce your anger can be reviewed and practiced while you are stopped at red lights on your ride home. Memorize your lines or write them on a note card for use at red lights.

One of the most important things to ask yourself is "What is it that I have to do?" It is also helpful to say, "This may upset me, but I know some ways to deal with it." Other useful phrases include "I'll try not to take it too seriously" and "There is no need for an argument." As you approach the situation, remind yourself: "Time for a few deep breaths and relaxation. I feel more comfortable, relaxed, and at ease." As you get out of your car, you may say, "Easy does it. I'm going to keep my sense of humor." The last phrase is very important. It is hard to be angry when one is laughing.

In this example, we could prepare for an encounter with people who are not respecting our rights and find that they are not home. Many times, what we expect never happens. By saying the positive statements we have just reviewed, you can keep yourself calm while you wait and prepare for the potential event.

What you tell yourself before you enter anger-provoking situations is just as self-fulfilling as what you may say before anxiety-invoking situations. We need to strive to make our prophecies full of calm assertiveness, rather than blood and guts.

## AND IN THIS CORNER . . .

Next we can learn to cope with aggressive feelings by knowing what to say if our anger starts to build. In a boxing match this buildup may start when the announcer says, "And in this corner . . ." At this point, we start to feel tense and ready to fight. We may get still angrier when we wonder whether we will be disqualified or at the last minute our opponent will not show up. These pessimistic ideas not only increase our anger but also can become self-fulfilling prophecies.

Take the example of someone who is accusing us of something we did not do. As we start to feel tense, it is helpful to say, "My muscles are starting to feel a little tight. Time to relax. Time to slow down." In addition, we might repeat the words, "My anger can remind me of what I need to do. Time to help myself." If a person begins to tell us all the wrong things we have done, it is easy to get angry. It is more helpful to say, "Let's take this point by point." As a person goes into a tirade, you can often help keep your own anger from getting out of hand by saying, "Maybe we are both right. Let's try a cooperative approach."

As the person's behavior begins to get under our skin and we begin to think of words to put him in his place, it is useful to say to yourself, "Arguments lead to more arguments. Let's work constructively." Sometimes, however, we feel that our self-esteem is on the line, and we have difficulty admitting that we are wrong. This reaction can come from the irrational belief that we need to be perfect or right all the time. Remember, usually it is a question of what is right, not who is right. Sometimes it is helpful to remind the other person of this fact.

Often it is best to let the other person run out of steam before beginning interactive discussion. By taking this time to relax, we can decrease our stress and allow the other person to become more receptive to discussion and arbitration.

In some situations, people provoke us in order to show that we have poor self-control. Even if this is not the case, many people have helped themselves by saying, "He may want me to get really angry.

> Be quick to listen, slow to speak, and slow to become angry.
>
> —JAMES 1:19

Well, I'm going to try to disappoint him." These positive statements should help you cope better when your feelings start to build.

## When Your Back Is Against the Wall

When someone provokes or insults you, you may find your feelings starting to overwhelm you. At times, we are all caught off guard. A driver can cut in front of us in traffic, for example, or someone may damage something that is important to us. Our feelings may overwhelm us before we have had a chance to prepare or even recognize that they are starting to build. In other situations, we may have been preparing for our feelings as they started to build, but in the middle of the event our feelings overwhelm us. Just as in anxiety management, we need to know what to say to manage anger.

One of the best things to say is "The more I keep my cool, the more I'm in control." We may believe our anger will help us control the situation, but it usually does just the opposite. In addition, others will respect your ability to keep cool and stay in control.

When someone insults us, it is important to remember that we don't have to prove or defend ourselves. Positive talking will help remind us. Try using "I don't need to prove myself." It will be helpful to have the following phrase at the tip of your tongue: "I don't want to make more out of this than I have to." Another way to deal with insults is to say, "No need to doubt myself—what he says may not matter."

Anger-producing situations may arise that do not involve insults or provocations. If someone is cheating us in business or sold us poor-quality merchandise, our feelings of anger may become strong. In these cases, it is often helpful to say, "I'll think of what I want to get out of this." This self-talk helps us to focus on what we need to do in order to get what we desire. Often it is helpful to remind ourselves, "Look for the good parts of this. I don't want to assume the worst and jump to conclusions."

## And the Winner Is . . .

After the situation is over and your anger has passed, it is important to know how to reward yourself. Just as in anxiety management, this is a unique opportunity for positive self-talk. It helps us to put the situation in perspective and reward ourselves for our accomplishments. When we get a reward for doing something, we are more likely to meet future challenges in the same way. If we reward ourselves for positive self-talk, we are more likely to use this skill again and avoid blowing up in other situations.

An example is if someone fails to pay back a loan or return something he has borrowed. You have coped successfully with your anger and asserted your needs to this person. The final step is to reward yourself by saying, "I'm doing better at this. I'm making progress." If you have done well but not as well as you had hoped, say, "I can be pleased with my progress." If you have done even better than you had expected, you might say, "That wasn't really as hard as I thought."

There usually are still some small feelings left over or some difficulties that are not resolved. In these cases, it is helpful to say, "I will try not to take it personally. These are difficult situations. They take time to straighten out."

## Common Problems: "I Always Have and I Always Will"

Just as in managing your anxiety, managing your anger requires that you try a new approach. One of the common problems is to get angry, blow up, and say, "I always have, and I always will." This response rewards the old ways and is not a productive way of managing your anger.

Just as in anxiety management, sometimes we are so angry that we cannot think positively. That is why it is very important to memorize the coping statements for each time phase of the event. If we are angry, it is often more difficult to remember what we want to say. That is why we must master and overlearn phrases so that they will be at our fingertips when we are angry.

Just as in anxiety management, some people find the phrases we suggest are not right for them. Write down your own phrases for the situation in which you hope to improve your coping. Again, be sure to include phrases that will prepare you for the event, some to help remind you to relax as your anger builds, some to help you cope with the anger when it starts to overwhelm you, and some to keep the situation in perspective and encourage yourself for the future.

## COUNTING YOUR TALKS (ARE YOU TALKING TO YOURSELF ENOUGH?)

Spend a little time each day going through the four phases for coping with anger on a different stressor. If you have only a few major stressors, you may want to spend more than a day on some of them. Go slowly and use your skill at visual imagery so that when you are working on these situations in real life, you will recall the statements and be able to cope more successfully. Make your "talkies" as clear and provoking as you can. It is helpful to exaggerate the anger-provoking events to test your skill. The more you practice your self-talk and imagery rehearsal, the better you will be able to cope with feelings in real life.

> *For every minute you are angry, you lose 60 seconds of happiness.*
> —BUMPER STICKER

## HELPFUL HINTS

Try to use periods of time during the day when you are waiting for a bus or checking out in a supermarket or have other free time. Again, it is often helpful to learn these phrases just before you go to sleep, and for this reason we recommend that you leave the list on your nightstand. Do not try to learn all the phrases or visualize all the scenes at one time.

If you still have difficulty with a situation, break it into phases, pick the one you have the most trouble with, and go over the statements for that time phase again. By continuing to do this, you will find yourself better and better able to cope with the anger that some situations evoke.

## TALKING CALMLY WORD-BY-WORD TO COPE WITH ANGER

### PREPARING FOR ANGER IN STRESSFUL SITUATIONS

| Effective Self-Talk | Less Effective Self-Talk |
|---|---|
| What is it I have to do? | I have to win this one. |
| This may upset me, but I know some ways to deal with it. | This is going to make me angry. |
| There may not be any need for an argument. | I know there will be an argument. |
| I'll try not to take it too seriously. | This one's for real. |
| Time for a few deep breaths and relaxation. I feel more comfortable, relaxed, and at ease. | I'm really ready for him. |
| Easy does it. Remember, I need to keep my sense of humor. | He's going to find out I'm serious. |

**COPING WHEN ANGER STARTS TO BUILD**

| Effective Self-Talk | Less Effective Self-Talk |
|---|---|
| My muscles are starting to feel a little tight. Time to slow down. | I'm really getting uptight. |
| My anger can remind me of what I need to do. Time to help myself. | This makes me mad. |
| Let's take this point by point. | He's wrong. |
| Maybe we are both right. Let's try a cooperative approach. | He's against me. |
| Let's remember, it's not who is right but what is right. | Only one of us is right, and it's me. |
| Arguments lead to more arguments. Let's work constructively. | Now he's in for an argument. |
| He may want me to get really angry. Well, I'm going to try to disappoint him. | I'll show him. |

**COPING WHEN ANGER STARTS TO OVERWHELM**

| Effective Self-Talk | Less Effective Self-Talk |
|---|---|
| The more I keep my cool, the more I'm in control. | He can't do that. |
| I'll think of what I want to get out of this. | I'll get even. |
| I don't need to prove myself. | I can't let him get away with that. |
| I don't want to make more out of this than I have to. | I'll take it to the top. |
| No need to doubt myself. What he says may not matter. | He can't say that to me. |
| Look for the good parts of this. I don't want to assume the worst and jump to conclusions. | This is going to be awful. |

**COPING WHEN IT'S ALL OVER AND THE ANGER HAS PASSED**

| Effective Self-Talk | Less Effective Self-Talk |
|---|---|
| These are difficult situations. They take time to straighten out. | That always happens. |
| I will try not to take it personally. | He still didn't see my point. |
| That wasn't really as hard as I thought. | That was awful. |
| I'm doing better at this. I'm making progress. | I should have said more. |
| I can be pleased with my progress. | I'll win the argument next time. |

## ANGER IS ONE LETTER SHORT OF DANGER

The key to success in learning to attack the irrational beliefs that control your anger is: Practice, practice, and practice. Benjamin

> To seek to extinguish anger
> is but a bravery of the stoics.
> We have better oracles:
> Be angry, but sin not.
> Let not the sun go down
> upon your anger.
>
> —FRANCIS BACON

Disraeli said, "Little things affect little minds." Exercising your mind with self-control and positive self-talk will turn your mind into a compass to guide you through the most challenging of times.

# EIGHTEEN

# The Dark Movies of Your Mind: Depression

*The mind is its own place, and in itself can make a heaven of*
*hell, a hell of heaven.*
—JOHN MILTON

HAVE YOU EVER BEEN DOWN IN THE DUMPS, TEARFUL, AND SAD?
An extended period of stress or acute event may have caused your
depression.

Almost one in five of us will qualify for a diagnosable major depressive disorder sometime in our lives. Almost twice as many
women, especially single mothers, suffer from depression as men.
Such a depression can steal your interest in all areas of life without
necessarily making your mood depressed. This is why many people are depressed without knowing it.

Along with a loss of interest and/or a depressed mood, depression may bring on too much sleep or too little sleep, overeating or

undereating, restlessness or sluggishness, a lack of concentration, self-blame, and suicidal thoughts. If you have had five or more of these symptoms for over a week, talk with your doctor; she may make a diagnosis of depression and provide treatment. Treatment may include medication, psychotherapy, or both.

The many forms of depression are matched by its many causes. These may include the prolonged stress involving a major loss by death or by misfortune, anger turned inward on oneself, financial or parenting stress, a decrease in pleasurable activities following life-changing circumstances, a poor fit between job and person, or an underactive thyroid. Major depressions tend to run in families and may be the result of genetic vulnerability to the effects of these kinds of prolonged stress.

## BURNOUT, RUST-OUT, AND DEPRESSION

Burnout can happen to any of us, whether we labor at work or school, or with a home and children. It often occurs among the overworked in helping professions. As the word "burnout" implies, the brightly burning flame of desire to help others is exhausted and goes out. Burnout is not a psychiatric term or disorder, but rather an occupational hazard.

For most, burnout involves exhaustion. It may not necessarily involve a loss of interest in all activities. If it is job-related burnout, then personal and home life may not be affected. If it involves caregiving to children and taking care of a household, then a part-time job and recreational activities may not be affected.

In certain job settings many employees rather than just a few often experience burnout. A change in duties or jobs can often relieve the symptoms of burnout. Nonetheless, what we have to say about depression can often be very helpful to a person with burnout.

Another related stressor may well be boredom or "rust-out." Again, many of the symptoms and treatments for depression will be useful. Some research suggests that boredom increases the inci-

dence of heart disease among workers. Given the relationship between anger and heart disease, the frustration and anger of boredom may explain this finding.

## DIAGNOSING DEPRESSION

If you have more than the occasional blues and it is interfering
with your work or your enjoyment of life, we strongly recommend a visit with your doctor. If clinical depression has set in, you
may benefit from counseling or other interventions.

One of our highly respected colleagues, Gene Bont, M.D.,
summed up the best options this way. Like old-fashioned water
pumps, a depressed patient needs to prime the pump to get it
moving. This can be done either through counseling, medication,
exercise, or all three.

Research has shown a 30 percent
reduction in depression among the
middle-aged when they began an
aerobic exercise program. Psychiatric hospitals commonly employed
their patients on farms until it was
declared an illegal labor practice.
Many hospitalized depressed patients benefited by both the meaningful workouts and the diversion
from their problems.

> *A man can be concerned
> with his serious problems
> and still walk with his
> chin up and a carnation in
> his buttonhole.*
>
> —DALE CARNEGIE

Depression may be less common in less industrialized countries where people physically work for their food. So if you are
feeling depressed, get moving!

## THE DEPRESSIVE DOZEN

Just as certain thoughts and images can evoke anxiety and anger,
other thoughts and images can lead to depression. By reviewing the

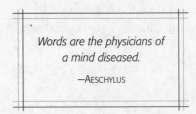

*Words are the physicians of a mind diseased.*

—AESCHYLUS

list that follows and becoming aware of your depressing thought patterns, you can prevent or lift many depressive moods. Some of our patients call this "cleaning up their stinking thinking."

1. **Labeling.** Do you call yourself or others "stupid," "lazy," "crazy," "sinful," "ugly," or "ridiculous"? Labels are best used on cans. No one is 100 percent any of these. Irrational, exaggerated thoughts bring on irrational, exaggerated feelings. It is also best to avoid confusing what you do with who you are.

2. **Absolute thinking.** Things are either all good or all bad when we think this way. If you are not loved, you are rejected; what you do is excellent or totally useless. This black-or-white categorizing leaves no room for the in-between, subtle shades of life.

3. **Arguing for the "toos."** It is often hard enough to get motivated without thinking that it is too something or other. Maybe you say you are "too old" or "too young," "too big" or "too small," "too tired" or "too wired," or "too hungry" or "too full."

4. **"Shoulding."** This guilt-inducing thought pattern includes the "shoulds," "oughts," and "have tos." Those who "should" on themselves may overuse the word "must" as a self-punitive motivation.

5. **Mind reading.** You assume the actions of another must come from negative feelings about you. If someone doesn't call, it means he or she doesn't like you.

6. **Regretful thinking.** What happened in the past and your "if onlys" dominate your thinking. It is hard to put

the past behind you if you are always looking in the rearview mirror of life.

7. **Fortune-telling.** You imagine the worst in the form of "what ifs" and become increasingly convinced about your bleak future. Whatever bad is in your life now is there to stay and will never improve.

8. **"Yes-butting."** No matter what good comes your way, you are able to deny that things could be improving. You tell people that their suggestions and support are good, but you usually say, "Yes, but . . ."

9. **Personalizing.** Whatever goes wrong, you insist on taking the full credit and argue that it was your fault and only your fault.

10. **Enlarging and shrinking.** Exaggerating the catastrophes in your life and minimizing the blessings keep you convinced how bad life is and how you always get the short end of the stick.

11. **Mood-based reasoning.** When you are deciding whether to do something or not, you decide on the basis of your feelings at the moment rather than your experiences in the past. For example, if you feel tired, you decide to put off starting your exercise program.

12. **Focusing on the little picture.** You find one small, lousy thing in your life and let it spoil everything else. Once something has gone wrong in the morning or even the early afternoon, the rest of the day is ruined.

## LEARNED HELPLESSNESS

Research conducted by Martin Seligman, Ph.D., found that when animals were trained to escape the shocks from an electrical grid by jumping a barrier and found that the other side was also electrified, they jumped a few times, but then became depressed. Later,

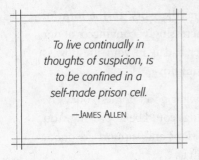

*To live continually in thoughts of suspicion, is to be confined in a self-made prison cell.*

—James Allen

when placed into a cage where they could escape shock by jumping the barrier, they still withdrew into the corner. They had "learned" that they were helpless.

This "learned helplessness" paradigm offered a model for human depression. Challenging our distorted attributions of problems (to ourselves, to unchanging conditions, and to everything in our lives) leads to an important approach to overcoming depression—learned optimism.

## Depression, Disease, and Death

All of us have down days where we feel blue or depressed, but this becomes a risk factor when it persists. One study showed that death from cancer was predicted seventeen years earlier by scores on a test for depression. Those who died of cancer seventeen years later were twice as likely to have previously had higher depression scores than those who developed no cancer at all. Another study showed that patients with AIDS-related complex who had weaker beliefs that they could do things to influence the course of the disease were less successful in fighting off AIDS. These studies suggest that persistent negative emotion can put you at greater risk of disease, depression, and death.

Heart disease patients with a pessimistic outlook about their ability to recover were more than twice as likely as optimists to have died one year later, even when the severity of heart disease was considered. Patients recovering from heart attacks who scored high on tests of sadness and depression were eight times more likely than optimistic patients to die within the next eighteen months.

Reducing pessimistic outlooks and negative emotions in the midst of negative life circumstances can be one of the most important stress management tools. Depressive thoughts can be overwhelming, and just possibly lead to disease and death.

## KEEPING THE BLACK DOG OUTSIDE

You have been learning new ways of dealing with anxiety and anger by positive self-talk. Depression is a little different from other moods because it tends to last longer. There have been many famous people who struggled with depression. In the Bible, Elijah complained to God that he was exhausted, couldn't eat, and wanted to die. Winston Churchill spoke about his ongoing struggle with depression and called it the "black dog."

Depression may differ from anxiety and anger, but many situations that can bring us down or add to our blues can be anticipated and rehearsed with positive self-talk and optimism to help us cope more effectively. The same four time phases we used to reduce anxiety and anger in earlier chapters can be utilized to rehearse self-talk that will help keep the black dog outside.

> *Our life is what our thoughts make it.*
> —MARCUS AURELIUS

## GETTING IN LINE FOR A BERGMAN FLICK

Just the titles of Ingmar Bergman's famous films, such as *Shame, Torment,* and *Through a Glass Darkly,* suggest that, like the horror movies and the shoot-'em-ups, what we focus on and think about determines our mood.

What you tell yourself before you enter depression-evoking situations is just as self-fulfilling as what you may say before anxiety- or anger-evoking situations. You have to watch your language! Fortune-telling is the thought pattern that may bring on the de-

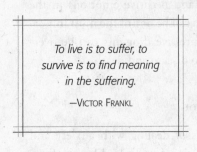

> To live is to suffer, to
> survive is to find meaning
> in the suffering.
>
> —VICTOR FRANKL

pression. We need to address our thought patterns while preparing for depression in stressful situations. What we expect or prophesy often comes true. We need to strive to make our prophecies full of calm and cautious optimism, rather than dark and overwhelming pessimism.

## A Note About Suicide

Suicide is the most serious and fatal complication of depression.

Depressive thinking, especially a false absolute belief that there are no other options to a never-ending problem, plays a prominent role. Ultimately suicide is an attempt to alleviate overwhelming emotional pain. For persons who are suicidal, talking with others, preferably a mental health professional, and applying the ABC's can help to alleviate the pain. Encour-

> I do not like the way the
> cards are shuffled, but
> yet I like the game and
> want to play.
>
> —EUGENE F. WARE

age them to get help. If you fear immediate danger to their life, call 911. Suicide is a permanent solution to a temporary problem. The pain will always pass given the opportunity. Let's learn some of the techniques to help prevent our pains from ruling our days.

## Managing the Darkest Hour

When the depression starts to build, take one thought at a time and find what's bringing you down. Ask yourself what just happened or what did I just tell myself. Study and rehearse the effective phrases below to help you conquer the thoughts that can lead to depression. Remind yourself, "I'm in control." Start challenging the negative self-talk.

## EXAMPLES OF EFFECTIVE AND INEFFECTIVE SELF-TALK FOR DEPRESSION

**PREPARING FOR DEPRESSION IN STRESSFUL SITUATIONS**

| Effective Self-Talk | Less Effective Self-talk |
|---|---|
| This is getting easier to handle. | This is always depressing, but I'll get through it. |
| I know ways to deal with this. | I think I can handle it. |
| I've made mistakes, but I'm learning from them. | I'm a loser, but something should go right soon. |
| I can find ways to reach out to others. | I can't stand being alone. Maybe someone will call. |
| I've enjoyed events like this in the past. | I shouldn't let my feelings get me down. |
| I can do something to make this better. | I should do something to make this better. |

## COPING WHEN DEPRESSION STARTS TO BUILD

| Effective Self-Talk | Less Effective Self-talk |
|---|---|
| I'm feeling a little blue. Time to dispute any negative thoughts. | Oh, no, the blues again. Time to distract myself. |
| One thought at a time. I can find what's bringing me down. | I have to stop bringing myself down. |
| I can improve my mood by improving my thoughts. | I should think positive thoughts. |
| I'm in control. I'll find a positive "what if" for each negative "what if." | Don't get down. I must get control of this. |

## COPING WHEN DEPRESSION STARTS TO OVERWHELM

| Effective Self-Talk | Less Effective Self-talk |
|---|---|
| Right now I feel blue. I'll think of a good time in my life and feel better. | Don't get sucked into the hole. You'll never get out. |
| It's OK to feel sad. It helps me appreciate the good things I enjoy. | I shouldn't get depressed. |
| I'll manage this feeling. | I've got to stop feeling so depressed. |
| I'll label my sadness from 0 to 10 so that I can keep it in a good range. | I'll label my depression from 0 to 10, so I can watch it deepen. |
| I'll see what I can enjoy today. | I shouldn't be depressed. |
| I don't want to make more of this than I have to. | I'm ready for a pity party. |
| Look for the good parts—I don't want to assume the worst and jump to conclusions. | This is going to be awful. |

**COPING WHEN THE DEPRESSION HAS PASSED**

| Effective Self-Talk | Less Effective Self-talk |
|---|---|
| The road back from sadness to joy has ups and downs. One fewer down to go through. | When will this end? |
| I felt better in some ways and I'll take comfort in this success next time. | I wasn't happy—maybe tomorrow. |
| That wasn't as hard as I thought it would be. | That was awful. |
| I'm doing better at feeling good. I'm making progress. | I didn't think I would make it. I hope next time is easier. |
| I can do this. | I hope I can do this. |

## Summary for Managing Your Darkest Hours

Depressive disorders make us feel exhausted, worthless, helpless, and hopeless. Negative thoughts and feelings make us feel like giving up. Realize that negative thinking is part of depression and does not accurately reflect the actual situation. Treatment is very successful and can include medication, exercise, psychotherapy, and self-help. In the meantime, while learning to manage the stress of depression:

> As I continued upward, I saw my life as a whole. I saw the pattern and the privilege of it, and the purpose of it, too. It was simply this: I was meant for a long, hard climb.
>
> —Lance Armstrong

- Do not set difficult goals for yourself.

- Do not take on a great deal of responsibility.

> *I have never known six happy days in my life.*
>
> —NAPOLEON

- Break large tasks into small ones.

- Set priorities, and do what you can when you can.

- Do not expect too much too soon. This will increase feelings of failure.

- It is better to be with other people than being alone. But avoid those who "should" on you.

- Participate in activities that may make you feel better.

- Exercise, go to a movie or sports event, or participate in religious or social activities.

- Don't rush it. Feeling better takes time.

- Do not make major life decisions or other important decisions until your depression has lifted.

> *Although the world is full of suffering, it is also full of the overcoming of it.*
>
> —HELEN KELLER

- Challenge your negative thinking. It is part of depression and can be disputed and changed as the depression lessens.

# SECTION V

## Communicating Your Needs and Feelings

*It was a foggy night. Out in the distance, a dim light broke through the misty mask resting above the ocean waters. Captain Smith, the master of a battleship, commanded his communications officer to send a message to the ship whose light indicated it was directly on a collision course. The message commanded the other ship to yield and pass on its starboard side. The reply suggested the battleship yield and pass far to port.*

*This infuriated Captain Smith who personally took the microphone and sternly spoke in a pompous and condescending tone, "I am the captain of a battleship, and I command you to move to the south."*

*A quiet, confident voice replied, "With all due respect sir, this is Second-Class Seaman Jones, but you need to steer to starboard and pass me on your port side." The angry captain yelled loudly and suggested that if Seaman Jones did not yield, the battleship would collide with him. The seaman calmly replied, "Sir, I would discourage you from not yielding, since my light is on top of the lighthouse."*

# NINETEEN

# What Is Assertiveness?

*I'm broken from bending.*
*I've lived too long on my knees.*
—LEONARD COHEN

WE HAVE PRACTICED A NUMBER OF TECHNIQUES FOR STRESS MAN-
agement. Some involved relaxing our bodies. Others involved
changing our thoughts, beliefs, and feelings so we could better
cope with stressful situations. Another way of managing stress is
through effective communication and assertiveness.

Sometimes we fail to draw lines, set limits, speak up, or say no
to people and demands in our lives. This difficulty can lead to
procrastination, suffering in silence, halfheartedness, sloppiness,
or forgetfulness, as we say no in unconscious or dishonest ways.

If we cannot refuse the requests of others, we may live our lives
according to other people's priorities rather than our own. We

then may have additional stress that can be harmful and unnecessary. If we fail to assert ourselves, we can stockpile anger and find ourselves mentally and physically uptight.

Sometimes we feel that the only way to get our needs met and keep from being pushed around is to fight for our rights. When we feel bullied or anticipate that we will be bullied, we may try to bully others. We may then find ourselves in a continuous and desperate struggle with a lion's share of stress from guilt and loneliness.

In living and communicating with others, we behave in many ways. It is helpful to look at our reactions to others and group them into three main ways of behaving. We can be assertive, aggressive, or passive. What do we mean by these words?

## PASSIVE BEHAVIOR

Passive behavior means giving up your rights by not expressing your honest feelings, thoughts, and beliefs. It often involves permitting others to walk all over you. It can also mean expressing yourself in such an apologetic way that you are overlooked. We behave passively when we do what we are told, regardless of how we feel about it. When we act passively, we often feel helpless, anxious, resentful, and disappointed with ourselves. The goal of passivity is usually to please others and to avoid conflict or rejection.

## AGGRESSIVE BEHAVIOR

When we are aggressive, we stand up for our personal rights and express our thoughts and feelings. But we do this in dishonest ways, which usually are not helpful and almost always step on the personal rights of others. Examples of aggressive behavior are blaming, threatening, and fighting.

When we are aggressive, we usually feel angry, frustrated, or self-righteous. We often feel bitter, guilty, or lonely afterward. The usual goals of aggressive behavior are to dominate, protect, win, humiliate, and force other people to lose.

## ASSERTIVE BEHAVIOR

Assertive behavior means standing up for your personal rights and expressing your thoughts, feelings, and beliefs in direct, honest, and helpful ways, which do not violate the rights of others. Assertiveness means respecting yourself, expressing your needs, and defending your rights. It also means respecting the needs, feelings, and rights of other people.

When we are assertive, we usually feel better about ourselves and more self-confident. Assertiveness does not guarantee winning, but it does increase the chances of a good compromise or a better result without making others angry.

The first step in assertiveness training is learning to recognize passive, assertive, and aggressive behavior. Read slowly through the charts on pages that follow. Notice that the first two charts clarify the verbal and nonverbal characteristics of these three types of behavior.

About 60 percent of all communication is nonverbal, so pay attention to these characteristics. To become aware of potential double messages, try to imagine using the verbal part of one type of behavior with the nonverbal part of another.

The third and fourth charts reveal what our goals, feelings, and payoffs may be. How do you feel most of the time? What are your goals and what are your payoffs?

The fifth chart shows the effects of the three types of behavior on others. What effects do you want to have on your family, friends, and fellow workers?

The sixth chart reveals the outcomes we can expect from such behaviors. Think of some recent events and their outcomes. Did your outcomes match the behaviors you used?

These charts can help you see meekness, withdrawal, attack, and blame for what they are—sadly inadequate strategies of escape that create more pain and stress than they prevent. Before you can achieve assertive behavior, you must face the fact that passive and aggressive behaviors have often failed to get you what you want.

## A COMPARISION OF PASSIVE, ASSERTIVE,
## AND AGGRESSIVE BEHAVIORS

| VERBAL BEHAVIORS | | |
| --- | --- | --- |
| PASSIVE | ASSERTIVE | AGGRESSIVE |
| You avoid saying what you want, think, or feel. If you do, you speak in such a way that you put yourself down. Apologetic words with hidden meaning, a smoke screen of vague words, or silence are used frequently. Examples are "You know," "Well," "I mean," "I guess," and "I'm sorry." You allow others to choose for you. | You say what you honestly want, think, and feel in direct and helpful ways. You make your own choices. You communicate with tact and humor. You use "I" statements. Your words are clear and objective. They are few and well chosen. | You say what you want, think, and feel, but at the expense of others. You use loaded words and "you" statements that label or blame. You employ threats or accusations and one-upmanship. You choose for others. |

| NONVERBAL BEHAVIORS | | |
| --- | --- | --- |
| PASSIVE | ASSERTIVE | AGGRESSIVE |
| You use actions instead of words. You hope someone will guess what you want. You look as though you don't mean what you say. Your voice is weak, hesitant, and soft. You whisper in a monotone. Your eyes are averted or downcast. You nod to almost anything another person says. You sit or stand far away from the other person. You don't know what to do with your hands, and they are trembling or clammy. You look uncomfortable, shuffle, and are tense or inhibited. | You listen closely. Your manner is calm and assured. You communicate caring and strength. Your voice is firm, warm, and expressive. You look directly at the other person, but you don't stare. You face the person. Your hands are relaxed. You hold your head erect, and you lean toward the other person. You have a relaxed expression. | You make an exaggerated show of strength. You are flippant. You have an air of superiority. Your voice is tense, loud, cold, or demanding. You are deadly quiet. Your eyes are narrow, cold, and staring. You act as if you could almost see through the other person. You take a macho fight stance. Your hands are on your hips, and you are inches from the other person. Your hands are in fists, or your finger is pointed at the other person. You are tense and appear angry. |

## YOUR APPARENT GOALS AND FEELINGS

| GOALS | | |
|---|---|---|
| PASSIVE | ASSERTIVE | AGGRESSIVE |
| To please, to be liked. | To communicate, to be respected. | To dominate or humiliate. |
| **FEELINGS** | | |
| PASSIVE | ASSERTIVE | AGGRESSIVE |
| You feel anxious, ignored, hurt, manipulated, and disappointed with yourself. You are often angry and resentful later. | You feel confident and successful. You feel good about yourself at that time and later. You feel in control, you have self-respect, and you are goal-oriented. | You feel self-righteous, controlling, and superior. Sometimes you feel embarrassed or selfish later. |

## YOUR APPARENT PAYOFFS

| PAYOFFS | | |
|---|---|---|
| PASSIVE | ASSERTIVE | AGGRESSIVE |
| You avoid unpleasant situations, conflicts, short-term tensions, and confrontations. You don't have to take responsibility for your choices. | You feel good. You feel respected by others. Your self-confidence improves. You make your own choices. Your relationships with others are improved. You have very little physical distress now or later. You are in touch with your feelings. | You get some anger off your chest. You get a feeling of control. You feel superior. |

## THE EFFECTS ON OTHERS

| THEIR FEELINGS | | |
|---|---|---|
| PASSIVE | ASSERTIVE | AGGRESSIVE |
| They feel guilty, superior, frustrated, or even angry. | They feel respected or valued. They feel free to express themselves. | They feel humiliated, depreciated, or hurt. |

| THEIR FEELINGS TOWARD YOU | | |
|---|---|---|
| PASSIVE | ASSERTIVE | AGGRESSIVE |
| They feel irritated. They pity and depreciate you. They feel frustrated or disgusted with you. They lose respect for you because you are a pushover. | They usually respect, trust, and value you. They know where you stand. | They feel hurt, defensive, humiliated, or angry. They resent, distrust, and fear you. They may want revenge. |

## PROBABLE OUTCOMES OF EACH TYPE OF BEHAVIOR

| PASSIVE | ASSERTIVE | AGGRESSIVE |
|---|---|---|
| You don't get what you want. If you do get your own way, it is by indirect means. You feel emotionally dishonest. Others achieve their goals at your expense. Your rights are violated. Your anger builds up, and you either push it down or redirect it toward other people who are less powerful. You may find yourself procrastinating, suffering in silence, doing things halfheartedly, being sloppy, or becoming forgetful. Others manipulate you. Loneliness and isolation may become common in your life. | You often get what you want if it is reasonable. You often achieve your goals. You gain self-respect. You feel good. You convert win-lose situations to win-win ones. The outcome is determined by aboveboard negotiations. Your rights and others' rights are respected. | You often get what you want but at the expense of others. You hurt others by making choices for them and infantilizing them. Others feel they have a right to get even. You may have increasing difficulty with relaxing and unwinding later. |

## EXAMPLES OF COMMUNICATION STYLES

| The situation you might be in | What you say and do |
|---|---|
| You are watching a movie, but people seated in front of you are making it hard to hear the sound. | You sit and fume, clearing your throat occasionally. (Passive) |
| At a meeting one person often interrupts you when you are speaking. | You look at the person and say firmly, "Excuse me, I'd like to finish what I'm saying." (Assertive) |
| You'd like a raise. | You shuffle into your boss's office and say, "Do you think that, ah, you could see your way clear to giving me a raise?" (Passive) |

| The situation you might be in | What you say and do |
|---|---|
| You have talked with your boss about a helpful suggestion for organizing the work in the office. He says that he thinks it is a good idea and he will ask someone else to put the change into effect. | You put your hands on your hips and shout, "This was my suggestion, and I won't stand for someone else getting all the credit for it." (Aggressive) |
| You are looking forward to a quiet night alone. A relative calls and asks you to babysit. | You communicate caring but strength as you say, "I put aside tonight for myself, and I won't be able to babysit." (Assertive) |
| Your parents or in-laws call and tell you they are dropping by, but you are busy. | In a loud voice you say, "You always call two minutes before you get here and expect me to drop everything." (Aggressive) |
| Two workers in your office have been talking about personal matters. The work is piling up. Others have been complaining. You are their supervisor. | You call the offenders together, lean toward them, and say, "I know how easy it is for time to slip by when you are relaxing and talking to your friends. But your work is piling up and I would like you to use the twenty-minute break for personal conversation." (Assertive) |
| You are the only woman (or man) in a group of men (or women). You are asked to be the secretary at the meetings. | You respond, "I'm willing to do my share and take the notes this time. In future meetings I'd like others to take their turn. (Assertive) |

| The situation you might be in | What you say and do |
|---|---|
| A date and time is being set for a weekly meeting. The time is not convenient for you, and it will be next to impossible for you to make the meetings regularly. | When asked about the time, you look down and almost whisper, "Well, I guess it's okay. I'm not going to be able to come very much, but if it fits everyone else's schedule, it's okay with me." (Passive) |
| A good friend is always late for things you plan to do together. You have not said anything for several weeks. | When your friend arrives, you look as though you are ready to explode. You say, "You're never on time!" (Aggressive) |

## LEARNING TO TAKE CHARGE OF YOUR COMMUNICATION

> All sensible people are selfish.
>
> —RALPH WALDO EMERSON

Being assertive is somewhat selfish since it involves expressing your rights and needs, but it means doing so in an adaptive manner meant to respect yourself and others. It is one of the most powerful interpersonal stress management tools.

> There are thousands of causes for stress, and one antidote to stress is self-expression.
>
> —GARSON KANIN

In the next chapter we will teach you different techniques to help with your personally challenging communication situations.

# TWENTY

# Rolling Up Your Sleeves and Becoming Assertive

*Most of the time we don't communicate,*
*we just take turns talking.*
—ANON

YOU HAVE TAKEN THE FIRST STEPS TOWARD ASSERTIVE BEHAVIOR.
You have learned the differences among aggressive, passive, and
assertive behavior. Now it is time to begin practicing assertiveness
skills.

The following step-by-step approach to assertiveness training
comes from the book *Your Perfect Right* by Robert Alberti, Ph.D.,
and Michael Emmons, Ph.D. Their book started the assertiveness
training movement. The steps involve reviewing your behaviors
and trying to be assertive in a situation with a high probability of
success.

First, write lists of mildly, moderately, and very difficult situations and categorize your responses according to whether they were passive, assertive, or aggressive. Look at what you say verbally and how you say it nonverbally. Write down your goals by referring to the chart "Your Apparent Goals and Feelings" in Chapter 19.

Perhaps you are trying to avoid conflict, please, dominate, or humiliate rather than communicate. Consider what you gain by being aggressive or passive and what you might gain by being assertive. You almost always have more to gain by being assertive. If necessary, review the effects on others of your behavioral options and their probable outcomes.

## PLANNING YOUR ASSERTIVENESS

Now that you have reviewed what you are currently doing and have chosen to become more assertive, it is time to decide how you might handle the situations better. A good way of finding a better method of coping with the situations is to observe someone who is handling it effectively. You may wish to write down a variety of responses that might be more effective than ones you are currently using. Later in this chapter, we will suggest many different assertive techniques.

## IMAGINING YOUR ASSERTIVENESS

The next step is to use visual imagery to imagine better ways of handling the problem. Imagine yourself acting in an assertive manner both verbally and nonverbally. Picture how the other person will react and your response. Envision a number of outcomes and how you can handle them.

## ROLE-PLAYING YOUR ASSERTIVENESS

Rather than jumping from imagining your new behavior to trying it out in the "cruel world," it is best to first role-play your assertive solutions. Role-playing means taking the role of someone who is acting in an assertive manner.

It is often helpful to use a mirror to check your nonverbal messages. Be sure that you are:

1. Facing the other person from a normal distance

2. Looking directly at the other person without staring

3. Keeping your head erect and body relaxed

4. Leaning toward the other person

5. Speaking distinctly and firmly, so as to be easily heard

Try taking the role of yourself and then taking the role of the other person. Finally, try your role once again. Imagine and rehearse all the possible outcomes.

When you role-play, be sure to use your relaxation techniques to calm yourself. This will also help you learn a relaxed, calm, and firm approach to assertive communication. You may also want to practice your new skills with someone in your family or with a friend. Be sure to switch roles and practice both roles several times.

## The Real Thing

The next step is to choose a situation that is likely to bring good results and build up your confidence. Talk over your difficulties with members of your family or a close friend. Ask them to help you deal with your problem by encouraging you and by praising you when you report back about your attempts. Then relax and take the plunge. Afterward, do not be blind to your progress. Reward yourself for acting assertively.

Remember, you do not have to succeed all the time. Just be sure to learn from your mistakes and then practice more effective behaviors in your imagination, your role-playing, and your daily life. It will take a good deal of practice before you can perform these behaviors naturally and automatically.

## TAKING THE STEPS TO ASSERTIVENESS

A young woman who was looking forward to graduating from college and getting married came to one of us for therapy because she was suffering from tension headaches. After she found some relief from relaxation training, it became clear that a major source of stress was her relationship with her fiancé, a senior medical student. Her fiancé often asked her to do more errands than she wanted to take on.

Following the steps suggested above, the woman began by reviewing her behavior. She described the situation that brought the problem to a head in the following way. The weekend before, her fiancé had spent one of his few days off fishing with his friends. He had been at her apartment a couple of hours before she returned from shopping with her mother. When he told her that he was hungry and asked why she was late, she was angry and disappointed that he had not started dinner, but she apologized and said she would begin cooking right away.

She correctly identified her behavior as passive. She had avoided saying what she thought, wanted, or felt. Her apology had a hidden meaning of anger, and she remembered being tense and hoping that he would see how tired she looked.

She realized how much she wanted to please her fiancé. At the same time, she felt resentful. Thinking back, she remembered how little respect her future father-in-law had for his wife, who had never stood up to him or refused his requests before their divorce. She vowed not to fall into the same trap.

This patient started to think of assertive behaviors that she might use. She talked with her friend, who was married to a medical student and seemed to have a very healthy relationship with her husband.

She then began using visual imagery and rehearsed new ways of responding to her fiancé's requests. She also imagined new ways of approaching him for a discussion about these issues.

She role-played new behaviors. But with a weak voice and her eyes turned downward, she did not look as though she meant what she was saying. As she watched herself in the mirror, she started to laugh, and she agreed to use a mirror to practice her nonverbal behaviors at home. She began role-playing some of the new approaches she wanted to use in her relationships. She practiced with her friend and then tried out her new skills with her fiancé.

As it turned out, he was very concerned that their marriage not end the way his parents' had. He was surprised at his actions when she expressed her disappointment and described what he did that troubled her. At the next session of therapy, she reported that she was proud of her assertiveness and that their communication was steadily improving.

## RESPONDING ASSERTIVELY TO THE REQUESTS OF OTHERS

The step-by-step approach we just covered is effective in situations in which you need to initiate an assertive behavior. But there are many situations that require you to respond to the actions of other people. We have found it important to practice these situations and role-play them repeatedly because in these stressful situations you may respond impulsively.

Let us take the example of a request made by an authority figure at work. Your immediate supervisor asks you to stay a few hours overtime and do extra work. You have special plans, and you do not want to give them up. First, you should ask for clarification. If you do not understand what is requested of you or its importance, it is difficult to make a decision either to fulfill the request or to refuse it. In this case, it would be important to clarify how pressing the work is and whether it is a task you might be reasonably expected to accomplish.

The next step is to decide where you stand on the issue. You need to take time to process the request and make a decision. Even in a situation such as the one just given, you may want to say that you need time to think it over and let your boss know when you will have an answer. Before responding, it is helpful to use a relaxation technique such as scanning.

Try to use the word "no" when turning down a request. "No" has a great deal of power and clarity. It is a lot better than "Well, I just don't think so . . . ah . . ." Along the same lines, it is important to be as brief as possible. Give your reasons for refusing the request, but avoid long, elaborate justification or explanation. Long excuses can become accusations or reveal your tendency toward overresponsibility. The other person can use these excuses to manipulate you.

Try to use "I" messages. In this case, you might say, "I won't work overtime tonight." This might be more effective than "I can't work tonight" or "I shouldn't work tonight." Using an "I" message makes it clear that you have made a choice.

## THE BROKEN-RECORD TECHNIQUE

You may find it necessary to refuse the request several times before the person "hears" you. In this case, you can use a technique that has been popularized by Manuel Smith, Ph.D. He called it the "broken record." To use the technique, you calmly repeat your no, with or without your original reason for declining. You do so as often as is required. You may find it helpful to practice the broken-record technique in your role-playing.

One of the best situations in which to use the broken record is when you feel entitled to something purchased or some type of service you have purchased. It is particularly useful with repairmen, waiters, salespeople, and landlords. In these cases, you continue saying no to any compromise that is unsatisfactory. Be sure to speak in a firm, relaxed manner. Role-playing these situations can help you to realize how frequently you may have to play your broken record in a situation.

## The Power of Silence

Silence is a very potent form of nonverbal communication. If someone continues to badger you after you have turned on your broken record, use silence. This technique is particularly useful on the telephone.

## Additional Approaches

You may also want to assert yourself about what is happening when you are being badgered. You may want to say, "I really wish you would stop pressuring me." Or you could try saying, "I'm not going to change my mind." If this does not work, you may need to tell the person what you are going to do next. You may say that you are going to change the topic, hang up the phone, or leave. And it may be necessary to follow through and do what you say you are going to do.

An additional approach, called the paradoxical statement, has the power of the unexpected. A paradox may lead to exactly the opposite of what you actually say. For example, just before you leave or hang up the phone, you may say, "I hope you will write me a letter or call me several more times about this matter. It is really helping me to practice my assertiveness." This response often disarms the person who is badgering you and leaves him without an offense.

## The Fogging Technique

Another major technique popularized by Dr. Smith is called fogging. The person trying to be assertive repeats what the other person is saying or asking for. In this way, before he says no, the person acknowledges the other individual's problem and shows that he understands what the other is communicating.

In relationships with important people, it is helpful to acknowledge the feelings that the other person may have about your refusal. You may want to reflect his feelings after he has stated them, saying something like "I know that you've been hoping that I would do it and that this may be a disappointment to you, but I won't be able to."

Try to avoid using the words "I'm sorry." Apologizing is often unnecessary and dishonest. It also tends to compromise your basic right to say no. You may wish to offer a compromise, but it is important that you realize you have the freedom not to compromise and not to work an hour extra or come in early the next day. Be sure to refuse the major request clearly and without feeling guilty.

Finally, you have the right to change your mind and refuse a request that you may have originally agreed to. You have to weigh the consequences, but if you find yourself hedging or feeling manipulated, you may want to reconsider your initial decision.

## PRACTICE SAYING NO

To practice saying no to requests and demands, use the following examples. First try them in your imagination and then role-play them in front of a mirror.

1. A friend asks you for a loan until next payday.

2. Your daughter asks if she may stay out until three o'clock in the morning.

3. You are on a committee and have done your work. Another committee member calls you at the last minute and tries to get you to do some of his or her work.

4. Your uncle tells you of his plan to visit you for a month. This is his third visit this year.

5. A person at work never seems to have a ride home. He asks you once again for a ride.

6. A salesperson pressures you to buy when you are still undecided.

7. You and your wife are out with friends who want to go for a nightcap. You are tired and want to go home.

8. A friend asks you to make cookies for a bake sale. You have already planned an evening with another friend.

9. Your boss asks you again to postpone your vacation.

10. A friend expects you to help plan a party.

## TAKING THE STRESS OUT OF CRITICISM

Criticism you receive from others is another major category of situations for which you may need to practice responding to others in an assertive manner. When someone criticizes you, you may find it helpful to use a brief relaxation technique such as taking a deep breath and saying silently, "Relax and let go." This will help you to listen to what the person is saying. If the criticism is vague or ambiguous, it may be helpful to ask the person to be more specific. The next step may be to state the criticism in your own words. This allows you to check out what you have heard and shows the other person that you understood the criticism.

At this point, it is often helpful to take a moment to relax and decide whether the criticism is accurate or useful. You may also want to get in touch with your feelings so you can share them with the person making the criticism. You may feel annoyed, angry, or scared. It is often helpful to share these feelings with the other person so that the person will know the effect the criticism is having on you. You may want to express your feelings about the timing, frequency, or accuracy of the criticism.

If the criticism is fair, you may find it helpful to ask for specific suggestions and alternatives. It is important to avoid excuses that may turn out to be self-accusations. Try to move toward the future and turn the person criticizing you in the same direction. When sharing your feelings about the criticism, it is important to use "I" statements so as not to put the other person on the defensive. Consider the difference between "You don't understand anything" and "It seems to me that you may not have understood what happened."

By using a relaxation technique, you can avoid an escalating sense of urgency and anger. If you try to match the pace and volume of the person criticizing you, an argument may develop. Try speaking slowly, calmly, and quietly.

Here are some examples of criticism to practice with:

1. Your boss says your work is sloppy.

2. Your supervisor says your work is never finished on time.

3. Your wife says you don't love her.

4. Your child says you don't understand him.

5. Your mother says you don't visit often enough.

6. Your boyfriend says you are a cheat.

7. Your teacher says your paper was confusing and meaningless.

8. A new acquaintance says, "Most women don't know what they're talking about."

9. Your students say your lectures are boring.

10. A customer says that what you have done or what you sell is useless.

## IRRATIONAL BELIEFS SUPPORTING PASSIVE BEHAVIORS

Another way of handling difficulties with assertiveness is to examine potential irrational beliefs about assertiveness. Lynn Bloom, Karen Coburn, and Joan Pearlman, in their excellent book *The New Assertive Woman,* review irrational beliefs that support passive behaviors. One of their chapters is entitled "What's the Worst That Could Happen: Irrational Beliefs." These irrational beliefs can support passive behaviors whether you are a man or a woman.

You may have unrealistic beliefs about the possible outcomes of a situation involving assertive behavior. Even if the outcome is negative, you may be blowing it out of proportion or assuming that you could not handle it. Some of the irrational beliefs and their rational counterparts are listed on page 245.

## IRRATIONAL BELIEFS SUPPORTING AGGRESSIVE BEHAVIORS

Aggression is appropriate for situations in which we are physically attacked. Fearing harm, we strike back to protect ourselves. Unfortunately, we may misperceive a situation as dangerous and become aggressive in unnecessary and ineffective ways. What we think and say to ourselves can determine what we see and do. This is especially true when we jump to conclusions without considering all the evidence.

Just as there are irrational beliefs that support passive behaviors, there are irrational beliefs that support aggressive behaviors. If you are trying to substitute assertive behaviors for aggressive ones, consider some of the false beliefs that often support aggressive behaviors. People in an anger management group we led held the irrational beliefs listed on page 246. Some of the rational counterparts which the group members found useful are provided next to each irrational belief.

## IRRATIONAL BELIEFS SUPPORTING PASSIVE BEHAVIORS

| Irrational Belief | Rational Counterpart |
|---|---|
| As soon as I am assertive, others will become angry with me. | Others may react positively, neutrally, or negatively. If assertiveness involves legitimate rights, the odds are that you will have a positive response. |
| As soon as I assert myself, people will become angry and I will be devastated. | I will be capable of handling it, and I am not responsible for another person's anger. It may well be that person's problem. |
| I want others to be honest and straightforward with me, but if I tell others what I feel or want, I will hurt them. | People may or may not feel hurt, and most people prefer to be dealt with directly. |
| If others are hurt by my assertive behavior, I am responsible for their hurt feelings. | Even if they are hurt, I can let them know I care for them in other ways, and they will survive. |
| If I turn down legitimate requests, other people will hate me. | Even legitimate requests can be refused. I can consider my own needs, and I cannot please everyone all the time. |
| I should always avoid making statements or asking questions that might make me look stupid. | I am a valuable human being. The people I want to associate with will accept me as a valuable human being. |

## IRRATIONAL BELIEFS SUPPORTING AGGRESSIVE BEHAVIORS

| Irrational Belief | Rational Counterpart |
|---|---|
| It's either him or me, and it's not going to be me if I can help it. | We can both win. Let's look for a compromise. |
| If I'm not aggressive, they will be. | Others may respond in many ways; odds are the ways will be neutral or positive. |
| It's a dog-eat-dog world. | What you expect is often what you get. |
| If I don't angrily turn down this request now, I'll have a flood of requests to contend with. | I can be assertive if people later try to take advantage of me. |
| If I don't let them know loud and clear, they won't do what they said they would. | First I'll see what they say to my firm request. I can always use other assertive techniques if they refuse. |
| You can't teach an old dog new tricks. I always get angry. | Always? Few "always" or "never" statements are true. |

Check and dispute your irrational beliefs. Some of them may be interfering with your right to be assertive. Review the chapters about thinking and feeling better if you have trouble recognizing and disputing them.

## WHEN IT IS BEST NOT TO BE ASSERTIVE

Assertive communication is direct and honest. But there may be times when it is best to be aggressive or passive. When you are stressed, the fight-or-flight response may be appropriate. You do not want to talk about your rights when a saber-toothed tiger is running toward you. Likewise, when a robber puts a gun to your head, it may not be the best time to be assertive. Pick your battles carefully and weigh the costs against the benefits of being assertive, passive, or aggressive.

> *Conflict is inevitable, combat is optional.*
>
> —MAX LUCADO

# SECTION VI

## Planning the Days of Your Life

*Some get spiritual 'cause they see the light
and some 'cause they feel the heat.*
—RAY WYLIE HUBBARD

# TWENTY-ONE

# Managing the Times of Your Life

*Life . . . struts and frets his hour upon the stage,
and then is heard no more.*
—SHAKESPEARE

*Organize and execute around priorities.*
—STEPHEN R. COVEY

HOW EFFECTIVELY WE ORGANIZE AND MANAGE OUR TIME MAY make the difference in how much we feel in control of our lives. If we do not have time for breaks, building relationships, quiet reflection, planning, taking care of our physical body, loved ones, and ourselves, then we may have a serious problem with how we prioritize and spend the twenty-four hours we are given each day. People who have "hurry-up sickness" and never seem to get caught up or do the important things are more prone to illness and chronic stress-related problems.

For many people their job occupies over one-third of their workweek time. If that time is spent feeling insecure, unhappy, competitive, unchallenged, or poorly compensated, then resentment and distress may build. Some people work to live; others live to work. Some people enjoy their work; others just put in the time. Some people feel they are growing professionally; others feel they are stagnating. Some feel they have a balance between work responsibilities, authority, and resources; others do not. Depending on how you view the time management part of your total stress management plan, you will either contribute to your overall distress or enhance your sense of wellness and health.

> The bird of time has but a little way to flutter—and the bird is on the wing.
>
> —OMAR KHAYYAM

## Do Not Try To Manage Time; Manage Yourself Instead

There is really no such thing as time management. We cannot manage time. We will never be able to "save" time, and time does not really "fly." Time marches on at a fixed rate, and all of us have exactly as much time as the most or least productive person in the world. Time is the one thing that we are all given in equal amounts. The rich and the poor all have the same number of minutes in an hour, hours in a day, and days in a year. But we can organize our time so that we do those things in life that we truly value.

How did you spend your twenty-four hours yesterday? Did you get a good rate of return on your investment? Did you spend it wisely, or did you throw it away? Did you do something to strengthen your family ties, your physical body, or your spiritual foundation?

Too often we spend our lives doing busywork, which is neither important nor urgent. At other times we may be occupied with "putting out fires," some of which are important and others unimportant. The goal for successful stress management is to spend most of our time on the important but not urgent issues of living.

Physical health care is best managed in this fashion. If you wait until you have a heart attack or stroke to stop smoking, lose weight, or start exercising, then it may be urgent but too little, too late. If you wait until your spouse wants a divorce, then it may be ur-

> *While I'm busy with little things, I am not required to do greater things.*
>
> —St. Francis de Sales

gent but too late to heal the scars from years of neglect. If you wait until you lose your job to change your attitudes or learn new skills, then you may experience needless stress and frustration.

## Not Seeing the Forest for the Trees

One of the best stories we know concerning the ineffective use of time is about a lumberjack. He had been raised around lumbering communities and admired the strong lumberjacks. He told the boss that he wanted a job. Seeing that the boy was large, strong, and healthy, the boss quickly agreed. The first day this lad chopped down ten large trees entirely by himself. This was quite an accomplishment, and the boss was very pleased. He complimented the boy on his energy and strength.

The next day, the boy seemed to work just as hard and just as long, but he only chopped down eight trees. This was still a respectable showing. The rest of the week passed, and each day the boy worked just as hard and just as long, but each day he produced less. On Friday, the boss called the boy into his office after noticing that he had yet to fell one tree. The sun was going down. The boy had worked vigorously all day. He was ashamed because he had produced so little, and tears began to roll down his face as he went into the office.

"Sir," he said, "I'm working harder and harder, but I'm afraid I'm a disappointment to you. I have yet to fell one tree today."

"Why do you do so little?" the boss asked.

> Either people know what they would like to have but can't seem to muster the perseverance or they persevere at what they're doing and don't know what they want.
>
> —EARL NIGHTINGALE

"I'm really trying, sir," was the response.

"Have you taken the time to sharpen your axe, boy?"

The boy answered, "No, sir, I really haven't had time because I have been so busy working."

The lesson: work sharper, not harder, and take the time to sharpen your axe.

## DANGER SIGNALS OF POOR TIME MANAGEMENT

There are various danger signals that suggest a person can benefit from better time management.

Respond to the statements in the scale below by recording the number from 0 to 10 that accurately reflects your time management situations and attitudes. Use these guidelines for choosing your answers and then total your scores: 0—never; 1, 2, 3—sometimes; 4, 5, 6—frequently; 7, 8, 9—most of the time; 10—always.

If you scored less than 35 total points, you may benefit from learning additional time management techniques, but your stress level is probably not significantly affected by time pressure. If you scored 36 to 60, you probably could use time-management training to reduce the risk of potential stress disorders.

If you scored above 60, your life may feel dangerously out of control. People who score over 60 often say they "don't have time" for training in stress or time management. They may put off indefinitely such important decisions as to stop smoking, begin exercising, spend more time with family and friends, or take vacations. We have a choice whether we wish to allow time to manage us or we wish to manage time.

## TIME MANAGEMENT SCALE

| STATEMENTS ABOUT MY SITUATIONS AND ATTITUDES | SCORE (0 = NEVER TO 10 = ALWAYS) |
|---|---|
| 1. I am indispensable. I find myself taking on various tasks because I'm the only one who can do them. | |
| 2. Daily crises take up all my time. I have no time to do important things because I'm too busy putting out fires. | |
| 3. I attempt to do too much at one time. I feel I can do it all, and I rarely say no. | |
| 4. I feel unrelenting pressure, as if I'm always behind and have no way to catch up. I'm always rushing. | |
| 5. I'm working habitually long hours, ten, twelve, fourteen, even eighteen hours a day, five, six, or seven days a week. | |
| 6. I constantly feel overwhelmed by demands and details and feel that I have to do what I don't want to do most of the time. | |
| 7. I feel guilty about leaving work on time. I don't have sufficient time for rest or personal relationships. I take worries and problems home. | |
| 8. I constantly miss deadlines. | |
| 9. I am plagued by fatigue and listlessness, with many slack hours of unproductive activity. | |
| 10. I chronically vacillate between unpleasant alternatives. | |
| **TOTAL SCORE** | |

## TIME WASTERS ARE TIME ROBBERS

An analysis of time wasters helps to build a firm foundation for good time management. A time waster is anything that prohibits us

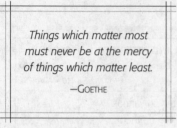

*Things which matter most must never be at the mercy of things which matter least.*

—GOETHE

from reaching our objectives most effectively. Time is a perishable asset, and if we are not careful, it can be taken away without our even noticing it is being stolen. Time wasters are robbers. They can be divided into two categories: major and minor.

Major time wasters stand between us and what we want to accomplish. They include problems with our attitudes, goals, objectives, priorities, plans, and abilities to make basic decisions.

Minor time wasters include distractions that hinder us once we are on the way to accomplishing our objectives. Minor time wasters can include interruptions that we face during the day, lengthy meetings of minor importance, needless reports, extended telephone calls, unexpected visitors, and many others.

## TAKING A TIME INVENTORY

Before examining steps to effective time management and analyzing time wasters, it is useful to take your own personal time inventory. To do this, you should make a chart of the day, broken into fifteen-minute segments, or use an appointment book either in paper form, on a personal digital assistant (PDA), or on your computer. If you have the technical skills to do a spreadsheet on the computer, this can help you evaluate your time inventory data.

*I recommend you take care of the minutes, for the hours will take care of themselves.*

—LORD CHESTERFIELD

Carry the time inventory sheet or appointment book with you during a typical day and fill it in as you go along. It is most helpful to complete this inventory as you go through a normal day.

You might find it difficult or impossible to try to accurately recall how you spent your time and how much work you actually accomplished in a particular day. Record your sleep time to help assess if you have too little or too much or if you have difficulties with sleep onset or early morning awakening.

Categorize the activities that suit your particular business or daily routine. We would like to suggest certain categories that you may find useful. Categories that are often helpful in taking a time inventory of the working part of the day include socializing, routine tasks, low-priority work, productive work, meetings, planning, and telephone calls. For homemakers, categories might include cleaning, straightening, transporting, cooking, home-schooling, and so on. Helpful categories for when you are not at work or homemaking include telephone calls, television, surfing the Net or reading e-mail, playing computer games, recreation, errands, commuting, shopping, household chores, eating, personal hygiene, and sleeping.

Modify these or add any categories that will help you better understand how you spend your time. Taking a time inventory can help you separate and examine the various categories of time and how you use them. You can then determine whether you want to spend more or less time in particular activities.

The next step is to make a satisfaction column and indicate whether you were satisfied, unsatisfied, or neither next to each fifteen-minute segment.

By taking a time inventory, some people learn that they need to limit phone conversations to five minutes, reduce the amount of time spent on preparation for breakfast and eating, shorten the time spent showering and preparing for work in the morning, and restrict the time spent watching television or playing on the computer. Some people, however, find that morning is their best time for relaxation. For them, a long, casual breakfast may be very effective in helping to manage stress.

Complete your time inventory and then add up the amount

of time spent in each category of activity. Consider doing a time inventory for both workdays and non-workdays to allow you to understand both areas of your life.

Once you have analyzed how you spend your time, we would like to encourage you to decide that you have a choice as to how you use your time. Taking responsibility for the way you use your time is no more and no less than taking responsibility for the way you live your life. Making this decision allows you to choose to spend your time in ways other than how you spend it now.

> *People are always blaming their circumstances for what they are. I don't believe in circumstances. The people who get on in this world are the people who get up and look for the circumstances they want and if they can't find them they make them.*
>
> —GEORGE BERNARD SHAW

## THE IMPORTANCE OF GOALS

A lack of important goals is a major time waster. Goals reflect our purpose in life and have a widespread impact on our lives.

Victor Fankl was a Viennese psychiatrist who survived the horror of the Nazi death camps in World War II. In his book *Man's Search for Meaning,* he described how those who had a purpose for living were able to withstand torture and starvation. The purpose for living could have been revenge, building a new homeland, or waiting for the Allied forces to arrive. Those without purpose, goals, or positive self-direction died quickly.

> *To live is to suffer, to survive is to find meaning in the suffering.*
>
> —VICTOR FRANKL

It has been said that two of the greatest tragedies are (1) to never have had a goal and (2) to never have reached it. Life is a se-

> *To have never have dreamed, is to never have lived at all.*
>
> —ELLIS PAUL

ries of ever-growing accomplishments, and few people have only one goal that they reach and then call it quits. Those who do so face a major change stressor. Consider the man who finally retires and has no new goals. The emptiness can be devastating. As you work through this section on goals, we would like you to consider your future in a number of different ways.

## LIFELONG GOALS

First imagine that you are very old and you overhear your grandchildren or relatives talking to their friends about you and your life. What would you want them to say about you and your accomplishments? Write down your thoughts on this subject.

Next, we would like you to write your own epitaph. An epitaph is an inscription on a tomb and is written as a tribute to the dead person. How would you want others to remember you?

As you list your future goals in this chapter, remember that people are goal seekers by design. We constantly adjust our self-image and subconscious to help us reach goals. Often our goals are not planned or they are dictated by negative self-talk such as "I can't do this very well" or "I just know she's not going to like me." Many people actually program themselves not to reach goals by using negative self-talk, failing to define goals clearly or neglecting to make plans for reaching well-chosen goals.

> *Slow down and enjoy life. It's not only the serenity you miss by going too fast. You also miss the sense of where you are going and why.*
>
> —EDDIE CANTOR

## GOAL SETTING

Goals must be obtainable, and objectives must be quantifiable. In addition, goals should be flexible in the event that they are blocked by other priorities.

We would like you to do an exercise involving two-minute drills. Use the listings in "Cues for Goal Setting," below, to help you think of categories of goals. Depending on where you find yourself in the cycle of life, you may place more emphasis on career or retirement, acquisitions or divestitures, growth or simplification. No matter where you find yourself in the cycle of life, do not forget to plan to get old. Few of us would prefer the alternative. Our society has changed in the last few decades, and more emphasis has been placed on the individual to plan for his or her own future.

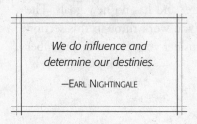

*We do influence and determine our destinies.*

—EARL NIGHTINGALE

First, we ask you to spend two minutes writing down all the goals that you would like to accomplish in the next five years. Limber up your imagination and write down anything that comes to mind. Spend only two minutes on this task.

Next, list all the goals you hope to accomplish next year. Spend only two minutes.

Spend only two minutes writing down all the goals you want to accomplish for the next six months.

Spend another two minutes writing down all your goals for the coming month. Include work priorities, self-improvement programs, recreational activities, social functions, family gatherings, and so on.

## CUES FOR GOAL SETTING

New home

Home improvement

Weight loss

Professional skill

Long vacation

Spiritual goals

New hobby

Closer friends

Coworker communication

Increase in earnings

New position

Family activity

Becoming more patient

Additional education or skills

Short vacation

Increase in savings

Paying off debts

Managing something better

Exercise

Stopping smoking

Stopping drinking

Starting to date

Family communication

New honor

Solving a problem

More spontaneity

Play with children

Community service

More marital satisfaction

Effective retirement planning

Long-term health care planning

Second career or new job

More discretionary time

Meaningful volunteer activities

Simplified lifestyle

Getting rid of "stuff"

## TOP-PRIORITY GOALS

Now that you have created these four lists of goals, we would like you to go back and prioritize each goal. Use an A, B, and C format.

A's will include all those items that you rank as being most essential and most desired. These are your "must-dos." They are often innovative and require creativity.

B's will include all those items that could be put off for a while but that you feel are still important. These are your "desirable-to-dos" or routine duties.

C's are items that could be put off indefinitely with little or no harm. These are your "can-waits" and are often trivial.

After you have prioritized your list, combine the three lists into one by including two A items from each of your long-term, one-year, six-month, and one-month goal lists. Write these down under the heading "A-Priority Goals."

The list you just made should indicate the most important goals you would like to accomplish in the next year. To ensure that this list contains your *most* important goals, we want you to complete another list.

For the next list, imagine you have been told that you have a terminal illness and you will die in one year. During your last year of life you will neither be incapacitated nor experience pain. You will be able to do everything you currently do. Now, write down your goals for the next year if you knew you would die at the end of the year. Title this list "My Goals if Next Year Is the Last Year of My Life."

> The necessity of not missing a train has taught us to account for minutes whereas among ancient Romans . . . the notion not of minutes but even of fixed hours barely existed.
>
> —MARCEL PROUST

Compare the last two lists you have constructed. If these lists are totally different, you may want to reconsider those goals and maybe strike them or add them to your one-year list to reflect your most important goals accurately.

Now that you have selected your current major life goals, it is essential to set up a timetable for each goal. Indicate time periods in which the goals can reasonably be attained.

You now have important goals to work toward and a timetable to guide you. These are your top priorities. Translate these goals and projects into small achievable monthly, weekly, and daily activities. Use these as a guide for your time management for a month.

At the end of the month, review your list to see if you need to make a new list. Sometimes goals are completed, and sometimes uncompleted goals remain high in importance. Other goals may drop in importance. Set aside time every day to work on your

A-priority goals. Emphasize the results that you want rather than the activity, and try to accomplish at least one step toward each goal every day.

The favorite time management experts of one of this book's authors is David M. Bailey. Bailey was a young corporate executive on the fast track to success. After a promotion and move he suffered with severe headaches, which his doctor initially said were probably just related to stress. The headaches became so intense that he decided to go to the local emergency room. After a series of tests and consultations with medical specialists he was given the diagnosis of brain cancer and a prognosis of living only six months. Bailey pursued aggressive treatment, dropped out of the corporate world, and turned to his first passion in life, singing and songwriting. After six years in remission, he continues to perform professionally and has won prestigious accolades for his moving and meaningful songs about life and living it fully while we are alive.

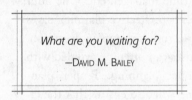

*What are you waiting for?*

—David M. Bailey

## Planning Today Means a More Relaxed Tomorrow

When a sailor is preparing for a voyage, he will chart his course toward his destination and determine what prevailing winds he may expect. Seldom will he be able to predict all the changes of weather, but the forethought of planning tells him which reefs to avoid. He will also plan and rehearse his actions should a sudden squall or prolonged storm appear. We may take an example from the real-life sailor as we sail on the sea of life.

Knowing what your goals and plans are gives you a better chance of recognizing the stressors you will en-

*Everyone says work before play, but no one says how much.*

—Anonymous

counter and how long you may
be exposed to them. Without
plans and goals, people never know
when they have done enough or
where they are on their voyage. It
is very hard to relax and take a
break if you don't plan for one or
forget when it is break time.

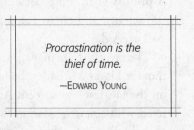

*Procrastination is the
thief of time.*

—EDWARD YOUNG

## An Ounce of Planning Is Worth a Pound of Work

The best way to work effectively toward your A-priority goals is to
plan your day successfully. Here is one of the most powerful rules

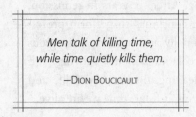

*Men talk of killing time,
while time quietly kills them.*

—DION BOUCICAULT

of time management: One hour
spent in effective planning saves
three to four hours in execution.
Crises can often be avoided with
proper planning. Proper planning will also ensure that the efforts you make during the day
are directed at your main priorities, the major goals that you have
set in your life. The only alternative to personal planning is react-
ing to the demands of others.

## Scheduling Interruptions and Quiet Periods

Build time into your daily schedule for interruptions, unforeseen
problems, and the inevitable fires that must be put out. If you schedule time for these, you can avoid rushing and feeling pressured.

You should be able to set aside periods each day for quiet times
when you can focus on relaxing and unwinding. These are times when
you should be interrupted only if there is an emergency. Schedule
quiet times in your appointment book or you may never find them.

## A Practical Lesson Worth $25,000: Sleep on It!

Dr. George Crane, a business journalist, wrote about a little-known incident in which $25,000 was paid for a practical lesson in time management. Charles Schwab, the chairman of Bethlehem Steel Company at the beginning of the twentieth century, once consulted a New York–based time management expert named Ivy Lee. Schwab said, "My friend, I'll pay you any price if you will just show us how to get more things done." Lee accepted the challenge and gave Schwab the following advice:

> *Come what may, time and the hour runs through the roughest day.*
>
> —Shakespeare

> *At night, spend five minutes analyzing your problems of the following day. Write them down on a sheet of paper, but place them in the order of their importance. Then tackle the first item as soon as you reach the office. Stick to it until it is finished; then shift to No. 2. Test this plan as long as you like; then send me a check for whatever you consider it worth.*

Shortly thereafter, Lee received a check for $25,000 and a brief note from the steel magnate. Schwab wrote, "This is the most practical lesson I have ever learned!" Schwab added that he had been putting off an important phone call for nine months, but after seeing Lee he had put it at the top of his first list. The call, he wrote, "netted us $2 million because of a new order of steel beams."

To optimize your performance, make a list of the five most important tasks that you want to accomplish during the next day. Create this list before you leave work. It may be practical to schedule quiet time during the last half hour of work. Review what you have accomplished for the day and decide on five important jobs that you want to do during the next day. Take this list home with you and review it before you go to bed.

Remember to plan your playtime and your weekend to make the most of your leisure time. This is very important for workaholics. On Friday, review your weekend plans just before you go to sleep. We emphasize planning, but remember the words of John Lennon: "Life is what happens to you while you're busy making other plans."

## Your Daily Calendar

Your appointment book or daily calendar can be a powerful tool for time management if you expand its uses. Consolidate all miscellaneous notes, phone messages, and memos in your book or calendar. The information will then be readily available for use now and retrieval later. List your activities and quiet periods for the following week.

Part of your appointment book can serve as a place for the to-do lists, relaxation cues, and meeting agendas. You can also schedule follow-ups on delegated tasks. Car and other maintenance schedules can be included for the coming year with reminders to make appointments. Anniversaries, birthdays, and other important dates can be entered with notes to purchase gifts or cards a week before. Several companies have developed both paper and electronic systems to help you keep your life more organized. See Appendix III for more resources to help you take charge of your time.

*Lost time is never found again.*

—Benjamin Franklin

## To-Do Lists

As you work toward the accomplishment of your goals, one technique to help you keep focused on important goals is to keep a daily to-do list. Break your larger goals into very small, short-term goals. Meeting some of these attainable short-term goals can be very reinforcing. It gives you an important sense of accomplishment and momentum.

Rate each item as A, B, or C. If you find yourself doing a C item such as cleaning out your desk, and your A items aren't finished, you can be certain that you are wasting your time. Often we do these little tasks as a way of putting off what causes us anxiety—our A items.

Find ways to overcome your anxieties and try to tackle the tough, important jobs first, not last. The following sections describe additional ways of managing your life to help you manage your time.

## Not-to-Do Lists

When you have a particularly tight timetable, you may find it helpful to write down specific things you do *not* plan to do. Write down the time wasters and time robbers you will avoid. For example, you may write down that you will not answer phone calls unless they are truly urgent, you will not accept visitors during certain hours, or you will not file anything today. Not-to-do lists can be almost as important as to-do lists.

## Saying No

One of the best things we can do for ourselves is learning how to say no. This is so important that we devoted an entire section about assertiveness training for refusing requests.

## The 80/20 Rule

The 80/20 Rule is a very important concept in time management. It is also called the Pareto Principle. This principle will help you to become more comfortable not doing C-priority items. Simply stated, only 20 percent of the tasks that we do produce 80 percent of the rewards. Another way of putting this is that most people spend 80 percent of their time doing duties that are related to only 20 percent of the total job results.

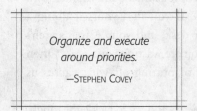

*Organize and execute around priorities.*

—STEPHEN COVEY

In a list of ten tasks, doing two of them will yield 80 percent of the rewards. Find these two tasks, because they are prime candidates for your A-priority list.

The C items and the B items that you have listed will probably not produce what you want to accomplish. Setting your sights on your A items and their related tasks will provide you with the best plan for reaching your true goals.

## DELEGATION

When you have many B and particularly C items to do, delegate them. Often they can be delegated to a secretary, hired help, spouse, parents, or children.

Diana Silox, a professional time management consultant and author of *Woman Time,* kept a time inventory when she was beginning to expand her consulting service. She found that she was answering every phone call, cleaning her house, doing her own laundry, and handling her own typing and filing. She reset her priorities so as to establish her right to a rich personal life as well as challenging professional life. She then hired a maid as well as a secretary and began sending out her laundry, shopping by phone or mail, and eating out more often.

Before you delegate, determine the time necessary to do the task and the time required to explain, instruct, and coordinate. Delegate tasks for which the time needed to complete the work is long in relation to the time required for instructing and supervising. Avoid doing things you should delegate, but be sure to avoid delegating jobs you should do yourself.

## Avoiding Reverse Delegation

Another important part of effective delegation is to follow up periodically on each task that you have delegated. Write down reminders in your appointment book. If a task is given back to you in unfinished or unacceptable form without a reasonable explanation or without sufficient time for redelegation, you are experiencing reverse delegation. Periodic follow-ups can help prevent reverse delegation and procrastination.

## One of the Best Places to Delegate

The garbage can is often the best place to delegate something. Ask yourself, "How terrible would it be if I just threw this away?" If your answer is "Not too terrible," delegate it to your garbage can.

If you find that you can't discard certain C items, set aside a special drawer or file for them. When the drawer or file gets full, file everything in an envelope or box and label it "C Items" along with the date. January 2 every year is a good time to go through these C files. Usually it is easy to throw things away when they have aged. If you still cannot throw them away, transfer them back to your selected drawer or file. Maybe you can delegate them to the wastebasket next year.

## The Once-Over

It is not always best to file your C's. To avoid accumulating paperwork, look at each item when you receive it. If at all possible, make a decision at that time.

The best example is dealing with mail, either regular mail, interoffice mail, or e-mail. Some mail

> *Do not squander time for that is the stuff life is made of.*
>
> —Benjamin Franklin

may not even need to be opened. Junk mail comes in both paper and electronic versions. Junk mail filters help you to never see the electronic junk mail. Standing over a garbage can while sorting regular mail may help minimize the time you spend dealing with these time wasters. Throw away any mail you feel you can do without. If the mail is electronic, then basically do the same. If you need an electronic file on your computer that says "C Items," then make the file and quickly get the low-priority e-mail items out of your regular mailbox. If you have friends that send you humorous but unimportant e-mails, then make a file to store them until you are done with your A items and have time for recreation. The barrage of electronic communications distracts many people. Don't fall into this trap.

## LIFE SIMPLIFICATION FOR TIME MANAGEMENT

We will offer many tips to manage your time more effectively in the twenty-first century, but this is the greatest tool yet—choose voluntary simplicity. Most of us show up at the office and have a dozen phone calls to return, a myriad of e-mail messages to read or discard, and many individuals or tasks wanting "just a minute" of our time. These are all followed by interruptions and crises. We continue to pursue that "petty pot of gold at the end of the plastic rainbow," because there is "too much month at the end of the money." Many stressed-out Americans who have struggled for years to balance work, family, and personal responsibilities are choosing to work less. This section is meant to make you consider if your life is too cluttered with poorly planned goals and in need of simplification. If you choose this time management tool, then recognize that it is a project that will take time.

Choosing to work less probably means collecting a reduced salary. The average American works nine full weeks more than our West European friends. We may be richer financially, but are we richer in terms of quality of life?

Simplifying life is a long-term process that will require preparation and determination. Look around your house, in your garage, in your yard, in your office, and in your rented storage space. Do you have too much stuff? Do you really

> *I wasted time, and now doth time waste me.*
>
> —SHAKESPEARE

need it all? Do you spend time earning money to have more stuff, only to find that you don't have time to play with your stuff? Use some of the books in Appendix III to guide your life simplification planning.

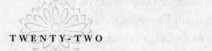

# TWENTY-TWO

# Saving Time with Technology:

*Focusing Your Laser*

*We can all make a living, or we can design a life.*
—Dennis Waitley

THE MAIN THRUST OF THIS CHAPTER IS HOW TO MANAGE YOUR time more effectively. Time is a major asset, and it should be managed just as we manage any other valuable asset. How satisfied are you with use of the time available to you?

Goals should be set for all areas of your life. Set business and professional goals, but also set goals related to family, physical health, educational development, life simplification, and spiritual growth.

Vividly imagine the accomplishment of your goals. The winners in life rehearse time and time again, seeing themselves being successful and attaining their goals. "Sharpen your axe" or "focus your laser" if you need new skills, knowledge, or technology. If your life does not lend itself to the high-technology suggestions in this chapter, remember that a simple lifestyle can be effective for many people, and attempts to add technology can be stressful. Assess if you would do well with incorporating PDAs, laptop computers, cellular phones, and wireless Internet into your life for more effective work and pleasurable play.

> *Carpe diem, lads!*
> *Seize the day.*
>
> —ROBIN WILLIAMS
> (in the movie
> *Dead Poets Society*)

Organize your space, both physical and electronic.

## TECHNOLOGY AND TIME MANAGEMENT: "FOCUS YOUR LASER"

In the last chapter, we talked about the importance of "sharpening your axe." What follows here can be be called learning to "focus your laser." The principle is the same as the lesson of the lumberjack, but in today's high-technology world, we may all need to make one of our most important goals continuing education and training in the utilization of time-saving technology. This can be intimidating if you are used to the paper-and-pencil world, but technology continues to become more and more user-friendly. Consider the possibilities below and take classes, hire professional trainers, or just teach yourself how to use the time management tools for this new millennium.

**Personal Digital Assistant (PDA)**   A personal digital assistant (PDA) is a handheld device that can be a combination of small computer, wireless cell phone, and Internet service. You can synchronize it with your desktop computer to back up and have additional access to your address book, calendar, and other important information and data. You can use it to wirelessly connect to the Internet, check e-mail, and retrieve information.

We emphasize nutrition and exercise as part of your stress management program in future chapters. Your can use your PDA to keep track of goals related to these important habits. There are software programs for your PDA that are powerful food and exercise diaries with over twenty thousand foods in databases to help you work out exactly what you need to do to shed pounds quickly and effectively.

**Consider a Laptop Instead of Desktop Computer**    Everything you can do on a PDA you can do on a laptop computer, and much more. Laptop computers have become less expensive, smaller, faster, and more powerful, with more storage and capability. In a relatively small package less than twelve square inches and weighing about five pounds, you can do everything you could with an expensive desktop from a decade ago, and more. With a laptop you can run most programs for work tasks, keep up with e-mail, organize your calendar and important files, wirelessly connect to the Internet for work and entertainment, retrieve files from a virtual storage space, read or listen to the latest novels or music, and watch movies.

**Internet Storage and Services**    Another advantage of living in this age of high technology is that you can always have your important files, phone numbers, calendar, and other important information just a click away. With the ability to store this information in a virtual domain, you can retrieve files and phone numbers, back up your files automatically for safekeeping, synchronize your laptop and desktop computers, and more from anywhere in the world when you have access to the Internet. See Appendix III for more information about this type of service.

**Data Protection for Effective Time Management**     An important part of time management is to do something well only once and then protect yourself from needlessly duplicating the completed task. On the beach it can be fun to build sandcastles, knowing that the tides will soon wash them away.

But who would want to build their own house in such a way that the big, bad wolf could huff and puff and blow their house down? Unfortunately, there are many "big, bad wolves" out there that can make our high-technology time management techniques more stress-promoting than stress-managing. We can make a mistake, technology can fail, electricity can surge, and viruses can sabotage. Whether you use a PDA, laptop, or desktop computer, you need to make certain your time management plan includes the following top-priority actions: always back up your data, always synchronize your data, always have the most current virus protection software, always have sophisticated junk-mail screening, and always—yes, always—back up your data!

**High-Speed Internet**     Consider spending the extra money for high-speed Internet capability. The time you can spend waiting for dial-up Internet to load the more complex Web sites may not be worth it. If you open only e-mail, then this may not be important, but if you find yourself waiting too long for your Internet service to respond, then consider upgrading to a faster Internet connection.

**Going Wireless**     Whether you use a laptop computer or PDA, consider going wireless. With a wireless network and Internet you can sit anywhere inside or outside your home or office, work on your important items, send files to print from a distant printer, or keep in touch with a friend or colleague. Most hotels now have wireless Internet in the rooms, and many coffee shops cater to the wireless workers of today.

**Instant**            If you spend a lot of time at your computer, then
**Messaging**          consider using an instant messaging service with
                       your Internet connection. This will save you time
with placing calls and playing telephone tag. Important colleagues
who are also online can ask and answer questions quickly. You can
also save long-distance phone charges.

**Cellular**           Cellular phones are replacing landlines for some in-
**Phones Versus**      dividuals. Better rates and reception continue to
**Landlines**          make cell phones more practical. Cell phones can
                       be answered anywhere, receive voice mail, connect
to the Internet, exchange instant messages, take photos and video,
and function as a two-way radio. You can roll your landline over
to the cellular phone, and answer as if you were sitting behind
your desk while you are really lounging at the beach.

**Telecommuting** Some companies allow employees to telecommute—
                       log in on their computers and work from home.
Some people do well with this technique, wasting no time commuting, dressing in business attire, and encountering distractions
at work.

Two dangers with telecommuting involve your control of time
and distraction parameters while at home. If you find you get
overinvolved in your work and extend your normal work hours,
then you may need to establish boundaries, schedule breaks, and
reprioritize personal goals into your calendar. If you find you are
distracted at home by television, children, and so on, then your
home environment may need to be engineered to give you the
workspace that will be conducive to high quality telecommuting.

Telecommuting is definitely something to consider if your job
and company are supportive of it. The ecology will appreciate one
less commuter, and your daily routine could lend itself to productive vocational pursuits with extra disposable time for recreational
or other activities.

**Get Hands-Free** Consider using a hands-free headset for your telephone or cellular phone. This will allow you to
work on projects with your hands free to do other things. It will
also prevent musculoskeletal pain from bending your head to one
side, awkwardly trying to hold the phone between your ear and
shoulder.

**Pay Your Bills**   A sure way to save time paying bills and organizing
**Online and**    your finances is the use of computer software to
**Use an**     keep your checkbook balanced. Once you enter the
**Electronic**    checks you can either print out a hard copy or pay
**Checkbook**    a bill electronically. This will allow you to easily rec-
oncile your account each month, summarize your
expenditures at the end of the year for taxes, and even transfer the
data over to tax preparation software. You can use this technology
to track investments, plan retirement, and organize assets.

**Technology**    If you have not taken advantage of the newer tech-
**and**      nologies related to computers and high-speed Inter-
**Recreation**    net access, then consider this as possibly one of the
most important areas to add to your repertoire of
coping tools. There is always time to be entertained and informed
by downloading music, recorded books, and periodicals from the
Internet to playback devices such as your computer, PDA, or
MP3 player. As one service suggests, "Make the most of every
minute in the car, at the gym, and on the go as spoken word audio
goes with you while you take on the world."

One service is Audible.com, which has over eighteen thousand
audiobooks, magazines, newspapers, and radio programs, including the *New York Times Audio Digest*, the audio edition of *Forbes*
magazine, public radio programs such as *Car Talk,* and more.
Transfer audio from your computer to MP3 player, Apple iPod,
Palm Handheld, Pocket PC, computer desktop, or CDs you burn
yourself. You can download your audio in minutes and listen any-

where, anytime. Learn in your car. Hear a newspaper on your commute. Be entertained at the gym. See Appendix III to pursue this option further.

> *Habits are like a cable. We weave a strand of it everyday and soon it cannot be broken.*
>
> —Horace Mann

In today's world of wireless Internet communication, if you have a laptop computer and a wireless card, you can take Internet courses and even earn a degree while enjoying beverages in a local coffee shop. If you are technically inclined, then consider that a laptop may give you the freedom to do more of the important A-priority items in your life without being tied to a desk. One of the authors worked extensively on the new edition of this book while on his sailboat. Without the distractions of his everyday life, he was able to carry in a small device everything he needed to work on A items.

Perhaps one of your goals is to increase your correspondence with friends and family. Make use of the wait time spent in beauty shops, professional offices, and restaurants by keeping postcards and notepaper in your purse or briefcase. You may want to conserve time and meet some of your goals by learning how to speed-read. You may also decide to carry reading matter with you to make the most of small chunks of time. The other author worked on this edition by writing notes in the mass paperback edition while waiting in long lines in banks and supermarkets, as well as throughout a day of jury selection. Combining the results of setting your goals, taking a time inventory, and thoughtful planning can yield exciting and surprising possibilities.

## Organize Your Space

Frequently the people we work with have physical and electronic space that needs to be organized. See if your space is stressful. Do you have piles on your desk that you justify by saying, "But I know where everything is in there"? Do you have clothes and "stuff" in piles or scattered haphazardly? Do you have stacks of photos, magazines, and articles that you never file? Can you find the things you need to complete tasks at home and work, or do you waste time looking for things over and over again?

In her book *Organizing from the Inside Out*, author Julie Morgenstern used three main strategies to whip a living or office space into shape: "analyze, strategize, attack." Morgenstern also likens a cluttered schedule to a cluttered closet. For example, a closet is typically "crammed with more stuff than storage," and a schedule is often "crammed with more tasks than time."

Space and time management are learnable skills, but not skills taught in school. Morgenstern's "from the inside out" system explores the possible reasons for a failure of organization: having a complex organizing system that breaks down and is difficult to maintain, not enough space for your belongings, and psychological obstacles (such as fear of failure or success). Her system encourages you to find or buy things you might need (an extra clothes rod in your closet, crates for files you aren't using but want to store, etc.) before you embark on the cleanup.

After her analysis she proposes a plan that is more or less as follows: sort, purge, assign a home, and containerize. If your space is not organized, then explore Appendix III for helpful resources.

## Discover the Usable Scraps of Time

So many of our clients excuse themselves from practicing relaxation, taking time to play with their children, developing new job skills, reading self-help books, and taking charge of their lives because they "don't have time." And yet research shows how we all have lots of wasted time that could be used productively.

Usable scraps of time can be found right before our eyes. Research has shown that most Americans spend five years of their lives waiting in lines, one year searching for misplaced objects, six months sitting at traffic lights, six years eating, eight months opening junk mail, and two years trying to return phone calls to people who never seem to be in.

## SUMMING IT ALL UP

> *Know the true value of time.*
> *Snatch, seize, and enjoy*
> *every moment of it.*
> *No idleness, no laziness,*
> *no procrastination: Never*
> *put off 'til tomorrow what*
> *you can do today.*
> —LORD CHESTERFIELD

Time management is not a skill that you will acquire from reading this chapter or from reviewing the suggested materials listed in Appendix III. You may need to take courses or hire a personal organizational/time management coach. You must practice and live some of these techniques of time management. This may take you two months, six months, or more. Remember, as long as you are practicing the necessary techniques, you will accomplish what you are working toward.

TWENTY-THREE

# People Who Laugh, Last

*God respects me when I work, but he loves me when I sing.*
—RABINDRANATH TAGORE

IN CONTROLLED STUDIES, HUMOR HAS BEEN SHOWN TO INCREASE pain tolerance, reduce muscle tension and stress hormones, and even boost immune system function. People who use humor frequently as a way of coping with stress consistently have higher levels of antibodies to protect them from diseases and do not have a drop in immune functioning after exposure to stress. During a good hearty laugh your brain releases endorphins, the brain's natural opiates, which reduce pain.

The body's healing system responds favorably to positive attitudes, thoughts, moods, and emotions (love, hope, optimism, caring, intimacy, joy, laughter, and humor) and adversely to negative

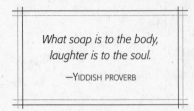

> *What soap is to the body,
> laughter is to the soul.*
>
> —YIDDISH PROVERB

ones (hate, hopelessness, pessimism, indifference, anxiety, depression, and loneliness). It is best to organize your life to maintain as positive a focus as possible. This does not mean you should avoid negative emotions. You need to find ways to express whatever emotions you feel. Failure to find effective ways to express negative emotions causes you to stew in your own juices day after day, and this chronic immersion in negativity appears to be harmful to health.

Future research may show that the power of recreation, laughter, and humor lies in their capacity to pull us out of the anxiety, anger, and depression caused by the constant stress in our lives, and to replace those negative moods with positive, optimistic moods that lower stress hormones and enhance the immune system.

## How Humor Helps Us Manage Stress

Laughter reduces muscle and psychological tension, which are the main goals of many stress management techniques. Positive emotions from recreation, laughter, and humor help your body's natural healing systems fully engage in the battle for your health. These positive emotions reduce the level of stress hormones, blood pressure, and pain. Positive emotions nurture hope and determination to overcome stressors. Minimizing negative emotions such as anger, anxiety, or depression, allows your positive emotions to energize you and work for your health, rather than against it. Anything you can do to sustain a more positive, upbeat frame of

> *This I believe to be the
> chemical function of humor:
> to change the character
> of our thought.*
>
> —LIN YUTANG

mind in dealing with the daily hassles and problems in your life contributes to your physical health and your ability to deal with stress.

## HUMOR AND SENSE OF CONTROL

Daily recreation and laughter can provide a sense of control over stress by giving you more control over your daily moods. They help you sustain an upbeat, optimistic frame of mind, even when life is tough. These more positive emotional states give us the resilience to cope with the next problem thrown our way. Finally, recreation, humor, and laughter provide a means of letting go of depression, anger, and anxiety associated with chronic stress.

## USING HUMOR TO COPE WITH STRESS

A perceived lack of control, or sense of helplessness, is probably the most important single cause of stress. Finding something to laugh at in the midst of problems helps

> *Those who get sick the most seem to view the world and their lives as unmanageable.*
>
> —BLAIR JUSTICE

you feel more in control, because you really are taking a kind of control over the situation—you are taking control over your emotional state. When you find something to laugh at despite stressful and difficult circumstances, you show yourself and others that you are superior to the stress and can choose your reaction.

When you learn to use your sense of humor in dealing with the hassles and stresses in your everyday life, you are training for the "big event." Your sense of humor grows stronger when used in managing the routine stress in your life, and then you have access to it when you're faced with greater challenges and stress. Remember the popular saying "It's easy to be an angel if no one ruffles your feathers."

## Playing with Language and Finding Humor in Daily Living

Dr. Paul McGhee says when we can come up with our own funny one-liners on the spot, we are really starting to use our funny bone to cope with stress. The puns we groan at are funnier when we are stressed and having a bad day. Practice looking for extra meanings in words. Coming up with a comment that connects with the "wrong" meaning can be a good beginning to witty "pun-up-man-ship." The more you practice doing this, the better you will get at coming up with puns and other spontaneous verbal humor.

> I've developed a new philosophy . . . I only dread one day at a time.
>
> —Charlie Brown
> (Charles Schulz)

Look for alternate meanings in newspaper headlines, church bulletins, signs, and anywhere else you see printed language. A sign in front of a church loudly proclaimed: "Don't let today's pace and stress kill you. Let the church help." And a church bulletin proudly invited: "At this evening's service, the sermon topic will be 'What Is Hell?' Come early and listen to the choir practice."

Look for humor everywhere, especially on your job or any other daily situation, which you may associate with stress. Look for road signs that can be interpreted in more than one way (e.g., "Slow children at play," "Draw bridge"). Finally, don't forget to look for humor in what young children say and do. The more you share your humor, the more "seeing funny" becomes a part of your daily perspective on life.

## Find Humor in the Midst of Stress: Using Humor to Cope

Finally, Dr. McGhee counsels us to develop good humor skills on the days when things are going well, so they will be there to serve us during the stressful times. You exercise your physical body to prepare for a stressful athletic adventure. You do not wait until the day you are actually running a marathon to get into shape! If you still struggle using your humor during stress, then your goal should be to keep trying. Start with predictable, everyday stressors to ease into the habit of seeing the light side regardless of what's happening.

> *Life is full of misery, loneliness, and suffering—and it's all over much too soon.*
>
> —WOODY ALLEN

Find some funny sayings, poems, or witty remarks to repeat to yourself whenever the going gets rough or you start feeling stressed.

> *More than any other time in history, mankind faces a crossroads. One path leads to despair and utter hopelessness. The other, to total extinction. Let us pray we have the wisdom to choose correctly.*
>
> —WOODY ALLEN

Try using humorous exaggeration to help put things into perspective. Expand situations into mock life-and-death proportions.

These sayings will give you a wry smile and serve as pick-me-ups. They can become old friends reminding you to see the humorous side, even when things don't feel very funny. The following guidelines, inspired by the wisdom of Dr. McGhee, will help you build these skills:

> *The art of medicine consists in amusing the patient while nature cures the disease.*
>
> —VOLTAIRE

- Make a list of normal, repetitive stressful situations and practice image rehearsal to lighten up the situations.

- Think about what it means

in stressful situations to see the glass half full instead of half empty.

- Look for humor in past stressful events. It may be easier to see the bright side after the stress has passed.

- Look for cartoons that are meaningfully connected to stress in areas of your life. The *Dilbert* cartoons have helped millions laugh about work situations, and the *Sally Forth* cartoons have helped millions laugh about parenting and family situations.

- Get a joke- or cartoon-a-day calendar to help you stay on the other side of stress.

Recreation and humor can be powerful medicines, and laughter can be contagious. It is reassuring in these days of deadly epidemics and sometimes painful, expensive medical treatments, that laughter is cheap and effective. And the only side effect is pleasure.

> *Life is too important to be taken seriously.*
> —OSCAR WILDE

If you are having difficulty finding written humor you may want to consult the *Directory of Humor Magazines and Humor Organizations in America (and Canada)*. This book is dedicated to helping people find humorous magazines, newsletters, newspapers, and organizations. It provides sample articles and descriptions of the publications or organizations to help you decide if you are interested in pursuing their style of humor. See Appendix III to find more resources for your recreation.

> *Seven days without laughter makes one weak.*
> —ANON

Resolve today to do the things that will begin to add recreation to your daily life. Do something just for fun every day. Develop a hobby or creative pastime. Let your friends and family know your playful side, and use humor to defuse stress and tension and increase your enjoyment of life.

> *When the circus comes to town, be there.*
>
> —Robert Fulghum

# TWENTY-FOUR

# Spiritual Stress Management

*It is not our economy we need to be worried about. What's imperiled today in America is her soul.*
—REV. JOSEPH LOWERY

*To believe in God is impossible; not to believe in Him is absurd.*
—VOLTAIRE

PHYSICIANS AND MENTAL HEALTH PROFESSIONALS ARE INCREASingly aware of the importance of our spiritual resources for healing and preserving physical and emotional well-being. The lead article in the December 2003 issue of the prestigious American Psychological Association's *Monitor* was dedicated to spirituality and mental health. Research indicates that the sense of hope, meaning, and spiritual support gained from including spiritual resources in mental health treatment helps individuals cope with stress more effectively.

## The ABC's of Spiritual Stress Management

If stress is our emergency response to anything we perceive as dangerous, demanding, or demoralizing, how do our spiritual beliefs and practices help us to manage stress? Activating events (A's) can trigger healthy spiritual beliefs (B's), which lead to less dangerous perceptions and calmer emotional consequences (C's).

For example, healthy spiritual beliefs can help us cope with anxiety. Beliefs about grace and forgiveness can diminish our regrets of the past and fears of the future. Most religions and wisdom traditions propose and encourage similar beliefs to help manage the stress of living.

## Fellowship for Stress Management

Faith has an "outer structure," which involves relationships of trust, reliance upon others, attachment, commitment, and loyalty. These relationships are tied together by shared values. Communities of faith may form around volunteer activities such as youth programs, visiting people who are shut-ins, blood drives, or assistance to the needy. Homes get built and repaired by these communities. Model programs offering a breadth of services to the needy are often known as assistance ministries. Such community-based programs have united multitudes of divergent faith groups and service organizations into alliances to serve their communities.

Support groups for the challenges of divorce, death of a spouse, and other losses help people experiencing stress find an affiliation to help them cope. The very successful twelve-step recovery programs that began with Alcoholics Anonymous endorse a Higher Power, foster a process of deep spiritual awakening within participants, and provide self-help meetings for over fifteen million Americans. The loneliness of addictions and lives without meaningful relationships can be dangerous.

Numerous population studies have shown that the lack of a strong social network can be as much or more of a risk of premature death as cigarette smoking. Beyond our scientific understanding of why prayer, faith, and fellowship reduce stress, the spiritual benefits of belief may be even more significant.

## WORK AND SPIRITUAL STRESS MANAGEMENT

Martin Luther King Jr. said, "No work is insignificant. All labor that uplifts humanity has dignity and importance and should be undertaken with painstaking excellence. If a man is called to be a street sweeper, he should sweep streets even as Michelangelo painted, or Beethoven composed music, or Shakespeare wrote poetry. He should sweep streets so well that all the host of heaven and earth will pause to say, 'Here lived a great street sweeper who did his job well.' "

We heard a story once about three different bricklayers. Each was working on the same project, and all were doing the same basic job. When one was asked what he was doing, he replied that he was just laying bricks. The next bricklayer responded to the same question by saying that he was making money to support his wife and three children. The third responded that he was building a cathedral where people could worship God and sing praises to his glory. Why you do something may be more important than how you do it!

## A PURPOSE-DRIVEN LIFE WITH MEANING

Faith is a journey by which persons seek the meaning of their lives. Victor Frankl wrote a book called *Man's Search for Meaning*. Frankl was a Viennese psychiatrist who was a victim of the Nazi concentration camps in World War II. He observed fellow Jews who came into the horrifying death camps. He watched while some died prematurely and others lived long beyond the time they should have succumbed to starvation, cruelty, and disease. Except for himself and his sister, his whole family died in the extermination ovens.

His whole existence was controlled by his Nazi captors, but "out of the night" that covered him he discovered his "unconquerable soul," a soul that possessed the "last of the human freedoms." Within Frankl grew the freedom to decide how he would respond to all the atrocities. He disciplined his mind, emotions, and morals through his memories and imagination. In his mind's eye he could teach class, inspire his family, and build personal dignity while his body was in the most indecent of situations. He sought and found a deep and profound faith, and a purpose for his life. Fortunately, we do not all have to go through such dark hours to find our purpose.

Rick Warren in *The Purpose-Driven Life* lays out a program to help explore the question "What on earth am I here for?" He starts off with a quote from Proverbs: "A life devoted to things is a dead stump; a God-shaped life is a flourishing tree." He starts from the premise that a faith-based life is like a tree planted next to a river. These trees are not bothered by long months of drought or heat. Their leaves remain green and their fruit sweet because their roots are able to reach deep for the nourishment they need.

You may reach all your goals and be a huge success and still not enjoy the resistance to life's stress offered by a purposeful life. Within the context of your beliefs, take time out to explore what a meaningful life will be, and begin to live it.

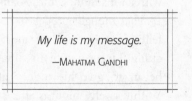

*My life is my message.*

—MAHATMA GANDHI

We invite you to use resources from Appendix III and consider developing your Life Purpose Statement. This summarizes what you think God's purposes are for your life, pinpoints direction in your life, defines "success" for you, and clarifies your role and unique spiritual gifts.

## You Only Get to Keep What you Give Away

Exploring your contribution to life may help provide a stress resistance to face life's challenges. This is based on your unique talents, abilities, personality, and experience. Each of us would benefit from choosing how to serve.

> To help, to serve, to care, to guide, to heal, these words were all used to express a reaching out toward our neighbor whereby we perceive life as a gift not to possess but to share.
>
> —Henri J. M. Nouwen

### Learning to Give

John D. Rockefeller made a fortune in oil. He donated millions of dollars to start and sponsor the University of Chicago. He helped rebuild war-torn countries after World War I. He gave millions of dollars to medical research and to the training of doctors. He spent millions on world missions.

Rockefeller's life could be summarized by two passions: getting and giving. He spent the first half of his life making money, a gift he said came from God. At the age of fifty-five, however, he was in bed dying when an article by millionaire Andrew Carnegie caught his attention. Carnegie said it was sinful for a wealthy man to die with all his money in the bank.

That thought propelled Rockefeller into one of the most exciting adventures of his life. He began to give his money away. Within twelve months after starting a program of giving he was a well man. He lived forty more years! To what did he attribute

> We make a living by what we get, but we make a life by what we give.
>
> —Winston Churchill

this miracle? He said that learning to give allowed him to live. His benevolence during a time when he felt he had little time to live seemed to give the gift of life—to himself and others.

## HEAVEN OR HELL

A rabbi asked the Lord about heaven and hell. "First," answered the Lord, "I will show you hell." The Rabbi found himself in a room where a dozen people were seated around a large round table. The people were moaning from the pain of starvation. In the middle of the table there was a great pot of stew with more than enough for everyone. The delicious smell of the stew made the rabbi's mouth water. The people around the table held spoons with very long handles. Each could reach the pot to take a spoonful of

> *Unhappiness is the hunger to get; happiness is the hunger to give.*
>
> —WILLIAM GEORGE JORDAN

the stew, but because the spoon handles were longer than a man's arm, no one could position the food back into their mouth. Some were so frustrated they were hitting one another. The rabbi saw that the suffering was terrible.

"Now," said the Lord, "I will show you heaven." The rabbi entered another room identical to the first. There was the same large, round table and the same big pot of stew. The people were holding the same long-handled spoons, but here they were all well nourished and healthy, laughing and talking. For a moment the rabbi was confused.

"It is simple," said the Lord. "You see, they have learned to feed each other."

## SERVING OTHERS

Martin Luther King Jr. said, "Life's most urgent question is, what are you doing for others?" "Consciously or unconsciously," said

Mahatma Gandhi, "every one of us does render some service or other. If we cultivate the habit of service deliberately, our desire for service will steadily grow stronger, and will make not only for our own happiness, but for that of the world at large." Almost all the great religions of the world place service and giving among the most central and important points. When history reflects upon really great people, it is almost always those who have enriched the lives of others.

A Rotary Club set up a Once-a-Year Service Committee to help awaken the spirit of service. Some members were very busy in their professions, but this committee encouraged the members to make a commitment of just one single act of service in an entire year.

One day the club president called a member and told him this was the day for him to perform his one annual act of service. The member complained about how busy he was, but relented. The president told him that another member, a doctor, was attending a very poor woman who was about to have a baby. She had a five-year-old son and no one to leave him with while she had her baby. The president asked that the son be picked up and kept for a few hours while the mother had her baby. Seeing no alternative, the member rushed off to pick up the boy while the physician took the mother to the hospital.

As the Rotarian drove off with the boy in the passenger seat next to him, he began to feel the boy's eyes staring at him. Finally the boy asked, "Mister, are you God?" His answer was, "Don't talk nonsense, boy. Of course I'm not God." After a few minutes the boy asked again, "Are you God?" In a gruff voice the man replied, "That's ridiculous! What makes you think I'm God?!"

In a voice of innocence the small boy said: "Mama was crying and in lots of pain. She said that only God could help us. Then you came and helped us, and so I got to thinking that you must be God."

The member was silent. A change in his heart took place in

that very instant. He has never
since refused the chance to serve,
be useful, or to do something to
help his fellow man.

*The only ones among you
who will be really happy
are those who have sought
and found how to serve.*

—ALBERT SCHWEITZER

Twenty-five hundred years ago
Muhammad said, "Every good act
is charity. A man's true wealth
hereafter is the good that he does
in this world to his fellows."

## A LAMP UNTO YOUR FEET, A LIGHT UNTO YOUR PATH

There are many resources for spiritual growth, including places of
worship; pastoral counseling; telephone, radio, Internet, and television ministries; and books or recorded materials in libraries and
bookstores. The Bible and other guides for the great religions of
the world offer resources for managing life and, of course, stress.

We once heard a story about a young woman with Down syndrome who played God in a theatrical production. Every night
during the intermission she would remain on the stage while the
audience asked questions of "God." One night a lady in the audience said she prayed morning, noon, and night to get what she
wanted and never got it. The young actress thought only briefly
before responding, "I make the sky blue and the grass green. Some
things you have to do for yourself." So it is with development of a
lifestyle consistent with your faith, values, and principles. We each
have our rules for living based on our spiritual faith. We wish you
peace in whatever rules your day.

## AFFIRMATIONS FOR EFFECTIVE SPIRITUAL STRESS MANAGEMENT

Many of the principles we have discussed may be used for positive
affirmations to help develop healthy beliefs (B's) in your ABC

model for effective spiritual stress management. Consider focusing on relevant affirmations during your daily relaxation or prayer. No matter what faith you practice, the following demonstrate that there are many universal spiritual guidelines for service:

## POSITIVE AFFIRMATIONS FOR SPIRITUAL STRESS MANAGEMENT

*"Help thy brother's boat across and lo! Thine own has reached the shore."* —HINDU PROVERB

*"The sole meaning of life is to serve humanity."* —LEO TOLSTOY

*"What is hateful to you, do not to your fellow man."* —TALMUD (JUDAISM)

*"As you would that men should do unto you, do you likewise to them."* —LUKE 6:31 (CHRISTIANITY)

*"Hurt not others in ways that you yourself would find hurtful."* —UDANA VARGA (BUDDHISM)

*"Do naught unto others which would cause you pain if done to you."* —MAHABHARATA (HINDUISM)

*"Regard your neighbor's gain as your own gain, and your neighbor's loss as your own loss."* —TAI SHANG KAM YING RIEN (TAOISM)

*"What you do not wish yourself, do not unto others."* —ANALECTS (CONFUCIANISM)

*"You give but little when you give of your possessions. It is when you give of yourself that you truly give."* —KAHLIL GIBRAN

*"The only true gift is a portion of thyself."* —RALPH WALDO EMERSON

*"For to be carnally minded is death, but to be spiritually minded is life and peace."* —ROMANS 8:6 (CHRISTIANITY)

*"Service above self."* —MOTTO OF ROTARY INTERNATIONAL

## Summing Up Spiritual Stress Management

Many people consider faith a journey. Through the effort to rediscover or perhaps discover faith we may strengthen our ability to cope with stress and find a peaceful and purposeful life.

Research demonstrates the importance of a spiritually based lifestyle to help people find the inner strength and peace to face every one of life's challenges. We feel less distressed or alone when we have healthy faith, beliefs, and convictions to carry us through our darkest hours.

Perhaps we should ask ourselves if we are physical beings having spiritual experiences or if we are spiritual beings having physical experiences. We also might consider changing our relationship with our God. Perhaps God can be more than a spare tire for when things go wrong. Perhaps God can become a steering wheel and a source of ongoing guidance for our journey.

Consider the very practical advice and lifelong example of one of the great humanitarians of our times, Mother Teresa of Calcutta:

*People are often unreasonable, illogical, and self-centered; forgive them anyway.*

*If you are kind, people may accuse you of selfish, ulterior motives; be kind anyway.*

*If you are successful, you will win some friends and some true enemies; succeed anyway.*

*If you are honest and frank, people may cheat you; be honest and frank anyway.*

*What you spend years building, someone could destroy overnight; build anyway.*

*If you find serenity and happiness, they may be jealous; be happy anyway.*

> Whatever you have
> learned . . . put it into
> practice. And the God of
> peace will be with you.
>
> —PHILIPPIANS 4:9

*The good you do today, people will often forget tomorrow; do good anyway.*

*Give the world the best you have, and it may never be enough; give the world the best you've got anyway.*

*You see, in the final analysis, it is between you and your God; it was never between you and them anyway.*

# SECTION VII

*Enhancing Health and
Preventing Disease*

In the beginning, God created the heavens and the earth and populated the earth with broccoli and cauliflower and spinach, green and yellow and red vegetables of all kinds, so man and woman would live long and healthy lives. Then using God's great gifts, Satan created Ben and Jerry's and Krispy Kreme Donuts. And Satan said, "You want chocolate with that?" And man said, "Yeah," and woman said, "And another one with sprinkles." And they gained ten pounds. And the stockholders were very happy. And Satan smiled.

And God created the healthful yogurt that woman might keep the figure that man found so fair. Satan brought forth white flour from the wheat, and sugar from the cane and combined them. And woman went from size 6 to size 14.

So God said, "Try my fresh green salad." And Satan presented Thousand Island dressing, buttery croutons, and garlic toast on the side. And man and woman unfastened their belts following the repast.

God then said, "I have sent you heart-healthy vegetables and olive oil in which to cook them." And Satan brought forth deep-fried fish and chicken-fried steak so big it needed its own platter. Hilltop Steak House thrived! And man gained more weight and his cholesterol went through the roof.

God created a light, fluffy white cake, named it angel food cake, and said, "It is good." Satan then created chocolate cake and named it devil's food.

God then brought running shoes so that his children might lose those extra pounds. And Satan gave cable TV with a remote control so man would not have to toil changing the channels. And man and woman laughed and cried before the flickering blue light and gained pounds.

Then God brought forth the potato, naturally low in fat and brimming with nutrition. And Satan peeled off the healthful skin and sliced the starchy center into chips and deep-fried them. And man gained pounds.

God then gave lean beef so that man might consume fewer calories and still satisfy his appetite. And Satan created McDonald's and its 99-cent double cheeseburger. Then he said, "You want fries with that?" And man replied, "Yeah! And super-size 'em." And Satan said, "It is good."

And man went into cardiac arrest.

God sighed and created quadruple bypass surgery.

Then Satan created HMOs.

## TWENTY-FIVE

# Keeping Your Body Tuned Up and Energized

*We do not want in the United States a nation of spectators. We want a nation of participants in the vigorous life.*
—JOHN F. KENNEDY

THE BENEFITS OF REGULAR EXERCISE AND GOOD NUTRITION ARE popular topics of conversation today, and science is providing an ever-growing body of knowledge to make possible the separation of fact and fantasy. Exercise and nutrition are important in the effective management of stress, prevention of illness, and enhancement of health. This and the next chapter offer some reasonable guidelines to help you incorporate regular exercise and proper nutrition into your life. These are essential ingredients in combating the wear and tear of stress.

Physical fitness is to the human body what a tune-up is to an engine. It enables us to perform up to our full potential. We strive to look, feel, and do our best whether facing saber-toothed corporate tigers or the demands of raising children. Physical fitness is the ability to perform daily tasks vigorously and alertly, with energy left over for enjoying leisure-time activities and meeting physical emergencies. It is the ability to endure stress, to persevere in circumstances where an unfit person could not, and maintain good health and well-being. Physical fitness involves the performance of the heart and lungs, the muscles of the body, and our mental alertness and emotional stability.

As you undertake your stress management program, remember that fitness is an individual quality that varies from person to person. What fitness means to a world-class athlete is different from what it means to an average participant in the game of life. Fitness is influenced by age, sex, heredity, personal habits, exercise, and eating practices. You cannot do anything about your age, sex, or heredity (except lie!). However, it is within your power to change and improve your habits related to exercise and eating.

## The Benefits of Regular Exercise

Regular exercise has both physiological and psychological benefits. Advantages that have been associated with regular exercise in various research studies include:

- Weight control and increased physical fitness

- Healthier bones, muscles, and joints

- Greater stamina, endurance, and muscular strength with fewer injuries and stronger immune response

- Lowered risk for colon cancer and type 2 diabetes

- Improved blood pressure, cholesterol level, and efficiency of heart and lungs

- More energy and productivity, less stress, and improved sleep

- Increased mental acuity and ability to concentrate

- Elevated mood with reduced anxiety, depression, and hostility

- Increased sense of psychological well-being and self-esteem

- Weight loss, toned muscles, improved posture, and a firmer appearance, leading to an enhanced self-image

- Increased opportunities to make new friends and share activities with friends or family members.

If we had one medication that provided as many positive health benefits as exercise, people would be lined up to get their prescriptions!

## FACE THE FACTS OF OUR SEDENTARY LIFESTYLE

The following facts are based on information from publications prepared by agencies and offices of the U.S. Department of Health and Human Services, the Centers for Disease Control and Prevention, the National Center for Health Statistics, the Office of the Surgeon General of the United States, and the Office of Disease Prevention and Health Promotion.

Physical inactivity contributes to 300,000 preventable deaths a year in the United States. Some 40 percent of deaths in the United States are caused by behavior patterns that could be modified.

A study at the Centers for Disease Control and Prevention found that physically active people had, on average, lower annual direct medical costs than did inactive people. The same study estimated that increasing regular moderate physical activity among the more than 88 million inactive Americans over the age of 15 years might reduce the annual national direct medical costs by as much as $76.6 billion. Physically active people have fewer hospital stays and physician visits, and use less medication than physically inactive people.

Employers can benefit too. Workplace physical activity programs can reduce short-term sick leave by 6 to 32 percent, reduce health care costs by 20 to 55 percent, and increase productivity by 2 to 52 percent. Workplace wellness programs typically offer help in smoking cessation, managing stress, prenatal care, nutrition, and fitness.

Regular physical activity reduces morbidity and mortality from mental health disorders. The overall cost associated with these disorders is approximately $148 billion per year. Potentially, increasing physical activity levels in Americans could substantially reduce medical expenditures for mental health conditions. In adults with affective disorders, physical activity has a beneficial effect on symptoms of depression and anxiety. Research suggests that exercise may stimulate the growth of new brain cells that enhance memory and learning—two functions hampered by depression. Clinical studies have demonstrated that exercise is one of the effective treatments for depression in older men and women.

Significant health benefits can be obtained by engaging in just a moderate amount of physical activity (e.g., thirty to sixty minutes of brisk walking or raking leaves, fifteen to thirty minutes of running, forty-five minutes of playing volleyball). Additional health benefits can be gained through greater amounts of physical activity.

Physically inactive people are twice as likely to develop heart disease as regularly active people. The health risk posed by physical inactivity is almost as high as risk factors such as cigarette smoking, high blood pressure, and high cholesterol.

Poor diet and inactivity can lead to obesity and increased risk for high blood pressure, type 2 diabetes, coronary heart disease, stroke, gallbladder disease, osteoarthritis, sleep apnea, respiratory problems, and some types of cancer. Seventeen million Americans have diabetes, and sixteen million more have pre-diabetes. Each year, there are one million new cases of diabetes, and nearly two hundred thousand people die from the disease. The cost to the economy is $100 billion annually in direct and indirect medical costs.

Sixty-one percent of adults in the United States were overweight or obese in 1999. The cost to the economy in 2000 was estimated to be $117 billion in direct and indirect medical costs. A recent study demonstrated that obese individuals spend approximately 36 percent more than the general population on health services and 77 percent more on medications. The study found that the effects of obesity on health spending were significantly larger than effects of current or past smoking.

## EXERCISE AND THE STRESS RESPONSE

In the first chapter of this book, we reviewed the sympathetic nervous system's response to stress. If you recall, the body responds with preparation for fighting or fleeing. Our heart beats faster, our blood pressure soars, our breathing quickens, our perspiration increases, our muscles tense, and our body pours stored sugars and fats into the bloodstream. In addition, a signal originating from the hypothalamus contributes to the secretion of adrenaline.

Exercise provides a way of releasing muscle tension and the general physical arousal that accumulates in our responses to stress. Rather than fighting a tiger or fleeing from a bear, we can pretend we are Lance Armstrong riding to a win in the Tour de France or Carl Lewis jogging around a track.

## THE ROLES OF EXERCISE TODAY

As man became industrialized, he developed more and more labor-saving devices. Physical activity was no longer necessary for survival, and it became a form of recreation. When we discover play and enjoy body movement, we restore a sense of control and wholeness to our lives. Since you are the sum of your physical and mental activities, exercise can be self-enhancing and improve your responses not only to physical stressors but to social and mental stressors as well. Below are just a few of the benefits of exercise today.

**Exercise as**    One very important benefit of exercise is muscle re-
**Relaxation**     laxation. In response to stress, our bodies often be-
                   come tense. This tension can accumulate, especially
after a long day. One way to relax after a tense day is to engage in exercise. You will find that after exercising, your muscles are relaxed and calm. If you combine your workout routine with stretching and taking a whirlpool afterward, your relaxation will be enhanced even more.

**Exercise as**    Exercise can be used to clear your mind. One frus-
**a Mental**       tration you may face during the workday is having
**Release**        your mind become so cluttered that you cannot
                   concentrate. Problems may seem impossible to solve.
This is an excellent time to go for a walk, jog, or swim. People who exercise report that time away from working diligently on a problem gives them a chance to sort everything out in a more relaxed, creative way.

For example, a nurse reached an impasse while working on the development of a new health program. After working on crucial scheduling problems for several hours, she seemed no closer than when she'd started. In an effort to solve these problems, she went to a coworker to discuss the schedule. Still, no solution was reached.

At this point, the workday was over, and the two workers decided to exercise together. During their twenty minutes of jogging, they discussed the scheduling problems. By the end of the run, they had solved the problem. It is not clear whether this happened because the pressure was off or simply because their minds were more creative while exercising in another environment. But it worked! This is a common response among people who exercise regularly.

***Exercise Helps*** Research has demonstrated that exercise enhances
***Vitamins Fight*** the benefit of vitamins on the body's immune sys-
***Disease*** tem in its constant fight to ward off disease. Vitamins C and E improve immune functioning, but
exercise augments these effects. In this research, the exercise group
had more infection-fighting cells regardless of whether or not they
took the vitamin supplements.

***Fitness as a*** As our bodies age, we experience a number of phys-
***Fountain of*** iological changes. These so-called effects of aging
***Youth?*** include reduced aerobic capacity, weakened bones,
diminished muscu-
lar strength and endurance, decreased sense of balance, slowed
reaction times, and increased body
fat.

A wealth of data indicates that
such effects may be more a factor of
inactivity than of aging, and may be
minimized by regular physical activity. While activity may not hold

*For each hour of physical
activity, you can expect
to live that hour over—and
live one or two more
hours to boot.*

—RALPH S. PAFFENBARGER JR., M.D.

the miracles of the elusive fountain of youth, it can go a long way toward increasing longevity and improving activities of daily living as
you age. It is an excellent investment of your time.

***Exercise and*** Exercise decreases stress and relieves tensions. Exer-
***Self-Image*** cise builds physical fitness, which in turn builds
self-confidence, enhanced self-image, and a positive
outlook. When you start to feel good about yourself, you are more
likely to want to make other positive changes. People who begin
an exercise program find that their self-image improves, and they
get an emotional lift as well.

Many people find that their body image is a stressor. Whether
they are overweight, too flabby, or not as muscular as they

would like to be, the end result is that they are unhappy with themselves. As Richard Simmons says, "Plastic surgery may tighten up a few things, but exercise is Mother Nature's cheapest body lift."

**Sleep and**      Sleep and rest are great rejuvenators. Exercise can
**Rest**      help relieve problems with insomnia. Mild exercise during the day helps many people get a restful night's sleep. Exercising too close to bedtime may have the opposite effect, so schedule exercise at least several hours before you plan to sleep.

**Balance and**      Balance and agility are important capabilities often
**Agility**      taken for granted. Regular exercise can help to maintain or restore them. When muscles are not toned, weakness and unsteadiness can contribute to falls. Exercise can increase a person's reaction time and strength, and help them reduce the risk of injury from falls and accidents.

**Exercise for**      Obesity continued to increase dramatically during
**Weight**      the early years of the twenty-first century for Amer-
**Control**      icans of all ages, with nearly two-thirds of all adults classified as overweight or obese, according to data from the National Health and Nutrition Examination Survey published in the *Journal of the American Medical Association*.

When you take in more calories than your body needs, you will put on excess fat. When you burn more energy than you take in, you will decrease excess fat. The benefits of exercise are many, from producing physical fitness to providing an outlet for fun and socialization. Additional benefits may be seen in how exercise reduces appetite. When added to a weight control program, these benefits take on increased significance. The combination of exercise and diet offers the most effective approach to weight control.

## Use It or Lose It

Physiologists have repeatedly shown that a regular exercise program will improve endurance, reduce total peripheral resistance in blood circulation, lower both systolic and diastolic blood pressure, increase the inner diameter of arteries, increase the number of capillaries, lower blood lipids, and improve both lung capacity and muscular strength. This all adds up to an increase in health and endurance and a greater resistance to fatigue.

The heart becomes more powerful and more efficient with appropriate exercise. A well-conditioned heart beats more slowly at rest and during work. It also acquires a greater pumping capacity and the ability to recover more quickly.

A simple way to express this effect is summed up in the old phrase "Use it or lose it." Approximately 80 percent of the adult population today is not active enough to retard physiological decay. It actually requires very little time to obtain and maintain an adequate level of fitness. This is often misunderstood because when one thinks of a physically fit person, too often the athlete comes to mind. It is not necessary to endure the strenuous training of a professional athlete to be considered physically fit. How, then, does one define physical fitness?

## Components of Physical Fitness

A person is considered physically fit who engages in sufficient activities to maintain ideal levels of four fitness components: cardiorespiratory endurance, muscular endurance, flexibility, and body composition.

**Cardio-respiratory Endurance**  The ability to perform moderately strenuous large-muscle exercises for relatively long periods of time leads to cardiorespiratory endurance. A relatively long period of time is defined as thirty minutes.

These activities depend on the capacity of the heart and lungs to increase the ability to deliver oxygen and nutrients to tissues.

For adults, cardiorespiratory endurance is often considered the most important fitness component. The work of Dr. Kenneth Cooper in the area of aerobics is an example of an approach to exercise that emphasizes cardiorespiratory fitness. These activities are also the most helpful in reducing stress.

There are many activities that improve cardiorespiratory endurance. Examples include basketball, cycling, jogging, racquetball, jumping rope, ice and roller skating, snow and water skiing, swimming, tennis, and vigorous walking and dancing. All of these activities have something in common that causes an increase in cardiorespiratory endurance—they are aerobic.

**Muscular**        Muscular endurance is the ability of skeletal mus-
**Endurance**      cles to resist fatigue and to sustain repeated contrac-
                        tions. Push-ups are often used to test endurance
of arm and shoulder muscles. This goal is reached by stretching
your abilities a small increment each day. The isometric, tension-
without-movement exercises that Charles Atlas made famous increased strength, but only in the skeletal muscles. The fitness of
the heart and lungs was not a focus of many of these fitness programs.

**Flexibility**      Flexibility is defined as the range of motion about a
                        joint, or simply the ability to move a body part
from one extreme position to another. Touching your toes is an
example of the range of motion about the hip joint.

**Body**            This is often considered another component of fit-
**Composition**    ness. It refers to the makeup of the body in terms
                        of lean mass (muscle, bone, vital tissue, and organs)

and fat mass. Exercises will help you decrease body fat and increase or maintain muscle mass.

Muscle tissue weighs more than fat tissue, and exercise develops muscle. Muscular individuals with relatively little body fat invariably are "overweight" according to standard weight charts, but they are not at risk from the consequences of excess fat. If you are doing a regular program of strength training, your muscles will increase in weight, and your overall weight may increase. Body composition is a better indicator of your fitness than body weight.

## How Much Exercise Do I Need?

What about the "how often," "for how long," and "how hard" of exercise? Exercise specialists refer to these as the frequency, duration, and intensity of exercise. It may surprise you to learn how little time and effort are needed to obtain an adequate amount of exercise to develop cardiorespiratory endurance.

**Activity and** Our understanding of fitness has evolved since the
**Good Physical** fitness craze first took hold. Scientific evidence now
**Health** clearly indicates that regular moderate-intensity physical activity offers many of the health benefits traditionally associated with more intense exercise.

Based on this evidence, a panel of health and fitness experts convened by the Centers for Disease Control and Prevention, the American College of Sports Medicine, and the President's Council on Physical Fitness and Sports has urged Americans to establish the minimum goal to accumulate at least thirty minutes, and preferably one hour, of moderate-intensity physical activity over the course of the day This should be done at least five days per week, and preferably daily. Also, twenty minutes of vigorous physical activity at least three times per week is regarded as a respectable goal.

**Make Physical**  Including moderate amounts of physical activity in
**Activity a**  your daily life may become a welcome addition to
**Regular Part**  your stress management program. Aim to accumu-
**of Your**  late at least thirty minutes of moderate physical ac-
**Routine**  tivity most days of the week, preferably daily. No
matter what activity you choose, you can do it all at
once, or spread it out over two or three times during the day.

Moderate-intensity activity includes many of the things you
may already be doing during a day or week, such as walking the
dog or raking leaves. For many people, being more active may
simply mean taking advantage of or creating opportunities for activity. This is explored more fully later in this chapter. The goal is
to seize the physical activity opportunities you have and make the
most of them to accumulate thirty to sixty minutes of moderate-
intensity physical activity daily.

You can choose to do light, moderate, or vigorous exercise as
part of your stress management lifestyle. Higher-intensity activities require less time. Lower-intensity activities require more time.
Many exercise classes combine the different levels of intensity so
that periods of vigorous activity are combined with periods of
light and moderate activities. Use the guidelines on page 313 to
help categorize your exercises.

## Different Techniques to Assess Exercise Intensity

Intensity is not as easy to define as frequency and duration. There
are several techniques to measure intensity, some more scientific
than others. Professional athletes will utilize laboratories to help
measure oxygen consumption and blood chemistry as part of a
training program. Most of us do not need to go to such extremes
to build exercise and physical activity into our stress management
lifestyle. Review the techniques on page 313 to help understand
how to accomplish your fitness goals.

## ACTIVITIES WITH DIFFERENT LEVELS OF INTENSITY
## AND RECOMMENDED DURATION FOR FITNESS
## AND STRESS MANAGEMENT

| LIGHT INTENSITY 45–60 MINUTES DAILY | MODERATE INTENSITY 30 TO 60 MINUTES 5 TO 7 TIMES WEEKLY | VIGOROUS INTENSITY 20 MINUTES AT LEAST 3 TIMES WEEKLY |
| --- | --- | --- |
| Walking slowly | Walking briskly | Race-walking, jogging, or running |
| Golf, powered cart | Golf, pulling or carrying clubs | Swimming laps |
| Swimming, slow | Swimming, recreational | Mowing lawn, nonpropelled mower |
| Gardening or pruning | Mowing lawn with power motor | Tennis, singles |
| Bicycling, very light effort | Tennis, doubles | Bicycling more than 15 mph, or on steep uphill terrain |
| Light housework such as dusting or vacuuming | Bicycling 10 mph, level terrain or with a few hills | Moving or pushing furniture |
| Light stretching or warm-up | Moderate housework such as scrubbing floors or washing windows | Circuit training |
| Yoga | Weight lifting with machines or free weights | Calisthenics |

**Talk Test**   A simple test of intensity is how a person feels. If it is not possible to talk while exercising because you are breathing too hard (known as the "talk test"), you are exercising too vigorously.

**Heart Rate**   A more scientific and individualized indicator is your heart rate or pulse. The heart rate will increase in direct proportion to the intensity of the exercise. Exercise that does not raise your heart rate to a certain level and keep it there for twenty minutes will not contribute significantly to cardiovascular fitness.

The average heart rate is approximately seventy-two beats per minute. This rate varies a great deal from one individual to another, and it depends on many factors such as age, sex, level of fitness, and medications. How high should your heart rate be during exercise?

To achieve cardiorespiratory benefits, a person should work between 70 and 85 percent of **maximum heart rate.** To calculate maximum heart rate:

220 − your age in years = **maximum heart rate**

*Example:* If you are fifty years of age, 220 − 50 = 170 beats per minute. Your **maximum heart rate** is 170 beats per minute.

Now fill in the blanks and calculate your **maximum heart rate.**

220 − _____ = _____ beats per minute

The **target heart rate range** is 70 to 85 percent of the **maximum heart rate.**

Now fill in the blanks and calculate your **target heart rate range:**

.70 × _____ = _____ beats per minute

.85 × _____ = _____ beats per minute

During cardiovascular exercise, your heart rate should remain in your target heart rate range. When checking heart rate during a workout, take your pulse within five seconds after interrupting exercise because it starts to go down once you stop moving.

If you are just beginning an exercise program, it is a good idea to exercise in the lower part of the target heart rate range so that you will be able to maintain it for the recommended duration of twenty to thirty minutes. You may be surprised at how little exercise it takes to elevate your heart rate to the target range if your life has been sedentary. If you are taking medications that alter your heart rate, check with your physician for exercise guidelines.

**Perceived Exertion (Borg Rating of Perceived Exertion Scale)** A third method of determining physical activity intensity is the Borg Rating of Perceived Exertion. Perceived exertion is how hard you feel your body is working. It is based on the physical sensations a person experiences during physical activity, including increased heart rate, increased respiration or breathing rate, increased sweating, and muscle fatigue, rated on a scale of 6 to 20, where 6 means no exertion at all and 20 means maximal exertion. Scores from 7 to 12 are extremely light to light exertion. An example is walking slowly at your own pace. Scores of 13 to 16 are somewhat hard to hard exertion. An example of this level might be jogging relatively fast, but at a pace where you are still able to carry on a conversation. Scores from 17 to 19 are very hard to extremely hard exertion. A healthy person can still exercise at these levels, but the intensity feels very heavy, and talking may be difficult.

This is a subjective measure, but it may provide a fairly good estimate of the exercise intensity during physical activity. This is especially important for people with medical conditions and on medications that may alter heart rate.

Practitioners generally agree that perceived exertion ratings between 12 to 14 on the Borg scale suggests that physical activity is being performed at a moderate level of intensity. During activity, use the Borg scale to assign numbers to how you feel. Self-monitoring how hard your body is working can help you adjust the intensity of the activity by speeding up or slowing down your movements.

Choosing the number that best describes your level of exertion will give you a good idea of the intensity level of your activity, and you can use this information to speed up or slow down your movements to reach your desired range.

## OVERCOMING PROCRASTINATION

There are probably as many reasons as there are people to explain why so many who are well informed procrastinate about starting an exercise program. Research from the surgeon general's report *Healthy People* showed that although individuals knew that regular exercise was an important health habit, few were practicing it. If you feel you are too busy to exercise, refer to the chapters on time management and apply the techniques to help you get started.

Let's discuss some of the reasons frequently given for not exercising. Memories of pain after exercise keep some people from beginning to exercise again. Pain from exercise is unnecessary and is usually brought about by exercising incorrectly. If one properly warms up and cools down after exercise and does not do too much too soon, there will be little or no pain. You can improve your body's strength and endurance without causing pain. Use pain as a signal that you are doing too much. Stiffness and muscle pain should not be considered signs that you are getting stronger.

Expense may be another excuse often used for not starting an exercise program. Although some sports and activities do require an investment in equipment or a fee, not all exercise programs are expensive. In fact, many of the best exercises are free. It is important to remember when you are selecting an activity that the lower the costs in time, money, and inconvenience, the more likely you will be to continue the program.

Lack of knowledge about how to exercise properly is another concern of people who do not exercise. The information in this chapter is sufficient to help you start exercising. The books listed in Appendix III provide additional information from many experts. Another suggestion is to enroll in an exercise class. This has the advantage of providing you with information, as well as involving you in a support group of others who are also beginning an exercise program.

The more fun the exercise is for you, the more likely you will continue. Fitness does not have to be a lonely, torturous activity. In fact, finding another person with whom you can enjoy exercising helps tremendously. So find a buddy and arrange to meet this person on a regular basis. Not only will this person be a support for you, but you'll provide support for him or her as well.

Some people feel embarrassed when starting an exercise program. Find others at your same level of fitness with whom to exercise. Avoid being competitive, and avoid competitive events at the beginning of a fitness program. Competition often brings out a blind determination that may not be safe.

It is important that if weather or scheduling problems force you to miss a day of exercise, you do not give up altogether. Instead, return to the regular schedule as soon as possible. Exaggerating your "failure" and criticizing yourself will only add another emotional stressor.

A common misconception about exercise is that it will bring about fatigue. If approached sensibly, this is not true. People report that incorporating regular exercise raises their level of energy, increases their alertness, and makes them more relaxed.

## CHECKING YOUR HEALTH BEFORE STARTING A FORMAL EXERCISE PROGRAM

A few words of caution are necessary. Too much exercise too soon not only will discourage you but also will add another stressor to your life. Most adults do not need to see their health care provider before starting to become more physically active. If you are under thirty-five and in good health, you do not normally need to see a doctor before beginning an exercise program. But if you are over thirty-five and have been inactive for several years, you should consult your physician, who may or may not recommend a stress test or graded exercise test. This test of physical working capacity is performed while you walk on a treadmill. During the test, the physician is able to observe how your heart responds to various exercise loads.

If your mobility is limited as a result of a chronic or disabling condition, be sure to review exercise with your doctor. Other conditions that indicate a need for medical clearance are high blood pressure; heart trouble; family history of early stroke or heart attack; frequent dizzy spells; extreme breathlessness after mild exertion; osteoporosis, arthritis, or other bone problems; obesity; severe muscular, ligament or tendon problems; or other known or suspected disease.

Vigorous exercise involves minimal health risks for persons in good health or those following a doctor's advice. Far greater risks are due to habitual inactivity and obesity. It is important, however, to assess your personal level of fitness to avoid starting a program that is too difficult. Completing the following assessment will give you a good sense of where you are now and how to begin.

## Physical Fitness Assessment

Rate your activities on each item in the following chart by using a number from 0 to 10 that best describes your general activity level for the previous month. *Never* is a score of 0. *Rarely* is a score from 1 to 3. *Sometimes* is a score from 4 to 6. *Frequently* is a score of from 7 to 9. *Always* is a score of 10.

| PHYSICAL FITNESS ACTIVITIES | SCORE (0 TO 10) |
|---|---|
| 1. I currently participate in regular daily recreation, sport, or moderate physical activity. | |
| 2. I engage in muscle strength exercises twice weekly. These are at least twenty-minute sessions and include exercises for all the major muscle groups. | |
| 3. I engage in three muscular endurance exercise (thirty-minute) sessions each week. These may include exercises such as calisthenics, push-ups, sit-ups, or pull-ups. | |
| 4. I typically walk, climb stairs, park farther out in parking lots, or do other similar activities to build exercise into my daily activities. | |
| 5. I engage in daily exercises to warm up, cool down, and stretch to help keep me flexible. | |
| 6. I participate regularly (three or more times per week, thirty to forty-five minutes) in aerobic exercise, recreation, or work requiring modest to vigorous physical activity, such as jogging, exercise classes, or biking. | |
| TOTAL SCORE FOR PHYSICAL FITNESS | |

If you totaled 0 to 20, start your exercise program with about ten minutes of continuous activity each session. If you totaled 21 to 35, then start with the goal of accumulating thirty minutes of moderate-intensity physical activity over the course of a day, five days a week. Start charting your activities, duration, and intensity.

If you scored over 35, then your lifestyle seems to be active and you may already have a formal exercise program. Decide if there are areas you would like to improve (muscular strength, endurance, cardiorespiratory fitness, and/or flexibility) and create a plan. Try to consistently be physically active for thirty minutes or more, five to seven days each week.

## Permanent Lifestyle Changes Promoting Activity

Before looking at what kind of regular exercise program is best, consider how you can increase the amount of physical activity in your daily routine. Recreational pursuits such as gardening, bowling, family outings, dancing, and many others provide added exercise, are fun, and promote physical fitness.

Adding more action to your day will help manage stress and enhance your overall wellness. Try walking to the store instead of using the car, parking several blocks from the office and walking the rest of the way, or walking up the stairs instead of using the elevator.

Little pieces of action are cumulative in their effects. Each does not burn many calories, but together they can result in a sizable amount of energy used over the course of the days, weeks, months, and years of your life. They will help improve your muscle tone and flexibility at the same time. Instead of just thinking in terms of a specific exercise program, work toward permanently changing your lifestyle to incorporate more activity. Remember that muscles used in any activity, any time of day, improve your stress management and fitness. Virtual reality may contribute to an exciting movie, but it's best to get real in your active participation in life.

## The Fitness Formula for a Formal Exercise Program

If you are ready for a more formal exercise program and more vigorous activity, remember that "no pain, no gain" isn't exactly true. Many fitness resolutions have been ruined by too much enthusiasm on the first day, too many sore muscles on the second, too much trouble on the third, and too easily forgotten on the fourth.

Once you are in better shape, you can gradually increase your time or distance or increase the intensity of the activity.

For at least thirty minutes, preferably one hour, most days of the week, preferably daily, do any one or more of the moderately intense physical activities such as aerobic exercise class, walking, bicycling, basketball, swimming, or similar exercises.

## TIPS FOR EFFECTIVE EXERCISING

Once you begin your daily physical activity routine, remember the basics:

- Start gradually and choose activities you will enjoy.

- Set a regular time in your daily routine to exercise.

- Increase the amount of exercise daily, up to about thirty to sixty minutes, and keep a daily diary of your progress.

- Vary your exercise program.

- Build some rest days into your exercise schedule.

- Listen to your body. If you have difficulty breathing or experience faintness or prolonged weakness during or after exercise, consult your physician.

- Choose more than one type of exercise to give your body a thorough workout and to prevent boredom.

As you begin to feel and look better, you will enjoy a new enthusiasm for life. You will be rewarded many times over for your efforts.

## WHEN TO EXERCISE

The absolute best time to work out is the time that is most likely to find you still working out a year from now. Research has shown that statistically, more people who start a morning workout program are still working out at the end of a year when compared to those starting an evening workout program. But if you are not a morning person and really cannot imagine yourself continuing to get up early to work out, then do not pick morning workouts. Remember, you are not a statistic, and what's best is what works for you.

The hour just before the evening meal and the late afternoon are popular times to work out and may help dissolve the day's worries and tensions. Another popular time to work out is early morning, when the early start may energize you far better than that cup of coffee.

Among the factors you should consider in developing your workout schedule are personal preference, job and family responsibilities, availability of exercise facilities, and weather. It is important to schedule your workouts for a time when there is little chance that you will have to cancel them because of other demands.

## How to Stick to Your Exercise Plans

Patience is crucial. If you do too much too soon, you may quit before you have a chance to experience the rewards of improved fitness. You cannot regain in a few days or weeks what you have lost in years of sedentary living. Remember that a journey of a thousand miles begins with the first steps (literally). The prize is worth the effort.

You may find it helpful to consider the equipment you want as a reward to be earned by increasing everyday activities that you are capable of doing without a financial expense. This is a far better alternative than waiting until you can afford the expensive sports equipment. For example, it is usually better to begin brisk walking before jogging or skiing, so walk everywhere you can and make a chart to show your progress. Reward yourself after a certain number of days of such activity.

Participating in a sport that does not cause pain will help you stick to your exercise plan. Many people remember the fun of riding a bicycle as a child, and then discover as adults that their hands, neck, and seat hurt when riding a traditional bicycle. One of the authors rides a recumbent bicycle so that he can relax and enjoy the ride. The semireclined position of the recumbent rider provides a much broader distribution of body weight, similar to sitting in a comfortable reclining chair. The hands, arms, and shoulders are in a relaxed position, not bearing the weight of the torso. With the back in a reclined position, the abdomen is flat and straight, which allows full and easy expansion of the lungs. The head is held in a neutral position, looking forward, and the neck is relaxed. For a humorous explanation of why people are changing to recumbents, see Dr. Paul Nolan's story about the medical benefits of recumbent bicycles on the Internet, www.bikeroute.com/BentMedBenefits.html, or go to www.stresscontrol.com to learn more about this bicycle of the future.

Consider joining a gym and choose to pay for it in monthly installments. The monthly payment is a reminder to make full use of your membership.

Entertainment while exercising combats boredom and fatigue. Bring along a pocket radio or MP3, CD, or cassette player and find a place with pleasant scenery. Also, set up a treadmill or recumbent stationary bicycle in front of the TV and watch a movie while you exercise. Be sure to pat yourself on the back for every move in the direction toward better health.

## A Physical Workout Plan for the Total Person

How often, how long, and how hard you exercise, and what kinds of exercises you do, should be determined by what you are trying to accomplish. Your present fitness level, your age, your health, your skills, your level of interest, and convenience are among the factors you should consider when establishing your fitness goals. For example, an athlete training for competition would follow a different program than would a person whose goals are good health and increased energy.

Your exercise program should include something from each of the four basic fitness components described previously. Your workouts should begin with a warm-up and end with a cooldown. You may do moderate exercise daily, but as a general rule, space your vigorous workouts throughout the week and avoid consecutive days of hard exercise.

Remember, fitness can be defined in many ways, depending on your goals, your current level of activity, and how much time you have available. A program that includes aerobics, resistance training, and stretching will give you the greatest overall health benefits. But, if you can't do it all, don't sweat it! Remember the latest health advice: accumulating thirty minutes of moderate-intensity physical activity over the course of a day can add up to significant health benefits. The important thing is to do something, as opposed to nothing. If you can do more, terrific!

Start by walking; it can always be worked into your day. Most of us can do it any time, in almost any place, without any special equipment. The opportunities are plentiful: go for a walk after dinner instead of watching television, walk to work, walk to the store rather than driving, or take the dog or the children for a long walk. A moderately brisk pace is preferable, but build up to it gradually.

## COOLING DOWN

If you have been participating in vigorous physical activity, it is extremely important not to stop suddenly. Stopping abruptly interferes with the return of the blood to the heart and may result in dizziness or fainting. A minimum of two to five minutes of reducing the intensity of exercise is a good guideline.

Cooling down gradually slows down the heart's pumping action to prevent blood from pooling in lower muscles, which reduces blood flow to the heart and brain, and can cause faintness. Cool-down stretching can help prevent muscle stiffness and soreness by stretching muscles that are shortened during exercise.

## STRETCHING

Stretching, though often overlooked, plays a vital role in keeping muscles and joints strong and pliable and less susceptible to injury. That is why it is such an important part of warming up and cooling down. It is recommended that you do five to ten minutes of stretching exercises slowly and without a bouncing motion both before and after physical activity.

Spending a few minutes a day doing slow, deliberate stretches can also help you manage stress more effectively by giving you a chance to momentarily shut off outside stressors and focus, physically and mentally, on your activity. A good routine should work each of the major muscle groups.

## PUTTING ALL THE PIECES TOGETHER FOR TOTAL-PERSON FITNESS

Some activities can be used to fulfill more than one of your basic exercise requirements. For example, in addition to increasing cardiorespiratory endurance, bicycling builds muscular endurance in the legs, and swimming develops the arm, shoulder, and chest muscles. Your warm-ups and cooldowns help with your flexibility. If you select the proper activities, it is possible to fit parts of your flexibility, muscular endurance and strength, and cardiorespiratory endurance into one workout and save time. You may also combine

> *In a nutshell, physical activity is something you do. Physical fitness is something you acquire.*
>
> —MICHAEL PRATT, M.D.

your exercise with social, recreational, and family activities to help your total stress management program.

Here are some more suggestions to upgrade your fitness program as you progress. Set specific, short-term goals, and reward yourself when you achieve them. Change your activities to keep you motivated. Add new ones or increase old ones. Enlist the support of your family and friends, and keep them updated as you progress. Read books or magazines on fitness to inspire you. Go to fitness Web sites and study the material there. (See Appendix III for suggestions). Identify people you admire who are fit, and use them as role models. Associate with friends who believe in fitness for mutual support.

## MIND OVER IMMOBILITY

Today, there is a growing emphasis on managing stress, living longer, and looking and feeling good. Scientific evidence tells us that exercise is one of the keys to achieving these. You are never too unfit, too young, too old, or too anything else to get started.

Most people do not get enough exercise in their ordinary routines. The advances of modern technology have made life easier, more comfortable, and much less physically demanding. We have remote controls for doors and televisions. We have jobs sitting at computers. It takes little muscular power to steer our cars. We are driving more than walking or biking. Unfortunately, for all too many of us, as Erma Bombeck said, "The only reason I would take up exercise is so I could hear heavy breathing again!"

> It's easier to maintain your health than regain it.
>
> —KEN COOPER, M.D.

Our bodies need activity. Satisfying this need requires a definite plan and a commitment. You can probably come up with plenty of excuses for why you are not more active. You are too busy or too tired. But with few exceptions, excuses are irrational self-talk. The next time you think about getting fit and say, "I don't have time to exercise," ask yourself, "Why haven't I been choosing to use my time to exercise, because I really want to feel better?"

> *The goal in life is to die young—as late as possible.*
>
> —ASHLEY MONTAGU

The benefits of fitness and the risks of unfitness are clear. Statistics show that preventive medicine pays off. So do not wait until your doctor gives you an ultimatum. Take the initiative to get active now.

# TWENTY-SIX

# Stress Management Through Nutrition and Weight Control

*The major cause of death in the U.S. is food poisoning.*
—NATHAN PRITIKIN

*The two biggest sellers in any bookstore are the cookbooks and the diet books. The cookbooks tell you how to prepare the food and the diet books tell you how not to eat any of it.*
—ANDY ROONEY

IT IS SAID THAT THE JOURNEY OF A THOUSAND MILES BEGINS WHEN you take the first step. As you step into this nutritional chapter of stress management, we will introduce you to some basics about food and how it relates to your stress management plan.

The relationship between exercise and stress has been studied for years. Research into the relationship between nutrition and stress is more recent but certainly deserves equal attention. The January 2004 issue of the American Psychological Association's *Monitor* was dedicated to obesity and stated that "high stress rates play a major role in the obesity epidemic." Stress imposes extra nutritional demands on the body. The right foods can boost our immune system, promote health, prevent chronic disease, and provide the energy we need to perform at our very best while facing the ever-increasing demands of an uncertain and challenging world. First, let us explore how our eating habits are related to stress.

## THE RELATIONSHIP BETWEEN STRESS AND EATING HABITS

People respond to stress in different ways: some smoke, some drink alcohol, and some increase or decrease their food consumption. Why is it that more of us tend to overeat rather than under-eat in response to stress?

**The Stress-Food Cycle**   Researchers are discovering clues about why some foods are often considered "comfort food." Foods with lots of sugar, fat, and calories appear to calm the body's response to chronic stress. During stress, brain chemicals cause the release of adrenal corticosteroids, including cortisol, to prepare us to fight or flee. During chronic stress this system seems stuck in the on position, and the activity that is increased for fight-or-flight behavior may turn into "graze-and-gorge" behavior. With high sugar and fat consumption, the chemical that originally caused the adrenal gland response is reduced. With the reduction in this stressful brain chemical, we feel calmer.

The stress-food cycle is as follows:

- We experience chronic stress from our modern lifestyle.

- Comfort foods high in sugar and fat (e.g., chocolate cake, ice cream—you can probably add your favorite food) turn off the stress response and calm our nerves.

- We gain weight.

- We get frustrated and depressed about our weight.

- We read or hear advertisements about rapid weight loss programs where we can eat anything we want and lose weight.

- We try them but fail to lose the weight.

- We blame ourselves for poor self-control.

- We get more frustrated and depressed.

- Our frustration and depression become additional sources of stress.

- The cycle starts all over again.

The most important thing to realize about this cycle is that the episode of overeating did not solve the problem unless the stressor was hunger. In most cases, the stressor that triggered the person to eat probably still exists. We recommend the entire collection of coping techniques discussed in this book for helping individuals through stressful situations. As we will show you, maintaining a proper diet is also an important technique for managing stress.

**Stress and Alcohol**     Another response to stress is the consumption of alcoholic beverages. Using alcohol to manage or avoid stress is similar to overeating. Alcohol just adds another stressor. It fails to solve the original problem, has almost twice the calories per gram of protein or carbohydrates, and brings still more problems with it, such as the disease of alcoholism and its life-threatening effects!

**Stress and Fast Food**     Stress is often used as an excuse for not eating properly. A common example is the person who complains of not having enough time to take a lunch break. Instead of taking a break, candy bars or potato chips from a vending machine are consumed or the meal is skipped altogether. If you find yourself saying, "I don't have time to eat," we recommend that you study the chapters on time management and self-talk to help overcome these barriers to a healthy nutritional lifestyle. Also consider our recommendations for healthy meal replacements. Make healthy eating a lifelong priority and habit.

**Stress and Advertised Foods** Advertising plays a tremendous role in our eating habits. Unfortunately, foods that are heavily advertised and easiest to sell, transport, and manufacture are frequently low in nutrients, and high in sugars and fats. If, over a period of time, we do not consume adequate amounts of nutrients, the stores of these nutrients become depleted. We are then more susceptible to disease and less able to adapt to other stressors. People who overeat and are overweight are often undernourished because of the poor quality of food they consume and the extra nutrients needed for the metabolic tasks related to digesting the extra food.

> *Advertising may be described as the science of arresting the human intelligence long enough to get money from it.*
>
> —STEPHEN BUTLER LEACOCK

## THE FOOD-MOOD CONNECTION

Food is tied to our coping with stress in many ways from a temporary sedative to a power lunch. Food associations anchor our thoughts and emotions to associations of comfort, security, and enjoyable times. Does food interact with your moods as a comfort, reward, relationship builder, source of nurturing, or medicine?

## THE COST OF OUR NUTRITIONAL CHOICES

Four of the ten leading causes of death in the United States have links to diet; these cost over $200 billion annually in treatment and lost productivity. According to the Economic Research Service of the USDA, the average American diet is unbalanced, top-heavy with added sugars and fats and light on whole grains, fruits, low-fat dairy products, dark green vegetables, fish, and dry beans. It is no mystery why being fat in America (two-thirds of us are) has become a crisis for America in the last twenty years!

## WHAT MAKES UP A HEALTHY DIET?

In the pages that follow, you will learn about the essential nutrients from food and guidelines for healthy eating. We want your nutritional stress management program to be solidly based on research that has stood the test of time.

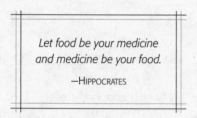

*Let food be your medicine and medicine be your food.*

—HIPPOCRATES

The guidelines we will propose for your stress management program are intended for the general population, specifically those who are free from disease. They may not be specific enough for people who are on a special diet for a diagnosed condition. There are certain diets that will help people with diabetes, and research has even demonstrated that specific diets may reverse some damage due to cardiovascular disease. Remember, no guidelines can guarantee health or well-being because health depends on many factors in addition to diet. Food alone will not make a person healthy, but good eating habits, combined with regular exercise and stress management, can improve your health and prevent disease.

## FEED YOUR MIND THE FACTS ABOUT FOOD

Food provides us with different sources of energy and nutrients. If you eat more than the body needs, it will store the excess as fat. And it is much easier for the body to store fat than to use it for energy. If you store more calories than you burn, you will gain weight.

From the early 1900s to the 2000s the energy in our food supply increased primarily because the fat and sugar content in our food supply increased. Each person, on average, consumed about 41 pounds of fat per year in the early 1900s; now we approach 80 pounds of fat. In the early 1900s we consumed about 80 pounds of sugar; now we take in over 150 pounds.

With two-thirds of Americans overweight, the U.S. government is encouraging Americans to eat less and exercise more. We will recommend dietary guidelines for your stress management program, but first let's learn what food is all about.

## Macronutrients, Micronutrients, and Water

Food can promote health or disease. What qualities of food can reduce our stress and promote health, or increase our stress and promote disease? First, food provides the nutrients essential to life, as well as non-nutritive substances such as fiber. These essential nutrients can be divided into three types:

1. **Macronutrients** are present in food in large amounts and include carbohydrates, proteins, and fats.

2. **Micronutrients** are present in small quantities in food and include vitamins and minerals.

3. **Water** is present in all foods.

Macronutrients provide energy, maintain our functioning, and repair tissue. Vitamins regulate the body's chemistry, while minerals assist the vitamins and help in the maintenance and formation of new tissues such as bones, teeth, and blood. Water is the most essential nutrient. It is present in all cells, provides the transport for other nutrients, plays a role in chemical interactions, helps remove waste, lubricates the joints, and helps regulate our body's temperature. The next section will help you to understand more about these essential nutrients in our food as well as nonessential ones, and how they may relate to your management of stress.

**Carbohy-**     Carbohydrates are the most efficient fuel for your
**drates**      body. Carbs are easily broken down for energy. First
     they are converted to glucose; what is not immediately needed is stored as glycogen in your muscles and liver, and the excess is stored as fat.

Complex carbohydrates are better than simple carbohydrates. Simple carbohydrates, such as sugars, provide energy but little else in the way of nutrients. Foods high in complex carbohydrates, such as beans, vegetables, whole-grain breads, cereals, and grain products, contain many essential nutrients, in addition to energy.

Refined carbohydrates, such as white bread, white rice, and pasta made from white flour, as well as certain vegetables such as potatoes, can be very quickly broken down to glucose to give energy to the body. These types of carbohydrates increase glucose levels in the blood more than whole grains do, and may be great if you are running a marathon. Eating a boiled potato raises blood sugar levels higher than eating the same amount of calories from table sugar. The rapid increase in blood sugar stimulates a release of insulin and can increase triglycerides and lower "good" (HDL) cholesterol.

**Protein**     The word "protein" is derived from a root word
     meaning "of first importance." Protein is the basic material of our muscles and organs and is an important nutrient required for the building, maintenance, and repair of tissues in the body.

When we eat protein-rich food, the digestive system breaks it down into essential amino acids to be used as building blocks. If a food supplies all the essential amino acids, it is considered complete; if not, it is incomplete. All animal protein is complete, but the protein in some fruits, grains, and vegetables is incomplete when consumed individually. Healthy plant-based protein consumption is accomplished by eating combinations of plant foods.

The average American consumes about double the protein needed, and usually from animal products, which are high in fat and saturated fat. For the average person the recommended protein intake usually ends up equivalent to a piece of meat, poultry, or fish about the size of a deck of playing cards.

Protein needs are higher for children under eighteen, for women who are pregnant or breast-feeding, and for active persons. People in these groups typically meet their increased protein needs through a larger intake of food.

**Fats**          Fat provides energy, but not as readily as carbohydrates. The energy from fat can come from fat we consume in food or the fat we have stored from an excess of food we have consumed in the past. Any dietary fat that is not burned by our activities is typically converted to body fat.

Most people know about saturated fats, but some may be confused about trans fatty acids, also known as trans fats, found mostly in partially hydrogenated vegetable oil. These are created by applying extreme heat to vegetable oil and adding hydrogen to distort the fat molecule in a way that makes it solid. The benefit of this hydrogenation process is that the solidified fat becomes almost impervious to spoilage. Foods could have a long shelf life, be transported for long distances, and develop a texture that does not crumble. Saturated fats (e.g., butter and lard) became demonized, and these trans fats (margarine or partially hydrogenated fats) became the fat of choice. In the first years of the twenty-first century, about 40 percent of the foods in supermarkets contained trans fats.

Now research has shown that these trans fats increase the risk of heart disease even more than the saturated fats. It seems the trans fats increase triglycerides and "bad" (LDL) cholesterol.

There are two main types of cholesterol. Low-density lipoprotein (LDL) is popularly known as "bad cholesterol" because it can build up on the inner walls of arteries. High-density lipoprotein (HDL) is called the "good cholesterol" because it seems to carry cholesterol away from the arteries to be broken down in the liver. Americans, whose diets are high in saturated fat, trans fats, and cholesterol, tend to have high total blood cholesterol and LDL levels, which increase their risk of heart attack. Current research has suggested that total dietary fat intake may be a poor indicator of heart disease risk. What is more important is the type of fat consumed. Replacing saturated fat with monounsaturated and polyunsaturated fat improves the good-to-bad cholesterol ratio and may reduce heart disease. Contact your physician to find out your cholesterol levels and obtain specific recommendations.

To avoid too much saturated fat, trans fats, and cholesterol:

1. Choose lean meat, fish, poultry, dried beans, and peas as your protein sources.

2. Limit your intake of eggs and organ meats such as liver.

3. Limit your intake of butter and cream. Eliminate hydrogenated margarines and shortenings as well as foods made with these products. Use monounsaturated and polyunsaturated fat, such as extra-virgin olive oil.

4. Trim excess fat off meats, and remove skin from poultry.

5. Broil, bake, or boil rather than fry foods.

6. Read labels carefully to determine both the amount and types of fat contained in foods.

## FIBER: THE NON-NUTRITIVE NUTRIENT

Fiber is considered a non-nutritive nutrient, because when swallowed, it stays in the digestive tract and is not broken down by digestive enzymes, nor does the body absorb it. Fiber is most commonly found in unrefined or unprocessed plant-based foods.

Ultimately, fiber is like a physiological scrub brush within your body's system. It scrapes, brushes, and pushes material through your GI tract, sweeping out what is no longer needed. Whole grains, fruits, and vegetables are high in fiber. There is convincing evidence that fiber intake can help reduce your risk of gastrointestinal cancer.

## THE FLAWS OF THE ORIGINAL FOOD GUIDE PYRAMID

In 1992 the U.S. Department of Agriculture (USDA) released the Food Guide Pyramid to help the American public make good dietary choices that would reduce the risk of chronic disease. The original pyramid was an outline of what to eat each day based on USDA and Department of Health and Human Services guidelines. It promoted certain healthy nutrition recommendations, especially a high intake of fruits and vegetables. It encouraged reduction of total fat intake but may have led Americans to eat fewer of the healthy unsaturated fats and more refined starches. The foundation of the original pyramid did not differentiate refined bread, cereal, rice, and pasta from those products made from whole grains. The top of the pyramid indicated sparing use of all fats and oils, but certain fats are necessary to the body and even promote health.

The messages "Fat is bad" and "Carbs are good" became the mantras from the original pyramid. Unfortunately, this approach was an oversimplification, and studies have demonstrated that polyunsaturated and monounsaturated fat, such as that found in vegetable oils and fish, reduces "bad" (LDL) cholesterol and increases "good" (HDL) cholesterol.

Another flaw in the original USDA pyramid was its failure to recognize the important health differences between red meat and the other foods in the protein group (poultry, fish, legumes, nuts, and eggs). High consumption of red meat has been associated with an increased risk of coronary heart disease, type 2 diabetes, and colon cancer.

This pyramid may have also promoted the overconsumption of dairy products. This advice has been justified by dairy's calcium content, which is believed to prevent osteoporosis and bone fractures. But the highest rates of fractures are found in countries with high dairy consumption. Calcium is an essential nutrient, but the requirements for bone health may have been overstated.

As a consequence of these research findings, the old food pyramid's generic emphasis on higher carbohydrates and reduced fat may not have been the best approach to the much-needed healthy diet.

## A HEALTHIER PYRAMID

Walter C. Willett and Meir J. Stampfer are professors of epidemiology and nutrition at the Harvard School of Public Health and professors of medicine at Harvard Medical School. In 2003, their studies suggested a new pyramid that significantly reduces the risk of cardiovascular disease for both men and women.

The revised pyramid emphasizes weight control through exercising daily and avoiding an excessive total intake of calories. This pyramid recommends that a diet should consist of healthy fats (liquid vegetable oils such as olive, canola, soy, corn, sunflower, and peanut) and healthy carbohydrates (whole-grain foods such as whole-wheat bread, oatmeal, and brown rice). Vegetables and fruits should be eaten in abundance, along with moderate amounts of healthy sources of protein (nuts, legumes, fish, poultry, and eggs). Dairy consumption should be limited to one to two servings a day. The revised pyramid recommends minimizing the consumption of red meat, butter, refined grains (including white bread, white rice, and white pasta), potatoes, and sugar.

Margarine or partially hydrogenated fat does not appear at all in their pyramid because the researchers feel it has no place in a healthy diet. A multiple vitamin and mineral supplement is suggested for most people, and moderate alcohol consumption can be health-promoting if it is not contraindicated by specific health conditions.

There are other food pyramids proposed for vegetarians and ethnic groups, such as the Mediterranean Pyramid, that attempt to promote healthful food choices. If you are interested in exploring other food pyramids, see Appendix III for more information.

We have taken the liberty of modifying some of the research-based and government dietary guidelines and propose a reasonable approach to a healthy nutritional lifestyle to help you cope more effectively with stress. Our recommendations are based on research, clinical experience, and review by expert nutritionists. Guidelines include these areas of advice: general fitness (which includes exercise and weight management), a healthy base of foods as the foundation for your nutritional lifestyle, and a daily multiple vitamin/mineral supplement. The following guidelines are what we propose to help maintain and promote your physical health so you can cope with stress more effectively. After the general guidelines, we present proven strategies to help you tailor this approach to overcome your unique nutritional and emotional challenges.

## The Stress Management Food Guide Pyramid

Our Stress Management Food Guide Pyramid proposes reasonable guidelines for people in good health. If you incorporate the information from the sections that follow, with guidance from your health care professional, then you will be on your way to making healthy nutrition one of your most effective stress management tools.

## THE STRESS MANAGEMENT
## FOOD GUIDE PYRAMID

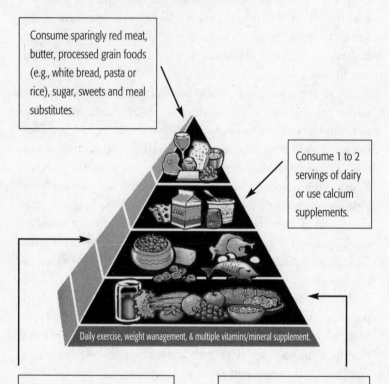

Consume sparingly red meat, butter, processed grain foods (e.g., white bread, pasta or rice), sugar, sweets and meal substitutes.

Consume 1 to 2 servings of dairy or use calcium supplements.

Daily exercise, weight wanagement, & multiple vitamins/mineral supplement.

Consume 1 to 5 servings from protein sources per day. If you choose a vegetarian lifestyle, then use plant-based sources of protein, including nuts, legumes, beans, bean curd (tofu), etc. If you choose to eat meat, select very lean meats, or eat skinless chicken or fish. If you eat eggs, limit yourself to 1 per day or use egg substitutes.

Consume from the whole-grain breads, cereal, and pasta, brown or wild rice group prepared with only plant oils, especially extra-virgin olive oil (avoid all partially hydrogenated fat), and vegetables at most meals; 2 to 3 servings of fruits and 6 to 8 glasses of water per day.

# The Base of the Stress Management Food Guide Pyramid: Weight Maintenance, Exercise, and a Multiple Vitamin/Mineral Supplement

**Maintain a Healthy Weight**   A healthy weight is key to a long, healthy life and helps us cope more effectively with stress. The average American gains one-half to one full pound per year between the ages of twenty and fifty. Keep an eye on these creeping pounds, which result from what some have called our country's "thorn of plenty"!

**Be Physically Active Daily**   Choose a lifestyle that combines sensible eating with regular physical activity. Physical activity and nutrition work together for better health and more effective stress management. Use the chapters on exercise and time management in this book to make your physical fitness a top priority.

**Dietary Supplements for Stress Management**   Research has shown that the body uses nutritional reserves when a person is under stress. The reserves most clearly depleted are protein, B vitamins, vitamin C, and vitamin A. These reserves can be replaced and maintained by consuming balanced meals. We recommend that you "eat as if your life depends on it," but consider supplementing your diet as necessary to ensure adequate intake of micronutrients.

Select a daily high-quality multiple vitamin/mineral supplement. Supplements should contain antioxidants such as vitamin C, vitamin E, the carotenoids, and selenium to boost the immune system and neutralize free radicals. Oxygen, an essential element for life, can create damaging by-products during normal cellular metabolism. Antioxidants counteract these cellular by-products, called free radicals, and bind with them before they can cause damage. If left unchecked, free radicals may contribute to heart damage, cancer, cataracts, and a weak immune system.

Depending on the foods and multivitamin you consume, other individual supplements may include vitamin C; B complex, including vitamins B5 (pantothenic acid) and B6; and vitamin E. Your health care professional might also recommend individual supplements that include additional antioxidants, such as bioflavonoids and proanthocyanidins, as well as minerals such as zinc, calcium, and magnesium.

Take your supplement with meals, since food is needed to help your body absorb certain vitamins. Let your pharmacist and physician know what supplements you are taking, since they can interfere with prescription medications. Other recommendations may be given by health care professionals for your specific needs.

### FOOD SOURCES TO REPLENISH MICRONUTRIENTS DEPLETED DURING STRESS

1. **Ascorbic acid (vitamin C):** citrus fruit, rose hips, acerola, alfalfa sprouts, leafy green vegetables, cantaloupe, strawberries, broccoli, tomatoes, green peppers, kiwi fruit, cabbage, potatoes

2. **Carotenoids (vitamin A):** orange vegetables such as carrots, sweet potatoes, and pumpkin; dark green leafy vegetables such as spinach, collards, and turnip greens; orange fruits such as mango, cantaloupe, and apricots; tomatoes

3. **Antioxidants:** fruits and vegetables, with the highest concentrations found in the most deeply or brightly colored fruits and vegetables (spinach, carrots, red bell peppers, tomatoes)

4. **Choline:** egg yolks, brewer's yeast, whole grains, dried beans and peas, fish, lecithin

5. **Chromium:** clams, whole grains, brewer's yeast

6. **Folate:** dried beans and peas, peanuts; oranges and orange juice; dark green leafy vegetables such as spinach, mustard greens, romaine lettuce; green peas

7. **Iron:** organ meats, egg yolks, fish, oysters, clams, whole grains, dried beans and peas, green vegetables

8. **Magnesium:** vegetables, whole grains, dried beans and peas, seafood, nuts

9. **Vitamin B5 (pantothenic acid):** brewer's yeast, eggs, dried beans and peas, sweet potatoes, whole grains, salmon

10. **Potassium:** lean meats, whole grains, sunflower seeds, bananas and plantains, white or sweet potatoes, green leafy vegetables, winter squash, dried fruits such as apricots and prunes, orange juice, dry beans and peas

11. **Tryptophan:** nuts and seeds, brown rice, carrots, beets, celery, endive, dandelion greens, fennel, snap beans, Brussels sprouts, chives, alfalfa

12. **Vitamin B6:** yeast, whole grains, egg yolks, dried beans and peas, green leafy vegetables, liver, muscle meats

13. **Zinc:** sunflower seeds, seafood, mushrooms, brewer's yeast, soybeans, eggs, whole grains

If you examine these food sources carefully, you will note that most of the nutrients we need to deal with stress come from whole grains, fruits, and vegetables. It is not an accident that these make up the foundation of our Food Guide Pyramid for Stress Management.

## SELECTING FOODS FOR OPTIMAL STRESS MANAGEMENT

What is the best solution for eating in times of stress? Replace saturated fats with healthy plant-based fats such as extra-virgin olive

> *Scientists, who once saw foods as mere collections of individual nutrients, are now vigorously beginning to explore their larger pharmacological complexities.*
>
> —JEAN CARPER

oil combined with high fiber; choose complex-carbohydrate-rich meals with plenty of whole grains, fruits, and vegetables. These can soothe us without sapping our energy, give us the nutrients we need to boost our immune system, and keep us from developing a weight problem. Here is a guide to help you include and avoid foods so that you manage stress more effectively.

### FOODS TO INCLUDE FOR EFFECTIVE STRESS MANAGEMENT

- **Whole-grain carbohydrate-rich foods.** Complex carbohydrates may help the brain to produce serotonin, a hormone that relaxes us. Pick whole-grain sources of carbohydrates, and avoid refined grains.

- **High-fiber foods.** Fiber is helpful in preventing late-night binge eating. Examples of healthy comfort food include baked sweet potatoes or sautéed vegetables over brown rice.

- **Fruits and vegetables.** Chronic stress can weaken our immune system. Increasing our intake of antioxidant-rich fruits and vegetables can minimize this damage. Carrots are a great source of the antioxidant beta-carotene. Citrus fruits provide vitamin C, another important antioxidant.

### FOODS TO MINIMIZE FOR EFFECTIVE STRESS MANAGEMENT

- **High-saturated-fat foods.** Fatty foods can make us feel tired and lethargic. This is not a good way to reduce stress when we may need energy for both physical and mental action. The lethargy can turn to inaction and avoidance, which may lead to increased stress.

- **Caffeine.** Cutting back on caffeine and stimulants can help with both sleeping problems and nervousness.

- **Sugar.** The problem with sugar is that it enters and leaves the bloodstream rapidly, causing us to "crash." More-complex carbohydrates can soothe without bringing us down.

- **Salty foods.** Salt is a necessary part of our nutrition, but almost all processed foods, such as processed meats and cheese and snack foods, contain an overabundance of salt. Excess salt may induce stress by increasing the number of brain-cell receptors for the stress-triggering hormones. The chemical part of the stress response that sustains alertness may also make the body stockpile salt.

> *My own view is that evidence in favor of fruits and vegetables in helping to prevent cancer is overwhelming.*
>
> —Dr. Gladys Brock

## The Foundation of Your Stress Management Meal Plan

There are many ways to create a healthy eating pattern, but they all start with whole-grain foods, fruits, and vegetables. Enjoy meals that have brown rice, whole-wheat pasta, whole-grain tortillas, or whole-grain bread at the center of the plate, with plant-based fat such as extra-virgin olive oil, plenty of fruits and vegetables, a moderate amount of low-fat foods from the meat and beans group, and limited amounts of dairy products or a calcium supplement. Go easy on foods high in saturated fat or sugars.

**Protein**          Nutritionists may recommend adding small amounts of animal protein to plant foods to boost the protein quality. For example, one may add a light meat sauce to whole-wheat pasta, or milk to breakfast cereal.

If you choose to eat meat, be certain to limit red meat since it is usually high in saturated fats. Instead, eat skinless chicken or fish to minimize the extra fat you consume. Omega-3 fatty acids—the fat found in some types of fish—can be health-promoting, but recent concerns about the quantity of mercury in fish have influenced us to place more emphasis on plant-based protein.

> *Diet is the key to wiping out the epidemic of heart disease in the country. Today I eat defensively. Fish, pasta, vegetables, fruits, and cereal grains are the staples of my diet.*
>
> —WILLIAM CASTELLI, M.D.

Legumes are among the most versatile and nutritious foods available. They are good sources of protein and can be a healthy substitute for meat. Legumes are a class of vegetables that includes beans, peas, and lentils. Legumes typically are low in fat and high in fiber, protein, folate, potassium, iron, and magnesium. Legumes have an abundance of phytochemicals, which may help prevent chronic illnesses such as cardiovascular disease, cancer, and diabetes.

Soybeans are unique among beans because they contain all of the amino acids needed to make a complete protein, just like meat. They also contain isoflavonoids, a plant-based compound that may reduce the risk of some types of cancer.

**Calcium**          Many people choose to avoid milk because it contains fat, cholesterol, allergenic proteins, and lactose. Keeping strong bones depends more on preventing the loss of calcium from your body than on boosting your calcium intake.

Some cultures consume no dairy products and little calcium per day but generally have low rates of osteoporosis. Many scientists believe that exercise and other factors have more to do with osteoporosis than calcium intake does. How rapidly calcium is lost depends on many factors:

- Diets that are high in protein, caffeine, and sodium cause more calcium to be lost through the urine.

- Protein from animal products is much more likely to cause calcium loss than protein from plant foods. This may be one reason why vegetarians tend to have stronger bones than meat eaters.

- Alcohol inhibits calcium absorption.

- Exercise slows bone loss and is one of the most important factors in maintaining bone health.

Exercise and a diet moderate in protein will help protect your bones. People who eat plant-based diets and who lead an active lifestyle probably have lower calcium needs. However, calcium is an essential nutrient for everyone. It is important to eat foods rich in calcium or take a supplement daily.

**Moderate Intake of Sugars**
Estimates indicate that, on the average, Americans consume more than 150 pounds of sugar a year—not only sugar in the sugar bowl, but the sugars and syrups in jams, jellies, candies, cookies, soft drinks, cakes, and pies. Sugars are also found in breakfast cereals, catsup, flavored milk, and ice cream. The ingredient label frequently provides a clue to the amount of sugar in a product. Ingredients are listed in descending order from the greatest to the smallest quantity. If a product lists sugar as the third of fifteen ingredients, you can be sure the food is high in sugar.

**Meal Substitutes**  We realize that many people have busy lifestyles and may have difficulty eating well at every meal. Even eating a fast-food salad may take more time than we feel we can afford on some days. There are meal replacement supplements that may assist you, and they are certainly better than grabbing a bag with a burger and fries. Be sure to select meal replacements that have a balance of macronutrients (fat, carbohydrates, and protein), are fortified with vitamins and minerals, and are high in fiber and low in sugar.

**Alcoholic Beverages**  Alcoholic beverages can be high in calories and low in other nutrients, but current research has suggested that some alcohol consumption may promote health. One or two drinks daily appear to cause no harm in adults. If you drink, you should do so in moderation. Even moderate drinkers may need to drink less if they wish to achieve ideal weight.

## THE MANY HEALTHFUL EATING PATTERNS FOR STRESS MANAGEMENT

Different people like different foods and like to prepare the same foods in different ways. Culture, family background, religion, moral beliefs, cost and availability of food, life experiences, food intolerances, and allergies affect people's food choices. Use the Stress Management Food Guide Pyramid as a starting point to shape your eating pattern. It provides a good guide to make sure you get enough nutrients. Make choices from each major food group and combine them however you like. For example, those who like Mexican cuisine might choose whole-grain tortillas from the grains group and beans from the protein group, while those who eat Asian food might choose steamed brown rice from the grains group and tofu from the protein group.

If you usually avoid certain types of foods—for example, if

you're a vegetarian—be sure to get enough nutrients from other foods. If you don't eat milk products, choose other foods that are good sources of calcium, and be sure to get enough vitamin D. Meat, fish, and poultry are major contributors of iron, zinc, and B vitamins in most American diets. If you choose to avoid these, be sure to get enough iron, vitamin B12, and zinc from other sources.

## How to Take Charge of Your Nutritional Lifestyle

We have given you the latest information about nutrition and a model to guide your food selections. Now it is time to create a plan of action.

Remember the Type C personality we described for you in an earlier chapter? We described a person who had learned to take charge of her life through commitment, challenge, and control. That is the basis of taking charge of your eating and nutrition. The recipe to develop Type C eating activities is not easy but ultimately follows a certain behavior modification pathway. First commit to the following:

1. Record food choices, calories, and exercise daily, follow the guidelines we have recommended, and accept that calories do count in weight maintenance.

2. Keep a weight chart in either written or electronic form, or at your doctor's office.

3. Identify conflicts leading to problem eating.

4. Address challenges and explore choices to overcome self-defeating behavior.

5. Develop control over behavior by making your habits conscious.

6. Recognize that external events cannot always be controlled.

7. Explore commitments by rehearsing new behaviors over and over until they become habits, and utilize positive self-talk when you are struggling.

8. Make compromises to increase flexibility and avoid rigidity. Examine each situation to make exceptions if needed.

9. Know that long-term compliance will create new habits and help you to take charge of your life.

We all share similar challenges when attempting to control our food consumption, such as eating schedules; food choices and aversions; eating in the company of others, or not; choosing places in which to dine, or grabbing a quick meal; eating a nutritionally diverse diet; and eating on the run or sitting and savoring meals; to name a few.

We encourage you to take the Type C approach when taking charge of your life and targeting habits that you need to change. Write down your plan of action.

## SERIOUS EATING DISORDERS ASSOCIATED WITH STRESS

Frequent binge eating, with or without periods of food restriction, may be a sign of a serious eating disorder. Other signs of eating disorders include preoccupation with body weight or food (or both), dramatic weight loss, excessive exercise, self-induced vomiting, and the abuse of laxatives. Seek help from a health care provider if any of these apply to you.

## PROFESSIONAL CONSULTATION FOR YOUR NUTRITIONAL LIFESTYLE

If you are struggling to enhance your nutritional lifestyle, then consider a consultation with a registered dietician, nutritionist, or similar health professional. Your family physician may be able to offer suggestions and make a referral. Use the references in Appendix III to guide you to sources of rational information about your nutritional lifestyle. If you have consulted with professionals and still find it difficult to follow a healthy nutritional lifestyle, then you may want to explore other professional options. Some weight loss programs offer sensible advice about nutrition and provide a support group and counseling to help you accomplish your goals. Some psychologists specialize in weight loss and behavior change for addictive and compulsive difficulties. Of course, dieticians, nutritionists, personal trainers, physicians, and chiropractors may also offer expertise in nutrition.

> *The great publicity given to such spectacular medical procedures as open heart surgery and organ transplants tends to make us forget that many of these patients would not have been hospitalized if preventive measures had not been severely neglected.*
>
> —John Knowles, M.D.

Taking charge of your nutritional lifestyle is an important part of your overall stress management plan for taking charge of your journey from birth to death that we call living.

## Relaxation and Stress Management for Healthy Nutrition

Just as relaxation techniques help you manage stressful situations, they can also help you get through the times when you are tempted to eat in response to anger, frustration, boredom, loneliness, depression, and other negative emotions. Try to eat slowly, chew your food thoroughly, and relax between bites. Breathing from your stomach area will not only relax you but also help you to become aware of signals that you are full.

You can succeed, but it takes time, effort, and persistence. The quick gimmicks—the fat burners and blockers, the screen stars'

> *Americans are people who laugh at African witch doctors and spend 100 million dollars on fake reducing systems.*
>
> —LEONARD LOUIS LEVINSON

secrets, the single-food diets, the appetite suppressants, and the magic pills—won't do it for you, but increasing your knowledge of nutrition and gradually modifying your thoughts and behaviors will. As Bela Karolyi told his world-class gymnasts, "You can do it!"

# SECTION VIII

# Putting It All Together

*Success in the long run depends on endurance and perseverance.
All things come to him who has learned to labor and wait.*
—Sir William Osler

# TWENTY-SEVEN

# Complementary and Alternative Medicine for Stress Management

*The learned man knows that he is ignorant.*
—VICTOR HUGO

MOST OF THE STRESS MANAGEMENT TECHNIQUES YOU HAVE BEEN exposed to in this book originated from the scientist-practitioner model of clinical psychology. This means that the techniques are scientifically studied and then refined in clinical trials and treatments. But stress is so vast in its effects, knowing no cultural, ethnic, or belief-based barriers, and our society is so diversified that it is important to recognize that for many people different systems of conceptualizing and treating stress-related disorders may offer an effective option. Alternative approaches to stress management may emphasize the interrelationship among mind, body, and spirit. Although some alternative approaches have a long history, many remain controversial. The National Center for Complementary and Alternative Medicine (NCCAM) at the National Institutes of Health was created in 1992 to help evaluate alternative methods of treatment and to integrate those that are effective into mainstream health care practice. The following brief descriptions of other resources to help you learn more effective stress management techniques reflect the work of NCCAM.

## Conventional, Complementary, and Alternative

There are many terms used to describe approaches to health care that are outside the realm of conventional medicine as practiced in the United States. The National Center for Complementary and Alternative Medicine defines some of the key terms used in the field of complementary and alternative medicine (CAM).

*Complementary medicine* is used together with conventional medicine. An example of a complementary therapy is using massage for relaxation or to help lessen a patient's discomfort following surgery.

*Alternative medicine* is used in place of conventional medicine. An example of an alternative therapy is using a special diet to treat cancer instead of undergoing surgery, radiation, or chemotherapy that has been recommended by a conventional doctor.

*Integrative medicine* combines mainstream medical therapies and CAM therapies for which there is some high-quality scientific evidence of safety and effectiveness.

NCCAM classifies CAM therapies into five categories, or domains:

1. *Alternative medical systems* are built upon complete systems of theory and practice. Examples of alternative medical systems that have developed in Western cultures include homeopathic medicine and naturopathic medicine. Examples of systems that have developed in non-

Western cultures include traditional Chinese medicine and Ayurveda.

2. *Mind-body medicine* uses a variety of techniques designed to enhance the mind's capacity to affect bodily function and symptoms. Some techniques that were considered as CAM in the past have become mainstream (for example, patient support groups and cognitive-behavioral therapy). Other mind-body techniques are still considered CAM, including meditation, prayer, mental healing, and therapies that use creative outlets such as art, music, or dance.

3. *Biologically based therapies* in CAM use substances found in nature, such as herbs, foods, and vitamins. Some examples include dietary supplements, herbal products, and the use of other so-called natural but as yet scientifically unproven therapies.

4. *Manipulative and body-based methods* in CAM are based on manipulation and/or movement of one or more parts of the body. Some examples include chiropractic or osteopathic manipulation, and massage.

5. *Energy therapies* involve the use of energy fields. Some forms of energy therapy manipulate biofields by applying pressure and/or manipulating the body. Examples include qi gong, Reiki, and therapeutic touch. Other therapies involve the unconventional use of electromagnetic fields.

NCCAM is the federal government's lead agency for scientific research on complementary and alternative medicine. NCCAM's mission is to explore complementary and alternative healing practices in the context of rigorous science, to train CAM researchers, and to inform the public and health professionals about the results of CAM research studies. Below are some of the different

CAM therapies that may promote themselves as helpful with stress-related disorders.

## Hypnosis

Hypnosis is very similar to relaxation training. Both usually involve physical relaxation, focused attention, and openness to suggestions. Relaxation training limits the suggestions to relaxation and mental rehearsal. Hypnosis includes many other suggestions, including, for example, pain relief, recall of memories, and habit change. Hypnosis is best provided by licensed health care practitioners who limit their hypnotic work to their areas of expertise.

## Massage Therapy

Massage therapy is a well-known drugless therapy for reducing stress and promoting relaxation. It is the manipulation of the soft tissues and includes kneading, pressing, or stroking with the use of pressure and movement. Massage can help loosen contracted muscles and provide gentle stretching to both the muscles and the connective tissues that surround and support the muscles and other parts of the body.

Massage doesn't just feel good. Research shows it reduces the heart rate, lowers blood pressure, improves range of motion, and increases endorphins, the body's natural painkillers. Therapeutic massage may also help people feel less anxious and stressed. Stress-related syndromes of anxiety, headaches, insomnia, digestive disorders, arthritis, asthma, carpal tunnel syndrome, and minor aches and pains are some of the problems that can respond to massage therapy.

> *Massage therapy is beneficial for almost all diseases. Eighty percent of disease is stress-related, and massage reduces stress.*
>
> —Sandra McLanahan, M.D.

## AROMATHERAPY

Aromatherapy involves the use of essential oils (extracts or essences) from flowers, herbs, and trees to promote health and well-being. These are often combined with other types of CAM therapies such as massage therapies.

## CHIROPRACTIC MEDICINE

Chiropractic medicine is a CAM alternative medical system, although many chiropractic practitioners have adapted their practices to be complementary of more traditional medicine. The chiropractic system focuses on the relationship between bodily structure (primarily that of the spine) and function, and how that relationship affects the preservation and restoration of health. Chiropractors use manipulative therapy as an integral treatment tool, but increasingly are treating the whole person with the adjunct of nutrition, exercise, massage, etc. Such practices may incorporate medical doctors, physical therapists, psychologists, personal trainers, etc. Since many stress disorders manifest in muscle tension and pain disorder, chiropractic practitioners often see stress-initiated complaints.

## DIETARY SUPPLEMENTS

Congress defined the term "dietary supplement" to include vitamins, minerals, herbs or other botanicals, amino acids, and substances such as enzymes, organ tissues, and metabolites. Dietary supplements come in many forms, including extracts, concentrates, tablets, capsules, gelcaps, liquids, and powders. Dietary supplements are considered foods, not drugs. Since stress impacts the adrenal glands and other parts of the physical body and endocrine system these practitioners may utilize supplements to help a person manage the results of stress.

## NATUROPATHIC MEDICINE

Naturopathic medicine is a CAM alternative medical system in which practitioners work with natural healing forces within the body, with a goal of helping the body heal from disease and attain better health. Practices may include dietary modifications, massage, exercise, acupuncture, and various other interventions.

## OSTEOPATHIC MEDICINE

Osteopathic medicine is a form of conventional medicine that, in part, emphasizes diseases arising in the musculoskeletal system. There is an underlying belief that all of the body's systems work together, and disturbances in one system may affect function elsewhere in the body. Some osteopathic physicians practice osteopathic manipulation, a full-body system of hands-on techniques to alleviate pain, restore function, and promote health and well-being.

## QI GONG

Qi gong ("chee-GUNG") is a component of traditional Chinese medicine that combines movement, meditation, and regulation of breathing to enhance the flow of qi (an ancient term given to what is believed to be vital energy) in the body, improve blood circulation, and enhance immune function.

## REIKI

Reiki ("RAY-kee") is a Japanese word representing Universal Life Energy. Reiki is based on the belief that when spiritual energy is channeled through a Reiki practitioner, the patient's spirit is healed, which in turn heals the physical body.

## THERAPEUTIC TOUCH

Therapeutic touch is derived from an ancient technique called laying-on of hands. It is based on the premise that it is the healing force of the therapist that affects the patient's recovery; healing is promoted when the body's energies are in balance; and, by passing their hands over the patient, healers can identify energy imbalances.

## SELF-HELP

Self-help groups are an invaluable resource for stress management and are offered at some hospitals, clinics, and even corporations. Self-help generally refers to groups or meetings that:

- Involve people who have similar needs;

- Are facilitated by a consumer, survivor, or other layperson;

- Assist people to deal with "life-disrupting" events, such as moves, death, abuse, serious accidents, addictions, or other stressors;

- Are operated on an informal, free-of-charge, and nonprofit basis;

- Provide support and education; and

- Are voluntary, anonymous, and confidential.

## PASTORAL COUNSELING

Some people prefer to seek help for stress-related problems from their pastor, rabbi, or priest, rather than from therapists who are not affiliated with a religious community. Counselors working within traditional faith communities increasingly are recognizing the need to incorporate psychotherapy and/or medication, along with prayer and spirituality to effectively help some people with stress related disorders.

## ANIMAL-ASSISTED THERAPIES

Working with an animal (or animals) under the guidance of a health care professional may benefit some people with stress-related problems by facilitating positive changes, such as increased empathy and enhanced socialization skills. Animals can be used as part of group therapy programs to encourage communication and increase the ability to focus. Developing self-esteem and reducing loneliness and anxiety are just some potential benefits of animal-assisted therapy.

## EXPRESSIVE THERAPIES

Art, dance/movement, and music/sound therapies can help a person integrate the emotional, physical, and cognitive facets of the self and may provide stress management through the release of emotions. Research suggests that music stimulates the body's natural feel-good chemicals (endorphins). This stimulation results in improved blood flow, blood pressure, pulse rate, breathing, and posture changes. We have listed some possible beginnings for the use of music in stress management in Appendix I.

## CULTURALLY BASED HEALING ARTS

Traditional Oriental medicine (such as acupuncture, shiatsu, and Reiki), Indian systems of health care (such as Ayurveda and yoga), and Native American healing practices (such as the sweat lodge and talking circles) all incorporate the beliefs that:

- Wellness is a state of balance between the spiritual, physical, and mental/emotional selves.

- An imbalance of forces within the body is the cause of illness.

- Herbal/natural remedies, combined with sound nutrition, exercise, and meditation/prayer, will correct this imbalance.

Several of these culturally based CAM systems may be useful for stress management.

**Acupuncture and Acupressure**    The Chinese practice of inserting needles or applying pressure at specific points on the body is an attempt to manipulate the body's flow of energy to balance the endocrine system. This manipulation regulates functions such as heart rate, body temperature, and respiration, as well as sleep patterns and emotional changes. Acupuncture has been used in clinics to relieve stress and anxiety.

**Ayurveda**    Ayurveda is an alternative medical system that has been practiced primarily in the Indian subcontinent for five thousand years. Ayurvedic medicine is described as "knowledge of how to live."

Ayurveda includes diet and herbal remedies and emphasizes the use of body, mind, and spirit in disease prevention and treatment. It incorporates an individualized regimen, such as diet, meditation, herbal preparations, and other techniques, to treat a variety of conditions including depression, to facilitate lifestyle changes, and to teach people how to release stress and tension through yoga or Transcendental Meditation.

**Yoga and Meditation**    Practitioners of this ancient Indian system of health care use breathing exercises, posture, stretches, and meditation to balance the body's energy centers. Yoga is used in combination with other treatment for depression, anxiety, and stress-related disorders.

**Native**           Ceremonial dances, chants, and cleansing rituals
**American**         are part of Indian Health Service programs to heal
**Traditional**      depression, stress, trauma, and substance abuse.
**Practices**

**Cuentos**          Based on folktales, this form of therapy originated
                     in Puerto Rico. The stories used contain healing
themes and models of behavior such as self-transformation and
endurance through adversity. Cuentos is used primarily to help
Hispanic children recover from stress-related problems associated
with leaving one's homeland and living in a foreign culture.

Storytelling and the use of metaphor have regained popularity
in the past decade and can be an effective adjunct with stress management. Within this book we have used stories to facilitate stress
management, and Drs. Charlesworth and Nathan have a collection of "copelets" (short stories with healing themes) used for effective stress management (see www.stresscontrol.com).

## TECHNOLOGY-BASED APPLICATIONS

The popularity of television, radio, the Internet, and electronic
tools at home and in the office makes access to stress management
information almost instantaneous. A telephone call or a mouse
click can bring stress management advice from popular broadcast-
ing personalities such as Dr. Phil McGraw. Below are some ways
we can use technology to access stress management counsel.

Telemedicine can enable consulting providers to speak to and
observe patients directly. It also can be used in education and
training programs for generalist clinicians. For many people telephone counseling often is a first step to managing stress. Tech-
nologies such as the Internet, bulletin boards, and electronic mail
lists provide access directly to consumers and the public on a wide
range of information about stress. Another relative newcomer to

stress management, radio/television psychiatry and psychology was first introduced in the United States in 1976. Radio/television psychiatrists and psychologists provide advice, information, and referrals in response to a variety of stress management issues.

This chapter does not cover every alternative approach to stress management. A range of other alternative approaches, such as psychodrama, hypnotherapy, recreational, and Outward Bound–type nature programs, offer opportunities to explore mental wellness. Before jumping into any alternative therapy, learn as much as you can about it. It is crucial to consult with your health care provider about the

> *The doctor of the future will give no medicine, but will interest his patients in the care of the human frame, in diet, and in the cause and prevention of disease.*
>
> —Thomas A. Edison

approaches you are using to effectively manage stress and achieve wellness. Many physical disorders masquerade as stress disorders, just as many stress disorders masquerade as physical disorders. In addition to talking with your health care practitioner, you may want to visit your local library, bookstore, health food store, or holistic health care clinic for more information. Also, before receiving services, check to be sure the provider is properly certified by an appropriate accrediting agency. See Appendix III for more resources about CAM therapies for stress management.

# TWENTY-EIGHT

## Making It Work for You

*Think it the greatest impiety to prefer life to disgrace, and for
the sake of life, to lose the reason for living.*
—JUVENAL

THE HABITS OF A LIFETIME CANNOT BE CHANGED OVERNIGHT.
Change takes time—sometimes a year or two of dedicated practice. But if you do not take on the challenge of change, your
blood pressure elevation could become chronic, your weight
struggles could lead to diabetes, you could be plagued with
headaches, or you could suffer any number of other stress-related
disorders.

There is no magic to transform you instantly into a successful
stress manager. But we have seen thousands of people make
tremendous progress when they apply and practice the techniques
presented in this book.

What will happen if you stop practicing your stress management techniques? Will you immediately return to the chronic stress responses of your old lifestyle? First, even if you have dedicated yourself to practicing these techniques, there will probably be times when you forget to "relax and let go." We all get overconfident at times.

Both authors have been practicing, teaching, and researching various stress management techniques for more than three decades.

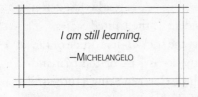

*I am still learning.*
—MICHELANGELO

They still find themselves tense and rushing at times. They recognize their stress faster now by listening to their bodies, and then they return to regularly scheduled stress management practice. The stress spiral can be broken!

Do not get discouraged if you find that you occasionally fail to handle certain stressors in the best way. If life is to be judged, it should be judged on a best-efforts basis. You may wish you had done something better. You can imagine, plan, and practice doing better. But looking back with discouragement is not a realistic way to approach life. Don't let initial failures or temporary setbacks stop you from trying.

## IS FAILURE A PART OF SUCCESS?

All of science is based on failures. Thousands of unsuccessful experiments were necessary to produce such discoveries as the lightbulb and pasteurized milk. Behind most successful people are numerous failures. The winners in life try to learn something from every experience.

The following is the history of one of life's winners who over-

*Never let the fear of striking out get in your way.*
—BABE RUTH

came many failures and personal hardships. He lost his job, suffered defeat in a campaign for the legislature, faced failure in business, won an election for the legislature, lost his sweetheart to a fatal disease, experienced a nervous breakdown, lost an election for Speaker in the legislature, lost in a race for congressional nomination, won an election to Congress, lost renomination, was rejected for the post of land officer, lost an election for the Senate, lost in a race for the vice presidential nomination, and suffered a second defeat in the Senate election. Two years after his last defeat, Abraham Lincoln was elected president of the United States.

We can all benefit from adopting the stick-to-it attitude of Lincoln. Accept initial failures or setbacks as part of the trial-and-error process that will bring you a little closer to being a successful stress manager. Most people don't fail; they just give up trying.

## Positive Self-Control

Dennis Waitley, the psychologist who wrote *Psychology of Winning*, lists the ten characteristics of successful people. He means much more than financial success. He studies people who succeed in managing stress and living satisfying lives. Waitley's emphasis is on mental health and not mental illness. His ten qualities of a winner include:

1. Positive self-awareness: understanding where you are coming from

2. Positive self-esteem: liking yourself

3. Positive self-control: making it happen for yourself

4. Positive self-motivation: wanting to succeed and deciding you can

5. Positive self-expectancy: deciding that next time you will do better

6. Positive self-image: seeing yourself changing and growing

7. Positive self-direction: having a game plan

8. Positive self-discipline: practicing mentally

9. Positive self-dimension: valuing yourself as a person

10. Positive self-projection: reflecting yourself in how you walk, listen, and talk

We highly recommend Dr. Waitley's books and tapes, as well as the books and tapes of Stephen Covey and Tony Robbins, who have all placed emphasis on the characteristics important for successful living. Dr. Waitley's characteristic of positive self-control means that winners say, "I make it happen for me." Losers say, "It always happens to me." Dr. Waitley's proverb for living is: "Life is a do-it-to-myself project. I take the credit or the blame for my performance."

## THE FREEDOM TO CHOOSE

Self-control means that you have the freedom to choose alternatives. If you believe your life is dictated by luck, fate, or circumstances, however, you are open to doubts and fears. In fact, you don't *have* to do anything in life. Hunger strikers, for example, decide they do not even have to eat. You can make the best choices among the available alternatives to help you reach your goals.

We hope you decide to break out of the habits of stressful living and into the skills of stress management. We know that you can. Positive self-control is a stress management skill and habit that puts you in control of your life. Not managing stress is also a habit. Habits take years to form, and habits die hard, or they die with the person. Nearly everything you do is a habit.

One of the best ways to break a bad habit is to replace it with a good one. Rather than concentrating on which stressful habits you are not going to do, begin to concentrate on which stress management habits you will practice and develop.

## MAKING EXCUSES VERSUS TAKING RESPONSIBILITY

If you are like most people, there will be times when you encounter difficulty in exchanging familiar habits for new ones. If you slack off practicing your new stress management skills, examine your excuses. We often hear excuses such as "I'm too busy today," "I'm too tired," or "This isn't working."

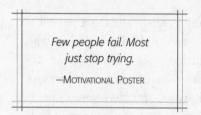

*Few people fail. Most just stop trying.*

—MOTIVATIONAL POSTER

Do not be lured by these excuses. Of course, they are partially true. You may be busy, tired, or progressing slowly. These excuses are also partially false. It is not because you are busy, tired, or progressing slowly that you cannot practice the exercises. Take responsibility for your decision to choose one activity over another by saying, "I am busy closing out the books for the end of the month. I could do the exercises, but I choose not to." Remember, you are in the driver's seat in your life.

The excuses you give for not rehearsing stress management techniques are probably the same excuses you have used for years to keep yourself locked into a stress cycle. Sometimes these excuses are based on faulty premises and misunderstood needs.

## UNDERSTANDING YOUR NEEDS

**Survival and Safety**  Most people have certain needs that must be met in order for them to feel comfortable. If your car leaked gasoline and caught fire, your strong need for safety would supersede any need to get to the destination toward which you were driving.

Psychologists, particularly Dr. Abraham Maslow, have helped us to understand that our needs are often hierarchical. Food and shelter are usually considered to be at the base of our need hierarchy. Next comes the need for physical safety. Most people in today's world can fulfill these basic needs. It may be helpful to acknowledge the role other needs play and how we try to fulfill them.

When we fail to recognize our other needs, we begin to feed our stress spiral. Recognizing your other needs will also help you to attack any excuses for not practicing your stress management skills.

**Security and**      The need for security and stability motivates people
**Belonging**      toward stable relationships, insurance policies, and
dependable jobs. A strong need for affiliation and belonging means we would value family, avoid disagreements, and attempt to have everyone like us.

Could strong needs for security and affiliation interfere with stress management? Yes. A middle-aged woman we worked with believed her family would reject her if she did not have all of her housework done before she practiced relaxation. Since the work of the homemaker is never done, she found little time to relax. She had a strong need to be appreciated. She wanted to be secure, not rock the boat, and have everyone like her.

Taking positive self-control of her life, she was able to examine her needs and discussed them with her family. She reread the material on assertiveness training. She discovered that her family did not reject her if she took time for herself; instead they wanted her to do so. In fact, her family had felt guilty because she was always doing things for others instead of for herself. She began meeting her needs for relaxing and replenishing her store of energy, and she sacrificed none of her needs for a secure family relationship.

Believe it or not, a strong need for the respect of others can also interfere with stress management. We worked with a lovely woman in her middle thirties who was in an important management position. Her need for the respect and admiration of others nearly prevented her from learning more about managing stress. She was not able to join the stress management class until she explored this need and brought it into balance with her other needs for a healthy body. Why? She was afraid someone would find out she was in the class, think she could not manage stress, and lose respect for her.

**Esteem**      If you are an energetic person who likes to succeed, you may have a strong need for achievement and accomplishment. Enthusiasm may push you to take on too many stress management exercises at once. You may overdo your practice at first as you strive toward a goal of perfect stress management in ten days. You may find that you have set unrealistic goals and your program is too rigorous. You may feel awkward or demand perfection and stop trying. The overachiever often feels guilty about not reaching goals, begins to lose interest, and makes excuses about already being overextended. Soon practicing the techniques is put off indefinitely, and the person has burned out even before getting a good start.

> *Change comes from the unfinished areas, not from pretensions of wholeness.*
>
> —MICHAEL MEADE

If you have a strong need for achievement, be sure to take stress management practice slowly. Don't expect too much too soon. You will begin to feel more energy as a result of relaxation training. Consider your long- and short-term goals. You may wish to use this energy for recreation and hobbies rather than funneling it back into still more work.

Another strong need that may interfere with stress management is the need for power and control. If you find that you cannot delegate enough responsibility to give you time to practice relaxation, review the time management and assertiveness chapters.

Rate the strength of your various needs. Use a number from 0 (no need) to 10 (extremely strong need) for each of the needs listed below.

_____ Power and control

_____ Achievement and accomplishment

_____ Esteem and respect

_____ Affiliation and belonging

_____ Security and stability

_____ Health and physical well-being

Now, ask yourself if, and how, your strongest needs may help or interfere with practicing what you have learned in this book. How strong is your need for a healthy body? For some people, the need for a healthy body is not stronger than the need for the things they gain by having a stress symptom!

In some cases, a spouse has to do the cooking, take out the garbage, or keep the house quiet if the person with the symptom is tired, suffers from a headache, or has elevated blood pressure. For others, a backache or an anger problem can offer power and control. How would your life be different if you did not have stress-related problems? Is there anything you might have to give up? What will happen if you don't choose to change your reactions to stressful challenges?

> *The history of man is a graveyard of great cultures that came to catastrophic ends because of their incapacity for planned, rational, voluntary reaction to challenge.*
>
> —ERICH FROMM

**The Highest Need on the Hierarchy**    If one has fulfilled the needs we have reviewed, then what is left to strive for? The highest need on Dr. Maslow's hierarchy is the need for self-actualization.

This is the need for self-fulfillment, for realizing one's potentials, and for becoming the person one is capable of becoming. As you learn to meet your other needs, strive to find the joy of self-fulfillment.

## REVIEWING YOUR PROGRESS

Have you already gained from practicing the techniques in this book? Could you gain more? Review this book and underline the techniques that worked for you. Review your scores on the self-assessment scales that helped you analyze the specific areas of stress in your life.

Do you need more work on relaxing your muscles? Could you benefit from biofeedback for headaches? Do you want to break a habit such as smoking? Is now the time to begin exercising? Should you select books from the reading list to gain further knowledge of time management?

You may find it helpful to set aside a few hours at the first of every month to review your stress management progress. Spend some time identifying the frequency and intensity of your stress responses. Look for the sources of your stress. These may be changes in your life such as new situations you are facing, new feelings you are experiencing, or new foods or drinks you have added to your diet.

Once you have reviewed your progress, develop a plan to cope with or to avoid the stressors. Consider using some or all of the techniques you have learned in this program. Finally, put your stress management plan into action.

This book and other books or recordings may not be sufficient to help you with all situations. You may want to become involved in an ongoing support group or obtain professional counseling to help you become a successful stress manager.

## Support Groups to Help You Through Crises in Living

In the past few years, many of our society's support networks have broken down. This is probably one of the reasons why we are experiencing such increases in stress today. Years ago, for example, people could count on a consistent and faithful family network that would help in times of crisis. In addition, we were much less mobile, and people tended to become very friendly with neighbors. The neighborhood was once a support network within itself.

Because support groups are often very important in helping people manage their stress, we have included in Appendix II a list of support groups and other resources. You may wish to refer to it during particular life crises and for stress-related disorders you face.

## Religion and Service: Sources of Strength

Religious fellowship, spiritual principles, and faith in a higher power can be major sources of strength for daily living and times of crisis. A sign we saw in front of a church reads, If God Seems Far Away, Who Do You Think Moved? Once again, the choice is ours.

Perhaps you could benefit from becoming more involved in a church or synagogue. If you have moved recently and need to find one in your new community, call the leader of the one you left and ask for a referral; most have national directories if you cannot get a referral to one in your area. You can also look in the yellow pages of the telephone book or SuperPages.com on the Internet under "Churches" or "Synagogues." If you are traveling, most hotels have a directory of nearby places of worship and the hours of their services. Most churches and synagogues have groups for single people, teenagers, and others in the congregation.

Community service organizations such as Rotary International, Optimists, Lions, Junior League, National Charity League,

Habitat for Humanity, Salvation Army, and Red Cross can also provide new social contacts and be sources of lasting friendships. Service groups are listed in the *Encyclopedia of Associations,* which can be found in most libraries. See Appendix II for more resources for group affiliation.

## PROFESSIONAL COUNSELING

If you find that you are continuing to struggle with serious conflicts and problems, we strongly recommend that you seek professional counseling or therapy. There are a number of mental health professions whose members offer the help you may need.

Mental health professionals include psychologists, psychiatrists, social workers, nurses, ministers, and counselors. Mental health professionals may be listed under their specialty in the yellow pages. Some work in mental health clinics or other institutions, which are also listed in the telephone book.

> *All of the truly important battles are waged within the self.*
>
> —SHELDON B. KOPP

To find the community mental health center in your area or other sources of both professional and paraprofessional help, you may need to look in the yellow or white pages of your telephone book or SuperPages.com on the Internet. Recommendations by friends or professionals who have knowledge of the therapist or institution are often informative and helpful. Most psychotherapists are listed in national registries. In addition, local county or state associations list names of their members by geographic areas and specialties. Local universities may also be a source of information. Finally, your health maintenance organization (HMO), preferred provider organization (PPO), or health insurance company may have a Web site and even counselors to help you find a therapist.

It is wise to ask what training the counselor or psychotherapist has had and what his or her specialty is. Never hesitate to explore the credentials of the professional you are interviewing. To ensure at least a minimal level of competency, be certain that the counselor is licensed. Make sure as well that the counselor has experience in dealing with your type of problem.

## AN INVITATION

We would very much appreciate hearing from you. One of the ways you can do this is to write us about this book. If there are parts you found difficult, let us know. If there are parts you found particularly helpful, let us know this as well. We would also like to learn about any additional ways you have found to manage stress and enhance your wellness. Dr. Charlesworth's Web site (www.stresscontrol.com) will allow you to contact us directly, and it is also a source for the latest information and resources for stress management. He has developed numerous booklets and recordings that may be used for specific areas of stress management. Begin to live your stress management techniques. Find guidance in the words of an eighty-five-year-old woman, Nadine Stair:

> *If I have my life to live over, I'd dare to make more mistakes next time. I'd relax. I'd limber up. I would be sillier than I have been this trip. I would take fewer things seriously. I would take more chances. I would take more trips. I would climb more mountains and swim more rivers. I would perhaps have more actual troubles, but I'd have fewer imaginary ones.*
>
> *You see, I'm one of those people who lived sensibly and sanely hour after hour, day after day. Oh, I've had my moments and, if I had it to do over again, I'd have more of them. In fact, I'd try to have nothing else. Just moments, one after another, instead of living so many years ahead of each day. I've been one of those persons who never goes anywhere without a thermometer,*

*a hot water bottle, a raincoat and a parachute. If I had to do it again, I would travel lighter than I have.*

*If I had my life to live over, I would start barefoot earlier in the spring and stay that way later in the fall. I would go to more dances. I would ride more merry-go-rounds. I would pick more daisies.*

This is not the end, but the beginning. The winners in the game of life have a game plan. We hope your plan includes finding excitement every day of your life.

Good luck, and may your stressors always be manageable. Remember, you are the one who writes your own story: "What goes in the plot, and what does not, is pretty much up to me."

### APPENDIX I

## Music for Stress Management

THE POWER OF MUSIC TO PROMOTE CHANGE IS NOT A NEW CON-cept. The Bible, Greek and Roman literature, and Egyptian records discuss music as a therapeutic device. Orpheus charmed wild beasts. Ulysses had his crew put wax in their ears to avoid hearing the song of the Sirens, which could lead them to destruction. The poets have written about the power of music to calm or stir the emotions and to inspire or suppress desire. Soldiers march off to war with a song on their lips. We respond affectively to music.

The ways in which music affects us are varied. There are many studies demonstrating physiological responses to music, including changes in breathing, blood pressure, blood supply, and galvanic skin responses. The first is attributed to a French musician, André Grétry (1741–1813), who took his pulse by placing the fingers of one hand on the artery in the wrist of his other hand and noted accompanying changes as he sang at different tempos. In 1880, Johann Dogiel tested the influence of music on the circulation of blood in humans by means of a device called a plethysmograph.

According to Charles Diserens, the following effects of music are generally accepted. Music increases bodily metabolism, changes muscular activity, affects respiration, produces marked effects on pulse and blood pressure, and affords the physiological basis for the creation of different emotions.

The field of psychoacoustics (studying the effect of sound on the human nervous system) is growing in knowledge and research. The right kind of music can influence a work environment, and a number of recent studies show that exposure to certain music can produce measurable short-term improvements in IQ, as well as positive changes in key neurotransmitters, hormones, and the immune system.

Possibly the greatest importance of music, as it relates to the study of stress management, is the range and intensity of its associational value. It can serve as a stimulus for a wide variety of reactions, both pleasant and unpleasant. Therefore, appropriately selected music can enhance the relaxation experience through calming images and can also promote physical relaxation.

Music in combination with lyrics can promote healing through emotional catharsis. Throughout this book you have probably noted that we quote songs to accentuate points. A few words from a song may trigger many emotions to help us discharge emotions, motivate us to action, stimulate us to consider options, grieve a loss, or soothe our feelings of restlessness and longing. Often music without lyrics will help us segue from tension to relaxation.

It is difficult even to define a musical category of music that will be beneficial for stress management when you go to purchase music. Some classical music has morphed into "healing/learning" music. This category may comprise a growing genre encompassing classical melodies and nature sounds. Therapists (psychologists, biofeedback practitioners, massage therapists, aromatherapists, etc.) use music during treatments, but they may select therapeutic music from the classical, New Age, world music, and healing sections in music stores.

We suggest that you try some of the selections listed below because research has shown that they can help most people to enhance their relaxation experiences. Since everyone responds differently, you should make your own evaluation of each recommendation. We have also included natural environmental sounds, which many people find calming.

## CLASSICAL INSTRUMENTAL MUSIC BY J. S. BACH

Concerto for Two Violins, "Largo"

Harpsichord Concerto in F Minor, "Largo"

English Suite #3, "Sarabande" from *Masters of the Guitar, Vol. 1*

Solo Harpsichord Concerto in G Minor, "Largo"

Concerto in G Minor for Flute and Strings, "Largo"

Solo Harpsichord Concerto in F Major, "Largo"

Solo Harpsichord Concerto in C Major, "Largo"

*Classical Relaxation,* Vols. 1–10

## MEDITATIVE LISTENING EXPERIENCES

Paul Horn, *Inside* (*The Taj Mahal*)

Paul Horn, *Inside 2*

Tony Scott, *Music for Zen Meditation*

Tony Scott, *Tibetan Bells*

Wendy Carlos, *Sonic Seasonings*

## ENVIRONMENTAL SOUNDS

*Environments 1: The Psychologically Ultimate Seashore*

*Environments 2: Dawn and Dusk at New Hope, Pennsylvania*

*Environments 8: Wood-Masted Sailboat and A Country Stream*

*Relaxation and Meditation with Music and Nature: Distant Shores*

*Relaxation and Meditation with Music and Nature: Ocean Dreams*

*Relaxation and Meditation with Music and Nature: Spring Showers*

*Relaxation and Meditation with Music and Nature: Mountain Streams*

APPENDIX II

# A Guide to Self-Help Groups and Service Organizations

*Important note: The descriptions of organizations and other resources that appear below are in most cases condensed from material made available by the sponsors or providers of products and services. The authors of this book and its publisher cannot be responsible for material contained on any Web site or in any other resource listed in this book. Please exercise caution and common sense in exploring and evaluating all information, recommendations, and instructions you come across in your research.*

## What Is a Self-Help Group?

A self-help group can provide valuable assistance and support to its members in dealing with their mutual problems and in improving their psychological well-being. People who share common life experiences and problems start most self-help organizations. Groups are usually controlled by their members and rely on the efforts, skills, knowledge, and concerns of their members as their primary way of helping.

## How Effective Are Self-Help Groups?

A survey of eighteen hundred outpatient psychiatric facilities in the United States found that about half (48 percent) make either frequent or occasional referrals to self-help groups. In evaluating the usefulness of self-help groups, about 85 percent of the professionals rated the effectiveness of the groups as very high, high, or average. This rating suggests that professionals generally view self-help groups favorably.

Self-help groups provide a social treatment that cannot only improve the quality of life for their members but also help prevent further difficulties. The groups offer their members information, comfort, emotional support, and a sense of belonging. The desire to avoid letting one's friends down and the hope of gaining the group's approval for success can be very positive and very powerful forces for many people.

Self-help groups also sponsor public information programs designed to remove commonly held prejudices and prevent discrimination against their members. In addition, they often support legislation and research of benefit to their members.

## How Can I Find a Self-Help Group?

There are several ways to find a self-help group that will meet your needs. If you know the name of the group, look it up in the telephone book or on the Internet. Many groups are also listed in the yellow pages under "Social Service Organizations." Some news-papers have a calendar or events section in which they announce the times and places of the local weekly meetings. Other sources of referral are friends or local professionals, who are usually familiar with area resources. In addition, a local social service directory may be available from your chamber of commerce or public library.

If you are unable to find a local group or chapter, contact the national headquarters listed below. Ask for the name, phone number, and address of the chapter nearest you.

## Does a Group Exist for My Problems?

You may find a group that meets your needs in the *Encyclopedia of Associations,* edited by Nancy Yakes and Dennis Akey, which is available in most libraries. It lists current addresses and telephone numbers.

You may also want to contact:

**National Health Information Center**
U.S. Department of Health and Human Services
Referral Specialist
P.O. Box 1133
Washington, DC 20013-1133
(800) 336-4797
(301) 565-4167
info@nhic.org
www.health.gov/nhic/

The National Health Information Center (NHIC) is a health information referral service sponsored by the Office of Disease Prevention and Health Promotion. NHIC puts health professionals and consumers who have health questions in touch with those organizations that are best able to provide answers. Using a database that contains descriptions of health-related organizations, NHIC staff refer people to the most appropriate resource.

If you still are unable to find a group, consider forming one. Find other people with the same problem and/or local mental health professionals who can help you start a group.

## TO GIVE IS ALSO TO RECEIVE: *A Guide to Service Organizations*

The following groups are not self-help groups, but service organizations where one may affiliate with like-minded individuals seeking a more meaningful and purposeful life through helping others. When evaluating service and volunteer organizations, be aware of the Better Business Bureau guidelines that only up to 35 percent of all donated funds may be used for administrative expenses. The lower the amount spent on administration, then the more that is going to benevolent assistance. Select organizations and causes based on your motivation for the cause and the efficiency of the organization to manage their affairs in a fiscally responsible fashion. Information about service organizations is provided here because there are times when helping others is the best way to help oneself.

> The only thing we get to keep is what we give away.
>
> —BRUCE COCKBURN

### The Association of Junior Leagues International Inc.
132 West 31st Street
11th Floor
New York, NY 10001-3406
(212) 951-8300
www.ajli.org

> If I am not for myself, who is for me? And if I am only for myself, what am I? And if not now, when?
>
> —HILLEL

The Junior Leagues are organizations of women committed to promoting voluntarism, developing the potential of women, and improving communities through the effective action and leadership of trained volunteers. The Junior League has been the driving force behind the kinds of initiatives and institutions that make communities healthier, more vital places to live: childhood immunization, family literacy, women's shelters, children's museums, historic preservation, leadership development, and more. The Junior Leagues offer members extensive training in areas such as leadership and organizational development, community needs assessment, strategic planning, communications, advocacy, and fund-raising. Explore this Web site to find out more about these opportunities in your area.

**Big Brothers Big Sisters of America (BBBS)**
230 N. 13th St.
Philadelphia, PA 19107
(215) 567-7000
www.bbbsa.org

Big Brothers Big Sisters has been a national youth-service organization for nearly a century. Their service is based on volunteers. Big Brothers and Big Sisters are friends to children and "share everyday activities, expand horizons, and experience the joy in even the simplest events." BBBS works closely with parents to match every child with the right Big Brother or Big Sister. See the Web site to find volunteer opportunities in your community.

**Goodwill Industries International, Inc.**
15810 Indianola Drive
Bethesda, MD 20855
(301) 530-6500
www.goodwill.org

Goodwill Industries International is a network of community-based, autonomous member organizations that serves people with workplace disadvantages and disabilities by providing job training and employment services, as well as job placement opportunities and post-employment support.

### Optimist International
4494 Lindell Blvd.
St. Louis, MO 63108
(314) 371-6000
(800) 500-8130
www.optimist.org

This international federation of business, industrial, and professional men's service clubs is dedicated to inspiring respect for law, promoting interest in good government, and aiding and encouraging the development of young people. Optimist Clubs conduct positive service projects aimed at providing a helping hand to youth.

### The Points of Light Foundation
1400 I Street, NW
Suite 800
Washington, DC 20005
(202) 729-8000
www.pointsoflight.org

The Points of Light Foundation and Volunteer Center National Network engages and mobilizes millions of volunteers who are helping to solve social problems in thousands of communities.

### Rotary International
One Rotary Center
1560 Sherman Avenue
Evanston, IL 60201
(847) 866-3000
www.rotary.org

Rotary is an organization of business and professional leaders united worldwide who provide humanitarian service, encourage high ethical standards in all vocations, and help build goodwill and peace in the world. The object of Rotary is to encourage and foster the ideal of service as a basis of worthy enterprise, the development of acquaintance as an opportunity for service, high ethical standards in business and professions, the recognition of the worthiness of all useful occupations, the dignifying of each Rotarian's occupation as an opportunity to serve society, the application of the ideal of service in each Rotarian's personal, business, and community life, and advancement of international understanding, goodwill, and peace through a world fellowship of business and professional persons united in the ideal of service.

**The Salvation Army**
National Headquarters
615 Slaters Lane
P.O. Box 269
Alexandria, VA 22313
www.salvationarmyusa.org

Adult rehabilitation centers are among the most widely known of all Salvation Army services and comprise the largest resident substance abuse rehabilitation program in the United States. Other major programs and facilities offered include emergency shelters, medical and counseling services for women suffering from substance abuse, homes for pre-delinquent adolescent girls, day care centers, and children's homes. Low-cost housing also is available to men and women living on pensions or social security.

**United Way of America**
701 North Fairfax Street
Alexandria, VA 22314
(703) 836-7112
www.unitedway.org

The mission of United Way is to improve people's lives by mobilizing the caring power of communities. Common focus areas include: helping children and youth succeed, strengthening and supporting families, promoting self-sufficiency, building vital and safe neighborhoods, and supporting vulnerable and aging populations.

For more information about service organizations contact:

**The National Assembly of Health and Human Service Organizations**
1319 F Street, NW
Suite 601
Washington, DC 20004
(202) 347-2080
www.nassembly.org

> *Life is short and we have not too much time for gladdening the hearts of those who are traveling the dark way with us. Oh, be swift to love! Make haste to be kind.*
>
> —HENRI AMIEL

The National Assembly of Health and Human Service Organizations is an association of national nonprofit health and human service organizations bound by a common concern for the effective delivery of health and human services to the American people. A review of its members will help you locate volunteer opportunities in such areas of service as children and family welfare, aging, cancer, blindness, mental health, missing and exploited children, crime prevention, mentoring, scholarships, and cerebral palsy.

APPENDIX III

# Suggested Web Sites, Books, Recordings, and Other Resources

*Important note: The descriptions of organizations and other resources that appear below are in most cases condensed from material made available by the sponsors or providers of products and services. The authors of this book and its publisher cannot be responsible for material contained on any Web site or in any other resource listed in this book. Please exercise caution and common sense in exploring and evaluating all information, recommendations, and instructions you come across in your research.*

We have listed below Web sites, books, prerecorded relaxation tapes/CDs, and other materials that you may wish to extend, deepen, and practice the material in most of the chapters in this book. Many of the books we have listed may be available in a recorded or electronic form. If the book (BK) is available as an audiocassette tape, then a (C) will be listed at the end of the reference. If the book is available as a compact disc, then a (CD) will be listed at the end of the reference. If the book has a video version available as a VHS or DVD, then a (V) will be listed at the end of the reference. We also indicate whether the book is available as an audio download (AD) or as an electronic book (EB) from the Internet. When a book is available in multiple formats, all applicable formats will be listed at the end of the reference (e.g., C/CD/V/AD/EB).

We invite you to visit our Web site www.stresscontrol.com for current self-help books and recordings, links to other Web sites that will be useful in searching for resources for stress management, and our e-mail addresses. In addition, we would welcome quotes for the soon-to-be published copelets collection, as well as resources you might suggest for inclusion on the Web site.

## RELAXATION TAPES

First, we recommend a cassette/CD stress management program developed by a team of psychologists, including the authors of this book. It consists of three cassettes or CDs. It includes instrumental music and environmental sounds that have been shown (in a controlled, published study) to increase its impact. Joe Wysong in *Psychotherapy Newsletter* reviewed the program. He wrote, "Of the recorded programs we reviewed, Edward A. Charlesworth's *The Relaxation and Stress Management Program* is by far the best. . . . We found [it] . . . to far outdistance any of the other recorded relaxation programs on the market. . . . [It was] the most effective."

The contents of this program include:

1. Progressive Relaxation

2. Deep Muscle Relaxation

3. Autogenic Relaxation: Arms and Hands

4. Autogenic Relaxation: Legs and Feet

5. Visual Imagery Relaxation

6. Image Rehearsal Practice

You may test this program for a fifteen-day, money-back trial period. For more information about these tapes and workshops by the authors, you may call (281) 890-8575, search the Web site at www.stresscontrol.com or write to Stress Management Recordings, Willowbrook Psychological Associates, P.C., 10609 Grant Road, Building B, Houston, TX 77070.

## SECTION I: LEARNING ABOUT STRESS AND YOUR LIFE

### Internet Resources

**American Institute of Stress**
124 Park Avenue
Yonkers, NY 10703
www.stress.org

**Dr. Edward A. Charlesworth**
Stress and Life Management Products Division
Willowbrook Psychological Associates, P.C.
10609 Grant Road, Building B
Houston, TX 77070
(281) 469-6395
www.stresscontrol.com

**National Institute for Occupational Safety and Health (NIOSH)**
Education and Information Division

4676 Columbia Parkway
Cincinnati, OH 45226-1998
(800) 35-NIOSH
Outside the U.S.: (513) 533-8328
www.cdc.gov/niosh

### Additional Resources

Brown, B. *New Mind, New Body.* New York: Irvington Publishers, 2000. (BK)

Charlesworth, E., and A. Peiffer. *Stress Management Training Program.* Houston: Stress Management Products Division of Willowbrook Psychological Associates, 2003. (C/CD)

Chopra, D., and D. Simon. *Grow Younger, Live Longer: Ten Steps to Reverse Aging.* Three Rivers Press, 2002. (BK/C/CD/V)

Goudey, P., J. Davidson, L. Deutsch, and P. Rosch. *The Unofficial Guide to Beating Stress.* Foster City, CA: IDG, 2000. (BK)

Moyers, B. *Healing and the Mind.* New York: Main Street Books, 1995. (V/AD)

Pelletier, K. *Mind as Healer, Mind as Slayer.* New York: Delta, 1992. (BK)

Robbins, J. *A Symphony in the Brain: The Evolution of the New Brain Wave Biofeedback.* Berkeley, CA.: Grove Press, 2001. (BK)

Sapolsky, R. *Why Zebras Don't Get Ulcers: An Updated Guide to Stress, Stress-Related Diseases, and Coping.* New York: W. H. Freeman & Co., 1998. (BK)

Selye, H. *Stress Without Distress.* New York: Lippincott, 1980. (BK)

Taylor, S. *The Tending Instinct.* New York: Henry Holt, 2002.

Witkin, G. *The Female Stress Survival Guide* (Third Edition). New York: Newmarket Press, 2000.

## SECTION II: RELAXING WAYS FOR A STRESSFUL WORLD

### Internet Resources

**American Massage Therapy Association**
820 Davis Street, Suite 100
Evanston, IL 60201
(847) 864-0123
www.amtamassage.org

**Dr. Edward A. Charlesworth**
Stress and Life Management Products Division
Willowbrook Psychological Associates, P.C.
10609 Grant Road, Building B
Houston, TX 77070
(281) 469-6395
www.stresscontrol.com

### Additional Resources

Benson, H., and M. Klipper. *The Relaxation Response.* New York: HarperTorch, 2000. (BK)

Bernstein, D., T. Borkovec, and H. Hazlett-Stevens. *New Directions in Progressive Relaxation Training: A Guidebook for Helping Professionals.* Westport, CT: Praeger Publishers, 2000. (BK)

Charlesworth, E. *Stress Management Training Program: Progressive Relaxation, Deep Muscle Relaxation, Autogenic Training, Visual Imagery Training, and Image Rehearsal Practice.* Houston: Stress Management Products Division of Willowbrook Psychological Associates, 2003. (C/CD)

Iknoian, T. *Mind-Body Fitness for Dummies.* Foster City, CA: IDG Publishers, 2000. (BK)

Naparstek, B. *Health Journeys: Stress.* New York: Time Warner Audio Books, 1993. (C, CD)

Sile, B. *The Pilates Body: The Ultimate At-Home Guide to Strengthening, Lengthening, and Toning Your Body—Without Machines.* New York: Broadway Books, 2000. (BK)

Yee, R. *Yoga: The Poetry of the Body.* New York: St. Martin's Press, 2002. (BK)

## SECTION III: OVERCOMING YOUR SPECIAL STRESSORS

### *Organizations and Internet Resources*

#### American Psychological Association
(800) 964-2000

"Talk to Someone Who Can Help," brochure about psychotherapy and choosing a psychologist from the American Psychological Association (free). (800) 964-2000

"Get the Facts: How to Find Help through Psychotherapy," a brief question-and-answer guide that provides basic information about psychotherapy and how it can help. Available at www.helping.apa.org/therapy/psychotherapy.html

"Find a Psychologist," information on how to be connected with the state psychological association referral network in your area. Go to www.helping.apa.org/find.html

"Coping with Terrorism" offers tips on managing this type of stress. Available at www.helping.apa.org/daily/terrorism.html

#### American Red Cross
www.redcross.org

The American Red Cross has several brochures available online, including "Helping Young Children Cope with Trauma," "When Bad Things Happen," "Disaster Preparedness for People with Disabilities," and "How Do I Deal With My Feelings." Go to www.redcross.org/pubs/dspubs/terrormat.html.

Local chapters of the American Red Cross may be able to direct you to additional resources. You can log on and enter your zip code where it says "Find Your Local Red Cross." The contact information for your local chapter will also be available in your telephone book.

**National Institute for Occupational Safety and Health (NIOSH)**
Education and Information Division
4676 Columbia Parkway
Cincinnati, OH 45226-1998
(800) 35-NIOSH
Outside the United States: (513) 533-8328
http://www.cdc.gov/niosh

*Additional Resources*

Fullerton, C., and R. Ursano (editors). *Posttraumatic Stress Disorder: Acute and Long-Term Responses to Trauma and Disaster.* Arlington, VA: American Psychiatric Press, 1997. (BK)

Johnson, S., and K. Blanchard. *Who Moved My Cheese? An Amazing Way to Deal with Change in Your Work and in Your Life.* New York: Putnam Publishing Group, 1998. (BK/C/CD)

Kushner, H. *When Bad Things Happen to Good People.* New York: Avon, 1997. (BK/C/CD/AD)

Matsakis, A. *I Can't Get Over It: A Handbook for Trauma Survivors.* Oakland, CA: New Harbinger Publications, 1999. (BK)

Nathan, S. *Troubled Times: Healing Trauma.* www.tip.net.au/~drsusan/. (C/CD)

Sheehy, G. *Middletown, America: One Town's Passage from Trauma to Hope.* New York: Random House, 2003. (BK)

Williams, R., and V. Williams. *Anger Kills: Seventeen Strategies for*

*Controlling the Hostility That Can Harm Your Health.* New York: HarperTorch, 1998. (BK)

Zimbardo, P. *Shyness: What Is It? What to Do About It?* New York: Perseus, 1990. (BK)

## SECTION IV: ATTACKING YOUR STRESSFUL BEHAVIORS, THOUGHTS, AND ATTITUDES

### Resources

Barlow, D. *Anxiety and Its Disorders: The Nature and Treatment of Anxiety and Panic,* second ed. New York: Guilford Press, 2004. (BK)

Bourne, E. *The Anxiety and Phobia Workbook.* Oakland, CA.: New Harbinger, 2000. (BK)

Burns, D. *Feeling Good: The New Mood Therapy.* New York: Avon, 1999. (BK/CD)

Carnegie, D. *How to Stop Worrying and Start Living,* rev. ed. New York: Pocket Books, 1990. (BK)

Davies, W. *Overcoming Anger and Irritability.* New York: New York University Press, 2001. (BK)

Ellis, A. *How to Control Your Anxiety Before It Controls You.* New York: Citadel, 2000. (BK/C/CD/AD)

## SECTION V: COMMUNICATING YOUR NEEDS AND FEELINGS

### Resources

Alberti, R., and M. Emmons. *Your Perfect Right: Assertiveness and Equality in Your Life and Relationships,* eighth ed. San Luis Obispo, CA: Impact, 2001. (BK)

Bloom, L., K. Coburn, and J. Pearlman. *The New Assertive Woman.* Gretna, LA: Wellness Institute, 2001. (EB)

Paterson, R. *The Assertiveness Workbook: How to Express Your Ideas and Stand Up for Yourself at Work and in Relationships.* Oakland, CA: New Harbinger, 2000. (BK)

## Section VI: Planning the Days of Your Life

### Organizations and Internet Resources

**Association for Applied and Therapeutic Humor**
1951 W. Camelback Rd.
Suite 445
Phoenix, AZ 85015
(602) 995-1454
www.aath.org

### Recordings

**Books on Tape, Inc.**
A Division of Random House, Inc.
P.O. Box 25122
Santa Ana, CA 92799-5122
(800) 88-BOOKS
www.booksontape.com

**Audible**
65 Willowbrook Blvd
Wayne, NJ 07470
(888) 283-5051 (United States and Canada)
(973) 837-2845 (International)
www.audible.com

**The Laughter Remedy**
3140 Wilmont Dr.
Wilmington, DE 19810
(302) 478-7500
www.laughterremedy.com

**Newstrack Executive Information Service**
140 South Broadway
Suite 3
Pitman, NJ 08071
(888) 639-7872
www.news-track.com

**Nightingale-Conant**
6245 W. Howard St.
Niles, IL 60714
(800) 560-5973
www.nightingale.com

### Additional Resources

Allen, D. *Getting Things Done: The Art of Stress-Free Productivity.*
New York: Penguin, 2003. (BK/C/CD/AD)

Blanchard, K., and S. Johnson. *The One-Minute Manager, Anniversary Edition: The World's Most Popular Management Method.* New York: William Morrow, 2003. (BK/C/CD/AD).

Bolles, D. *What Color Is Your Parachute? A Practical Manual for Job-Hunters and Career-Changers.* Berkeley, CA.: Ten Speed Press, 2003. (BK/C/CD)

Cousins, N. *Anatomy of an Illness as Perceived by the Patient.* New York: Bantam, 1991. (BK)

Covey, S. *The Seven Habits of Highly Effective People.* New York: Simon and Schuster, 1990. (BK/C/CD/AD/EB)

Donovan, K. *Growing Through Stress* (revised ed.). Berrien Springs, MI: Institute of World Mission, Andrew University, 2002. (BK)

Elgin, D. *Voluntary Simplicity: Toward a Way of Life That Is Outwardly Simple, Inwardly Rich.* New York: Quill, 1998. (BK)

Kabat-Zinn, J. *Wherever You Go There You Are: Mindfulness Meditation in Everyday Life.* New York: Hyperion, 1995. (BK/C/CD/AD).

MacCarty, S. *Stress Beyond Coping: Workbook, Instructor's Manual, and Powerpoint Presentations,* Hagerstown, MD: The Health Connection, 1997 (B/CD)

Morgenstern, J. *Time Management from the Inside Out: The Foolproof System for Taking Control of Your Schedule and Your Life.* New York: Henry Holt, 2000. (BK/C/CD/AD)

Naselli, M. K. *Little Guide to Happiness: How to Smile Again.* Bloomington, IN: 1st Books Library, 2002. (BK)

Popcak, G. *God Help Me: This Stress Is Driving Me Crazy.* Chicago: Loyola, 2003. (BK)

St. James, E. *Simplify Your Work Life: Ways to Change the Way You Work So You Have More Time to Live.* New York: Hyperion, 2002. (BK)

Tracy, Brian. *Goals: How to Get Everything You Want Faster than You Ever Thought Possible.* San Francisco: Berrett-Koehler, 2003. (BK/C)

Warren, Rick. *The Purpose-Driven Life: What on Earth Am I Here For?* Grand Rapids, MI: Zondervan, 2002. (BK/C/CD/AD/EB).

Winston, S. *Organized Executive: Classic Program for Productivity: New Ways to Manage Time, Paper, People and the Digital Office.* New York: Warner Books, 2001. (BK/C)

## Section VII: Enhancing Health and Preventing Disease

### *Organizations and Internet Resources*

**Center for Nutrition Policy and Promotion**
3101 Park Center Drive, Room 1034
Alexandria, VA 22302-1594
(703) 305-7600
www.usda.gov/cnpp

**Division of Nutrition and Physical Activity**
National Center for Chronic Disease Prevention and Health Promotion
Centers for Disease Control and Prevention
4770 Buford Highway, NE, MS/K-24
Atlanta GA 30341-3717
(770) 488-5820
www.cdc.gov/nccdphp/dnpa/

**Healthfinder**
P.O. Box 1133
Washington, DC 20013-1133
www.healthfinder.gov

Healthfinder links to information and Web sites from over 1,700 health-related organizations.

**Office of Dietary Supplements**
National Institutes of Health
6100 Executive Blvd., Room 3B01, MSC 7517
Bethesda, MD 20892-7517
(301) 435-2920
http://ods.od.nih.gov

**Physicians Committee for Responsible Medicine**
5100 Wisconsin Ave.
Suite 400
Washington, DC 20016
(202) 686-2210
www.pcrm.org

For alternative Food Pyramid models, including vegetarian and ethnic.

**President's Council on Physical Fitness and Sports**
200 Independence Ave., SW
Room 738-H
Washington, D.C. 20201-0004
Phone: (202) 690-9000
www.fitness.gov

The President's Council on Physical Fitness and Sports (PCPFS) serves as a catalyst to promote, encourage, and motivate Americans of all ages to become physically active and participate in sports.

### Additional Resources

American Heart Association. *American Heart Association Low-Fat, Low Cholesterol Cookbook: Heart-Healthy, Easy-to-Make Recipes That Taste Great.* New York: Times Books, 1997. (BK)

American Heart Association. *Fitting in Fitness: Hundreds of Simple Ways to Put More Physical Activity into Your Life.* New York: Times Books, 1997. (BK)

Anderson, R. *Stretching: 20th Anniversary Edition.* Bolinas, CA.: Shelter Publications, 2000. (BK)

Brownell, K. *Food Fight: The Inside Story of the Food Industry,*

*America's Obesity Crisis and What We Can Do About It.* New York: McGraw-Hill, 2003. (BK)

Burfoot, A. *Runner's World Complete Book of Running: Everything You Need to Know to Run for Fun, Fitness, and Competition.* Emmaus, PA: Rodale Press, 1999. (BK)

Cooper, K. *The Aerobics Program for Total Well-Being: Exercise, Diet, and Emotional Balance.* New York: Bantam, 1985. (BK)

Cooper, K. H. *Controlling Cholesterol the Natural Way: Eat Your Way to Better Health with New Breakthrough Food Discoveries.* New York: Bantam Books, 1999. (BK)

Ferguson, J. M., and C. Ferguson. *Habits Not Diets: The Secret to Lifetime Weight Control,* fourth edition. Boulder, CO: Bull, 2003. (BK)

Foreyt, J. P., W. Poston, K. McInnis, and J. Rippe (editors). *Lifestyle Obesity Management.* Malden, MA: Blackwell Publishers, 2003. (BK)

McGraw, P. *The Ultimate Weight Solution.* New York: Free Press, 2003. (BK/C/CD/AD/EB).

Willett, W., P. Skerrett, and E. Giovannucci. *Eat, Drink, and Be Healthy: The Harvard Medical School Guide to Healthy Eating.* New York: Simon & Schuster, 2001. (BK)

## SECTION VIII: PUTTING IT ALL TOGETHER

### Organizations and Internet Resources

**National Center for Complementary and Alternative Medicine at the National Institutes of Health (NCCAM)**
P.O. Box 7923
Gaithersburg, MD 20898-7923
(888) 644-6226
www.nccam.nih.gov

**Additional Resources**

Goldberg, B., J. Anderson, and L. Trivieri. *Alternative Medicine: The Definitive Guide,* second ed. Berkeley, CA: Ten Speed Press, 2002. (BK)

Lazarus, A., and A. Fay. *I Can if I Want To.* Essex, CT: FMC Books, 1999. (BK)

Waitley, D. *Psychology of Winning.* New York: Berkley, 1992. (BK/C)

**APPENDIX IV**

# Home Practice Chart

## HOME PRACTICE CHART

*DIRECTIONS:* Copy a Home Practice Chart each week of your stress management program and record the dates in the blank next to the week number. Space is provided to record your practice twice a day. The codes for what you practiced are defined below. Write the code of the technique you practiced in the appropriate blank next to session (1) and session (2) for each day. Next to the code, write the number of minutes you practiced. In the last two columns, write in your relaxation ratings. Remember, 0 means total relaxation and 100 means total tension.

CODES FOR WHAT YOU PRACTICED:

| Name of Technique | Code |
|---|---|
| Progressive Relaxation | PR |
| Scanning Relaxation | SR |
| Deep Muscle Relaxation | DM |
| Countdown Relaxation | CD |
| Autogenic Training | AT |
| Imagery Training | IT |
| Image Rehearsal | IR |
| Other Training | OT |

**WEEK #** _____  **DATE** _____   RELAXATION RATINGS (0–100)

| DAY/SESSION | WHAT YOU PRACTICED | MINUTES PRACTICED | Before | After |
|---|---|---|---|---|
| 1 (1) | | | | |
| (2) | | | | |
| 2 (1) | | | | |
| (2) | | | | |
| 3 (1) | | | | |
| (2) | | | | |
| 4 (1) | | | | |
| (2) | | | | |
| 5 (1) | | | | |
| (2) | | | | |
| 6 (1) | | | | |
| (2) | | | | |
| 7 (1) | | | | |
| (2) | | | | |

## INDEX

# ABOUT THE AUTHORS

EDWARD A. CHARLESWORTH, PH.D., is a clinical psychologist, director of Willowbrook Psychological Associates, P.C., president of Stress Management Research Associates, Inc., and an international consultant to corporations and hospitals. He is in demand as a speaker on topics of positive lifestyle changes and has inspired audiences from Switzerland to the Philippines. He is the author or coauthor of four books, *Stress Management: A Comprehensive Guide to Wellness, Stress Management: A Conceptual and Procedural Guide, Mind over Money,* and *Life Management,* and his numerous scientific articles include topics such as biofeedback and self-control, drug abuse, hypertension, cardiovascular disease, hypnotherapy, personality, and psychotherapy. He is the author of the popular audio-therapeutic recorded programs *The Relaxation and Stress Management Program* and *Stress Management Training Program*.

RONALD G. NATHAN, PH.D., is a clinical psychologist. Before entering private practice, Dr. Nathan was an award-winning professor of family practice and psychiatry at Albany Medical College and developed the country's first required stress management course for medical students. The coauthor of four books about stress, Dr. Nathan contributed the "stress" entry in recent editions of *The World Book Encyclopedia*. His work has been featured in *Men's Health, Cosmopolitan,* and *Family Circle.* For the past ten years, he has also served as an associate editor of the *American Journal of Health Promotion.* Recently, Dr. Nathan cocreated www.ChristMinder.com, an innovative Web site where visitors can download free software designed to integrate life-enhancing Bible verses and biblical affirmations into their personal computer activities.